A
STATE
OF
STRUGGLE

CLASS
WORK
UNIONS
SERIES
8

JOHN MCINALLY

manifesto

'A State of Struggle'
John McInally

First Published in 2025 by Manifesto Press
© John McInally
All rights reserved

MANIFESTO PRESS CO-OPERATIVE

Manifesto Press
Ruskin House
23 Coombe Road
Croydon CR0 1BD

Edited by Elaine McFarland and Jim Whiston
with Marine Picard and Nick Wright

Typeset in *Chaparral Pro* and *Neue Frutiger World*
Designed by *Corata Group*

All images by Andy Aitchison are reproduced in this book with the express
permission of the photographer.

Cover image: Andy Aitchison, Strike Day, 2012 © Andy Aitchison.

ISBN 978-1-907464-84-3
studio@manifestopress.coop
manifestopress.coop

Dedicated to John Lindsay Macreadie
19 September 1946–22 December 2010
Socialist and Trade Unionist

Contents

■ Andy Aitchison, *John McInally speaking outside the Treasury Building*, 2019 © Andy Aitchison

About The Author

John McInally was born in Glasgow in 1954 and grew up in the Easterhouse housing scheme. In 1977 he joined the Militant Tendency, forerunner of the Socialist Party, was active in the Labour Party Young Socialists, and organised campaigns with Unemployed Workers' groups.

In 1981 he was employed in the Unemployment Benefit Service (UBS), a forerunner of the Department for Work and Pensions (DWP). Within three months he was elected as a union representative for the Civil and Public Services Association (CPSA) at Easterhouse Benefit Office, going on to lead several campaigns and strikes on various issues. In 1988 he led the successful three-month Easterhouse staffing dispute and was a main organiser of the campaign in the West of Scotland against the introduction of the Youth Training Scheme (YTS) into the civil service.

Moving to Bristol in 1989, he was a founder of the Bristol Anti-Poll Tax Federation, playing an important role in organising protests and the non-payment campaign, led the Bristol health and safety dispute. He played an important role in the Bedminster Jobcentre dispute and in the subsequent anti-victimisation campaign against both management and the right-wing 'Moderate' leadership. As a member of the CPSA Group Executive Committee he organised strikes during the 1995–96 Employment Service pay dispute in Cardiff and Merthyr Tydfil. Subjected to years of harassment and victimisation, he fought off five serious attempts to have him sacked.

A long-term member of the CPSA Broad Left National Committee, he was a founder member of its successor, Left Unity, and, with the exception of one year, served on its National Committee until retirement in 2019.

McInally was elected to the Public and Commercial Services' (PCS) National Executive Committee (NEC) in 2002 and became vice-president from 2007 until 2017, playing a key organising role in the successful annual re-election of the left. He worked closely with general secretary Mark Serwotka and presidents Janice Godrich and Fran Heathcote, playing a significant role in the development of policy and strategy, especially on welfare, privatisation, organising campaigns, industrial action, and speaking at innumerable meetings throughout the United Kingdom. He served at various times as liaison officer for each of the devolved areas of Wales, Scotland and Northern Ireland, ensuring the voices of members in these areas were always heard. He played a very significant role in developing and delivering the union's highly regarded work in the Scottish independence referendum.

In 2018, along with other leading rank-and-file PCS activists, he was expelled from the Socialist Party for opposing its 'descent into sectarianism, opportunism and the embrace of prestige politics' and its abandonment of core principles, most particularly the United Front strategy. He joined the Labour Party under the Corbyn leadership but was expelled under Starmer.

He writes and speaks on political and cultural issues for socialist publications and organisations, principally the *Morning Star*.

He lives in Croydon with his wife and comrade, Helen O'Connor, a union organiser and political activist.

Acknowledgements

There are literally hundreds of CPSA and PCS activists who deserve to be recognised for their contribution in building the union and the left, but it is simply impossible to mention them all.

I must highlight two especially whose advice, constructive criticism and good counsel have been invaluable. Dave Watson, who for many years was Mark Serwotka's Policy Officer, and Frank Bonner, one of the principal figures in building the left in the union from the 1960s onwards. Sadly, Frank lost a long fight with cancer and died last year, he is sorely missed by me as a comrade and dear friend.

My gratitude to Nick Wright of Manifesto Press who offered to publish the book and for his hard work, advice and support. Thanks also to the rest of the team at Manifesto Press including Elaine McFarland and Jim Whiston whose excellent editing was invaluable. Many thanks also to Andy Aitchison for his generosity and great photographs.

And, of course, my thanks to Mark Serwotka for writing the Foreword, for his support for this project, and his comradeship and friendship during difficult times.

My thanks too to my wife and comrade, Helen O'Connor for her patience, support and encouragement.

Andy Aitchison, *Strike Day*, 2012 © Andy Aitchison

Preface

Capitalism is in irreversible crisis. The past forty years or more have seen an extended period of reaction in which the ruling class has waged unremitting class war to steal back all the gains won by the labour and trade union movement over generations of struggle.

The systemic failures exposed by the Covid-19 pandemic, with millions of unnecessary deaths, along with a major intensification of inter-imperialist conflict, are only two of the more visible indications that we have now entered a qualitatively different period in which multiple crises will follow one upon the other with little or no respite, and in which instability and insecurity for the vast majority in society will be the norm rather than the exception.

The age of reforms is long past. Reformism, the idea that concessions, in any meaningful and consistent form, can be won from employers and governments, has neither answers nor solutions now that the ruling class is no longer willing to share even the crumbs from its table.

Class struggle of the most intense character, even of a revolutionary nature, will be needed to defend workers' conditions and rights, let alone win gains – which can only be secured on a temporary basis before they again come under attack.

Business and service trade unionism, with the collaborationist partnership and sweetheart deals beloved of right-wing trade union leaders – the ruling class's surrogates in our movement – will be increasingly exposed and challenged as workers look to defend their terms and conditions, and through necessity organise to remove these fetters on their capacity to struggle.

This intensification of class war presents both opportunities and dangers for the primary democratic mass organisations of the working class – the trade unions. There is tremendous potential to build the type of democratic, militant unions with socialist leaderships from the workplace to their national leaderships. Trade unions can build effective resistance to defend and advance the interests of both their members and the wider working class, but only based on militant struggle and not the dominant 'strategy' of collaborationism that has seen union membership in Britain reduced by more than half in the past four decades.

Together with leading resistance and a fightback in the industrial arena, unions can, and must also be, the strongest advocates for a socialist alternative to the chaos of capitalism and for effective working-class political representation. The consequences of not grasping these opportunities will mean defeat, demoralisation and disorientation.

Karl Marx made this profound comment on the future of the unions in 1866. It is still as relevant today:

> Apart from their original purposes, they must now learn to act deliberately as organising centres of the working class in the broad interest of *its complete emancipation*. They must aid every social and political movement tending in that direction... They must convince the world at large that their efforts, far from being narrow and selfish, aim at the emancipation of the downtrodden millions.[1]

More than an observation or a declaration, Marx's comment is, for socialists and communists, a guide to action and the foundation stone of our programme in the trade unions.

The role of the trade unions is of the most critical importance in the struggle for 'the emancipation of the downtrodden millions'. It was not just Marx, but the British ruling class who knew and feared that trade unions could, given the correct direction and leadership, develop beyond their necessary but limited role of fighting on 'bread-and-butter' issues.

Trade unions are capable of playing the most positive role in the class struggle. If equipped with a militant perspective, programme and leadership, they are uniquely placed to unify other sections and elements of the working class: the unorganised within our communities together with social movements in the wider struggle for the socialist transformation of society.

But long experience tells us trade union leaders are also capable of playing the most divisive, backward and treacherous role.

So, what has all this to do with this contribution which is an 'activist's history' of a British trade union representing a relatively small and specific sector of the organised working class, mainly, if not exclusively, civil service workers?

If this contribution has one principal, over-arching and inter-connecting theme, it is this – the struggle between militant and collaborationist trade unionism.

And this is an issue of the most pressing concern and relevance to activists of all unions, and especially so for socialists and communists struggling to transform their unions, and society too.

It describes the industrial and political struggles that led to the formation of the Public and Commercial Services Union (PCS), the battles within it and its predecessors to defeat right-wing collaborationist leaderships, and to build a fighting, democratic union. It also highlights the role of the union's socialist leadership and activists in their struggles to defend and advance the interests of members, and the wider working class. Through this, the account strives to strike a serious balance that recognises the role of the union's socialist leaderships' and activists' achievements, but also the limitations and setbacks in conditions of isolated struggle over an extended period of reaction.

While recognising that there are features and characteristics specific to any trade union that determine its industrial and political development, they are of secondary importance in relation to the lessons of a general nature that can be drawn from the struggles in PCS. Real living events, in all their complexities, are described and analysed, which hopefully will be of use to socialist and communist activists in their own struggles within whatever union or working-class organisation they are active in.

This contribution provides an account and analysis of the development of the union from a Marxist perspective within the context of the wider class struggle. It is also a defence of the socialist and communist method in trade union work, it is therefore polemical in tone and makes no pretence to be an 'objective' history – there is no such thing: all histories are written from a class and political perspective, anyone claiming otherwise is either deluding the reader or themselves, or both.

The general themes addressed include the genesis of civil service trade unionism, the struggles of socialists and communists with the right wing, the role of the state, the proletarianisation of the workforce, the emergence of industrial militancy, and the election of PCS's socialist leadership in 2002–3 committed to organising against the neo-liberal policies of successive governments. It describes how the union organised resistance and opposition to the job cuts and privatisation agenda of the New Labour government, the coalition and Tory governments' austerity programmes, its advocacy of an economic alternative, and its campaigns for effective working-class political representation. It also discusses the question of how socialists and communists should organise, whether in the workplace or at other levels, including national disputes.

These events and issues have the sharpest contemporary relevance as Keir Starmer's Labour government embarks on yet another programme of attacks on our class which, unless opposed, will result in a qualitative intensification of the 'race to the bottom'.

The price of union inaction or collaboration will be severe. The destruction of the welfare state is at an advanced stage and the assault will continue. Deep cuts targeting the sick, disabled, unemployed and other recipients of state benefits have been announced, as have cuts in the NHS, in preparation for its full sell-off to American and European insurance oligarchs. For over forty years, public-sector pay policy has been defined by 'pay restraint' and 'freezes', and this will continue in one form or the other.

Therefore, this contribution is not just concerned with providing an industrial, political and historical analysis of past events but is intended as a guide to action in current and coming struggles.

Also discussed are the influence of socialist ideas and activism, the conflict between left and right – particularly the struggle to defeat the 'Moderate' right-wing bureaucracy, the building of an effective United Front and broad lefts, and the role of socialist organisations and parties. Other themes include the union's relations with the wider labour and trade union movement and its demand for united union campaigning, including coordinated industrial action to defend public services and public sector workers' terms, conditions and rights. The inter-connection between industrial and political campaigning is considered, including the union's interventions on wider class issues like anti-racism, national self-determination, and the form of political representation.

The destructive role of left sectarianism which exists, to a greater or lesser extent, in any workers' organisation, is also addressed, not 'theoretically' but by examining actual events and issues. This includes an account and analysis of how organisations and individuals under pressures exerted in an extended period of reaction abandoned not just a Marxist method in trade union work, but also militant trade unionism itself and capitulated to bureaucratism and collaborationism.

The book concludes with a brief consideration of potential directions for the British trade union movement and the many challenges, dangers and opportunities it faces in the current period of ever-deepening crises.

Although centred around an analysis of the struggles in PCS, the main purpose of this account is to demonstrate the potential to build our trade unions into organisations that can genuinely defend their members' interests, and those of the wider working class in this period of capitalist decline – the most serious challenge facing our movement.

Building the type of militant trade union movement that aims at 'the emancipation of the downtrodden millions' can no longer be understood as an aspiration for the future but as an imperative and urgent necessity for today.

Notes & References

1. 'Instructions for the Delegates of the Provisional General Council. The Different Questions', Karl Marx and Friedrich Engels, *Selected Works*, vol.2, Progress Publishers, Moscow, 1973, pp.82-83.

Foreword by Mark Serwotka

For over forty years, the civil service trade union movement was a key part of my life. On 10 March 1980, I started work as a clerical officer at the Department of Health and Social Security (DHSS) in Pontypridd, South Wales and applied for union membership on my first day. Within a month, I was elected to the branch committee, later being told that I must have been keen, having actively volunteered to join the union!

Twenty years later in December 2000, while working at the DHSS Sheffield, I was elected general secretary of the Public and Commercial Services Union (PCS). For all my working life, I had been active in the Civil and Public Services Association (CPSA), which became part of PCS in 1998.

As a lay activist and union representative in South Wales and then in South Yorkshire, I served at every level in the union, other than on the union's national executive. Attending conferences, meeting other activists, representing colleagues at work, negotiating with management, all the things any healthy union requires at the workplace level.

I also organised and led numerous local strikes, one of which was an all-out six-month strike at DHSS Caerphilly against the employment of casual workers and for permanent positions. It was in the mid-1980s, still in my early twenties, that I cut my teeth. This for me was an incredible part of my life, going on union courses, meeting other activists, including organised socialists. It was around this time that I met John McInally.

Having known John for four decades, I now consider him a good friend and comrade. Although now both retired, we remain in close contact. It was therefore a real pleasure to be asked to do this short foreword to a book that not only covers in detail such a key part of my life, but also one which examines thoroughly the extraordinary events in our movement's history.

John is now a friend; however, it was not always so. My first encounter with him came at a CPSA conference and then at the union's Broad Left conference. We certainly were not friends then but more like political opponents. Hailing from Glasgow and working in the Department of Employment, he was a leading voice in the Militant Tendency, and as such, active in the Broad Left. An excellent public speaker, he was seen by many as the hard face of Militant. On the other hand, I was viewed by John and his grouping as part of the ultra-left, belonging to a faction called the Socialist Caucus – a loose grouping of small left groups and left-wing independents.

Within the Broad Left, fierce debates and rows would occur where often we were on opposite sides of the argument. These rows were often bitter, but Militant's dominance of the Broad Left invariably meant I was on the losing side. But whatever our differences on the left, within the wider union we were allies fighting the hostile 'Moderate', or more accurately hard right-wing leadership of our union.

We actually had a lot in common, both former Catholics, both passionate about our union and, unlike too many of our peers, both with a record of 'walking the walk'. At a time when many on the left came under attack from the right wing as being out of touch with the membership, we both came from very well-organised branches, led lots of strikes and recruited hundreds of members and dozens of new activists. Our branches had high levels of member participation, meaning that when we spoke at conferences to challenge the right wing and call for national industrial action we could, and did deliver. It was these experiences, including victimisation both by our union and our employers, that shaped our vision for the future and what type of union we wanted to help build.

This is an important book. Books can perform a multitude of things, one of which is to set out an account of historical events. Books can also offer an analysis of how and why events took place. This book does both very well.

But for me that is not the main thing. The importance of this book is that it needs to be read not just as a historical account and political analysis, but as a tool and guide to action for trade union activists and socialists in navigating a path through these difficult times. It is necessary to take inspiration from victories, to learn from mistakes and to undertake the painstaking work required at the workplace level. Crucially, it is also vital to understand that the key to winning is the recognition that unions based on high levels of participation, with empowered activists, and with leaders prepared to fight and demand unity across our movement, can succeed in overcoming enormous challenges, becoming vehicles for political as well as industrial change.

And in these dangerous times this is crucial. For twenty years, I was a frontline activist alongside John. Then for the next twenty years, I was general secretary of PCS. Elected against all odds and in many ways at a time when many of the problems we faced were like the present, John became one of the most influential and important of the union's lay activists. Indeed, he served on the union's national executive committee (NEC) and as a senior elected lay officer in the role of national vice-president for almost the entire time I was general secretary.

We had gone from being vocal, respected activists fighting against a vicious right-wing CPSA hierarchy to leading a 300,000-strong union, PCS. This book looks at this period in considerable detail, setting out the fight to get elected to lead the union, as well as the struggle against firstly New Labour, and then the coalition Government and then the Tories. It deals with massive campaigns, huge strikes, government attacks, victories, defeats and score draws. It sets out the developments of politics within the union, and finally the dangers of sectarianism and bureaucratism.

It is written from the perspective of a prominent lay leader. Of course, in this period I was the leading elected full-time official, a very different role, and as such one in which my take or interpretation of events sometimes differs from John's. However, given everything the union faced, this book gives a thorough and accurate account of the key events as they unfolded. So why do I think this book is a useful tool to guide activists now?

Consider the events that it covers. The union was controlled by the most right-wing leaders in the whole trade union movement, with direct links and backing from the state. Many were in league with the employer and in some cases colluded with the victimisation of left-wing activists. Imperfect as democracy was under the Moderates, what did exist was totally ignored by them. If a policy democratically agreed by the union's conference did not suit the leadership's agenda, they simply rejected it. Elections were skewed to the existing leadership with right-wing electoral slates printed in full by tabloid newspapers, urging readers to 'keep the communists out'. Elections were overturned when, for example, the left candidate, John Macreadie, won the CPSA general secretaryship. Strikes were never called, cuts were accepted, partnership with employers became the policy.

Any of this sound familiar today? Are any unions currently operating on similar lines? If so, the book recounts the painstaking work required by activists to turn that situation around. We must remember that radical speeches at conferences are not enough, and that mobilising and involving members and building an activist cadre is essential.

There are no shortcuts. Having won power, the next issue covered in detail is how we, a left leadership, worked to build PCS into a union capable of seriously challenging both governments and employers. Recent history tells us that whether it is the unions or the Labour Party, winning is not enough. Indeed, unless fully prepared to do what is necessary after winning, victory can soon be followed by defeat, such defeat often resulting in setting radical policy and progress back years.

Preparing for battle, building structures that can deliver an organisation fit for purpose, galvanising activists for what is to come, and crucially being serious about winning can take time, but it is essential. This book details what was done and deals with mistakes as well as victories.

Being political as a union is crucial but it must be earned; if membership support is to be won, it too must be earned. Failing to deliver in your own backyard is a fatal mistake, still often made today.

John sets out the approach taken in PCS; one which successfully enabled a civil service union to become one of the most radical in the whole movement. Challenging New Labour demonstrated that PCS put its members first, unlike too many Labour-affiliated unions at the time. Challenging the coalition and Tory governments embodied a belief in the power of the organised working class, so different to the approach of many others. All this is detailed in the book, offering more invaluable lessons for today.

Being too timid lets down those members looking for the union to deliver on its promises. Being abstractly radical, being rhetorical without developing concrete, material strategies – in other words, failing to be serious lets down those same members.

This book honestly examines the judgements made at the time, some required now more than ever. Of course, other unions at the time fought some heroic battles. However, it was PCS that more than any other called for unity and coordinated action across the movement. It offered alternatives to austerity, took strike action and crucially called for and worked tirelessly to turn that action into joint strike action. The role of PCS, firstly in securing concessions from Labour on pensions, then building a two million-strong pensions strike across the public sector against the coalition, was remarkable.

It punched far above its weight precisely because activists across many unions and organisations saw PCS deliver action, provide solidarity, win disputes and argue for radical alternatives. This exposed the shortcomings of many other union leaderships and was at the time a significant threat to both them and the government.

The subsequent betrayal of the pensions dispute, however, demonstrated that the work done over the years in PCS had not been done elsewhere, allowing bureaucrats in the TUC and other unions to close down the dispute. Learning the lessons of this is critical for the battles that lie ahead.

PCS though had begun to develop weaknesses of its own. These sowed the seeds for problems ahead that were not always overcome. Years of the left being in power led to the neglect by some activists in maintaining a strong organisation in their own branches. Bureaucratism in the lay structures, arising in part due to Tory attacks on facility time, led to more meaningless meetings with management at the expense of independent union activity.

This was followed by an inevitable drift into sectarianism. John sets out these issues and they are in themselves worth considering carefully. Manufacturing difference, retreating from class to identity politics, failing to ensure that you could deliver in your own area were all features of the problems prevalent in PCS and other unions.

So, what of the future? What does this book help us consider?

First and foremost, we live in critical times. A dreadful Labour Government wedded to fiscal and political orthodoxy is attacking working-class people, whilst giving the richest a free pass. The rise of right-wing ideas and governments across the world is unleashing attacks on an unprecedented basis. The labour and trade union movement is not currently up to the task ahead. It is reminiscent of much of the period covered in this book.

However, the prospects are not encouraging. Social democracy has failed, and working-class people lacking a credible left alternative are increasingly attracted to populist right-wing parties. The obsession of many on the left with identity replacing class as their focus for radicalism has made things worse.

This is why this book makes essential reading. By focusing on participation, democracy and listening to workers, we can build organisations that are battle-ready. By being prepared to lead, even in the face of overwhelming odds, we can inspire people to fight, and to win.

John's book therefore deserves to be read, debated, and considered. The events it covers, the gains, the mistakes, the highs and the lows all need to be evaluated.

But here is the thing – most of all they should galvanise us to fight for the future of the working class.

1. Origins – historical, industrial and political overview

The state and the modern civil service

The Industrial Revolution in the early nineteenth century transformed Britain into the world's first great capitalist power. It also exposed the existing civil service as wholly unsuited for effective governmental and state control over an emergent industrial economy and empire. The civil service had developed over centuries in an ad hoc manner in the age of aristocratic ascendancy and feudal patronage, and comprised largely autonomous bodies or departments riddled with nepotism, bribery, corruption, and inefficiency.

The emergence of a reformed civil service as a reliable and efficient pillar of the state was driven by the ruling class's more far-sighted strategists who recognised the need to construct an effective, centralised bureaucratic superstructure capable of administering society in the interests of the profit system, including the planning and supervision of state resources and finance.

The state can be broadly defined as those institutions created, or evolved, often over considerable periods of time, to govern and administer class society. In Britain this includes the monarchy, Church, armed forces, police and security services, legal system, education and academia, parliament, government, and the civil service. To justify its power, the capitalist ruling class claims that the state represents an inviolable and inevitable natural authority, elevated above class interests and binding society together in the common interest, without which chaos would reign. In the final analysis, the state ultimately exercises its authority and power through armed force, arrogating to itself the right to use violence in defence of ruling class interests. Under feudal absolutism this was expressed as the God-ordained Divine Right of Kings, and under capitalism as the inalienable right to private property.

Throughout the early nineteenth century, the emergent working class, created by the Industrial Revolution itself, combined to form trade unions through a process of trial and error. Their aim was to win better wages and conditions, thus securing the basis of a civilised existence in the new brutal profit system. They developed the strike weapon – the withdrawal of labour – as the only truly effective method which could bring sufficient pressure on employers to extract concessions. Strike action resulted in some victories but often in setbacks and defeats.

One government after another, in league with the employers, used the full power of the state, including the legal system and the most violent physical repression, to try to crush the infant trade union movement. Many workers drew the conclusion that the government and state were not neutral but would always act in the interests of the exploiters. But also, that their trade unions, primary democratic organisations that had developed from necessity, must be defended and maintained if they were to win concessions and a better life.

In his 1899 article 'On Strikes', V.I. Lenin, with no-nonsense clarity and directness, defined the significance of the strike weapon in the class war: 'A strike opens the eyes of the workers to the nature, not only of the capitalists, but of the government and the laws as well'.[1] He went on, 'One German Minister of the Interior, one who was notorious for the persistent persecution of socialist and class-conscious workers, not without reason, stated before the people's representatives that behind every strike lurks the Hydra of revolution'. Lenin concluded, 'Every strike strengthens and develops in the workers the understanding that the government is their enemy and that the working class must prepare itself to struggle against the government for the people's rights'. This explains why employers and governments, along with right-wing union leaders and bureaucrats, liberals and newspaper columnists expend so much energy trying to convince workers that strikes do not work, while supporting every effort to break or betray them.

The role of the government and state in strikes, the sharpest expression of industrial struggle, inevitably led the more advanced working-class activists to recognise the class struggle as also political in nature. The first mass mobilisations of the British working class from the 1830s to the late 1840s saw demands for independent working-class political representation by the Chartist movement, conducting struggles which at their peak were of a revolutionary nature, including a major insurrection in South Wales and the world's first general strike in 1842. This was in pursuit of its demands for universal male suffrage, secret ballots in parliamentary elections, the removal of property qualifications for MPs, annual parliaments and other democratic demands. The movement was supported by many trade unions and counted many of them among its leaders and activists.

The Chartist movement receded in the 1850s, but despite the ebb and flow of class warfare and the balance of power in favour of the ruling class, the employers, government and state failed to decisively defeat the trade union movement.

The enormous social, political and industrial upheavals in Britain and revolutionary movements in Europe led colonial administrator and civil service reform advocate, Sir Charles Trevelyan, to summarise the problem facing the ruling class and the need for action, 'The revolutionary period of 1848 gave us a shake and created a disposition to put our house in order, and one of the consequences was a series of investigations into public office that lasted for five years'.[2]

The civil service was to play a critical and necessary role in implementing reform from above, within parameters set by the ruling class itself, to prevent revolution from below. The drive to create an 'integrated, efficient' civil service gathered pace from the 1850s due to increasing failures of government administration and scandals, perhaps most notably around disruption to the supply of essential equipment to the armed forces during the Crimean War – a consequence of endemic inefficiency and graft. In one telling illustration of the nature of the civil service before the period of reform, Major Graham, Head of the Board of Audit, offered a damning indictment of the sinecure system. Addressing a Select Committee in 1860, he said:

> I have made a return of fifty-five persons...who were nominated by the Treasury between 1836 and 1854... Several of them were incompetent from their ages... I found some perfectly unqualified...I also found persons there of very bad character: one person in that list had been imprisoned by the sentence of the court as a fraudulent debtor...Then with little regard to health, there was one man whom I was forced to keep in a room by himself, as he was in such a state of health that he could not associate with the other clerks...There was a case in our offices, in which a gentleman was appointed who really could not read or write, he was almost an idiot, and there was the greatest possible difficulty in getting him out of the office.[3]

Civil service reform extended throughout the remainder of the nineteenth century and into the twentieth in step with the rapidly changing nature of society. At the same time, industrial and technological change and the demands of the working class for improvement in living standards and democratic rights, presented challenges to the hegemony and control of the government and state itself.

The ruling class, through their press, academics and constitutional experts, sought to present the modern civil service as administering society in the interests of all by impartially implementing the democratic will of the people, as represented by the elected government. But it did not stand above class interests, on the contrary, it continued to reflect the character and nature of the capitalist society in which it was rooted. Its purpose remained, first and foremost, to serve the interests of the ruling class.

Struggles for unionisation

Civil service trade unionism first developed to any extent during the 1850s, another period of intense social, industrial, and political upheaval; it did not implant itself on an already fixed and defined civil service, but one evolving through enforced reform.

The same antagonistic relationship of the employer to the worker and the exploiter to the exploited that had driven the rise of industrial trade unionism in the factories, mines, and mills was also the moving force in the birth of civil service trade unionism. But there were also fundamental differences shaping how civil service unions developed. This was most notable in their campaigning methods, particularly in relation to the use of political campaigning rather than industrial action, which only became a central feature of civil service trade unionism in the late 1960s.

While industrial workers were employed by individual capitalist employers whose principal concern was to maintain and increase their profit margins, civil servants were employed at 'Her Majesty's Pleasure', or more accurately, in service of the state and government. The new layer of clerical workers rapidly developed their own distinctive political culture, arising from these specific work conditions and position in society.

Conditions were considerably better than for most industrial workers, apart from the skilled groups that constituted the so-called 'aristocracy of labour'. Wages were low but there was no back-breaking labour, no constant threat of unemployment as positions (with some exceptions) were generally permanent. At the end of a working life there was even the prospect of a pension, almost entirely unknown in industry. While there was disciplined management, it could not be compared to the crude oversight of the industrial workplace.

Expansion of the civil service was linked to improvements in education following the 1870 Education Act. Entry into the service on merit through examination and open competition opened the door for the lower middle classes, and eventually for the working class. This changed its social composition. Aware of working conditions outside the service, it also helped foster a progressive and even radical outlook, investing in social reform with a class-based contempt for patronage and nepotism. Not surprisingly, these developments caused serious concerns and even hostility towards civil service reform within the ruling class. They were not without foundation.

At any given time, the ruling class contains contradictory tendencies. There were those who understood the need for civil service reform to administer the developing state as a stable base for capital. On the other hand, there were those who regretted the unwelcome increases in public expenditure to finance large numbers of clerical workers as cutting into profits. Civil service expansion from the later nineteenth century onwards was also questioned in the reactionary press and by the political establishment. Some demanded to know why taxation should be wasted in employing such numbers of bureaucrats, evoking the good old days of 1787, when the entire civil service consisted of just 16,267 staff.

Descriptions of civil service workers as pen-pushing bureaucrats, accusations of wasteful public spending and demands for private sector efficiency – staples of the right-wing press and populist politicians ever since – found their earliest expression in this period and became deeply rooted. In 1921 Lord Rothermere, arch proponent of gutter journalism and later a pro-fascist propagandist, formed the Anti-Waste League in an effort to prepare public opinion to accept deep cuts both in the public sector and in workers' wages. A notorious recent example in 2004 was chancellor Gordon Brown's announcement of massive civil service job cuts as an 'efficiency measure'.[4]

The changing profile of the civil service workforce as a result of merit-based entry examinations and open competition also attracted hostile political comment. Reactionaries lamented that the prestige of the service would be diminished by the entry of the 'ill-bred middle class'. This reflected their worry that this new section of workers would inevitably raise grievances, demand better wages and combine – which is exactly what they did. In his evidence to the Playfair Commission of 1874–5, chancellor of the exchequer Robert Lowe, focused on the growth of trade unionism:

> One thing that we overlooked was the danger of collecting a very large body of persons together, having friends all over the country, having a particular interest, and that interest being to obtain better terms from the Government. I think we overlooked the political aspect of the question. Certain gentlemen have found it quite expedient to make political capital out of the alleged grievances of these writers [clerical workers]; and I now think that it is a pity that there were collected together some three thousand persons, or something of the kind, for this sort of employment. All having a common interest to press upon the Government – the raising of their wages.[5]

The ability of this newly constituted workforce to combine and establish collective bargaining was initially constrained by the existing grievance process, a legacy of the pre-reform civil service, in which issues were raised by petition on an individual basis. The right to collective petitioning was only grudgingly conceded in the face of vigorous challenges from workers and their unions. As early as 1855, attempts by management to restrict such collective petitions to internal departmental resolution were already coming under strain. Workers in their new organisations understood that only the Treasury, which controlled public finance, had the power to address certain grievances, including pay. Consequently, they demanded direct access to raise their demands with the real decision-makers – the government itself.

The tone of one group of workers when the Treasury tried to ignore their representations showed a combative as well as collective consciousness:

> With profound disgust and indescribable disappointment we have perused the insolent, pettifogging, and thoroughly contemptible reply of the Secretary

of the Treasury, conveying the refusal of My Lords to comply with the moderate prayers of the Officers of Inland Revenue, Excise Branch, for an increase of salary... we will never cease to urge the gentlemen engaged in the Excise to combine and organise their strength until they obtain what they have a right to – a fair wage for a fair day's work.[6]

Local groupings of workers, as well as wider combinations, grew during the second half of the nineteenth century and were concerned with wages, conditions, temporary posts, promotion, the establishment of all-service grades, civil and political rights and the right to permanent jobs.

Pressing demands were not restricted to collective petitioning. In 1859, the Surveyors' Committee, a predecessor of tax workers' associations, was attacked for publishing pamphlets in which an Excise Officers' committee complained in writing to MPs about a minor increase in salaries, which they claimed was unjust. The Board of Inland Revenue told the Treasury that such 'organised agitation' would not be tolerated. But despite vigorous attempts to restrict this form of political campaigning, these methods developed in the following decades as the key weapon, rather than strike action.

Demands for effective collective bargaining drove the development from loose, often temporary, or even issue-based combinations, to staff associations and toward recognisable trade unions. The strike weapon was not employed by these combinations, but this did not mean that it was never considered; in fact, a strike of telegraphists did occur in 1871, but was 'ruthlessly suppressed'. There were various factors that explained why these clerical workers looked to other avenues of pursuing grievances and advancing their interests, including better working conditions and the more variegated social composition of the workforce. These distinctions were deepened by a complex grading system, the underdeveloped nature of workers' combinations and their relationship to the government and state.

Organisation remained generally of a scattered, and sometimes isolated, nature. The idea that they were serving the public interest was strong within the new workforce, and this was ruthlessly exploited by politicians and the press, arguing that no matter how legitimate public sector workers' grievances might be, they should never take industrial action as it would hurt the public they serve. Serving the state was not regarded as the same as being employed in industry. As late as 1912, one commentator remarked in relation to a threatened Post Office strike that, 'Men who are employed by the public cannot strike. They can, and sometimes do, mutiny. They should be treated not as strikers but as mutineers.'[7]

When industrial workers went on strike, they had an impact on the operations and profits of a specific capitalist enterprise, but when employees of an elected administration with the full prestige and power of the empire behind it took industrial action, this could be viewed as a direct challenge to the state. Activists were also conscious that strike action by isolated groups of clerical workers could be easily handled by the government. They drew the conclusion that if strike action was ever to be effective, then inter-departmental and all-grade combinations were required. It was this very relationship with such a powerful employer that led and drove strategies based on political and public campaigning. These workers also had a vested interest in reform of the service itself. In general terms, progress was being made – gradual – but progress, nonetheless. The adoption of concerted campaigning methods did not just constitute the easiest route, but the most likely to yield results in a period of reform and general expansion of the service.

The radical nature of the workforce and their determination to fight for their rights and conditions was demonstrated in the 1870s, when the government began employing boys and women in the civil service to cut costs and help dilute militant sentiment. 'Boys will do more than half a man's work for less than a man's wages' was one claim, while senior civil servant Sir Algernon West informed the Ridley Commission that women, besides being quick, accurate and intelligent, 'are cheap and there is no superannuation.'[8] Ironically, both these groups rapidly organised and became among the union's most radical elements. Indeed, it was from the ranks of the 'boy clerks' that W.J. Brown arose, a socialist who went on to become one of the most notable and influential leaders of civil service trade unionism.

By the close of the nineteenth century, the social investigator Arthur Baxter remarked:

> ...it is impossible to blink the fact that no other class of the community are so loud or so persistent in calling attention to their grievances... They are, indeed, trade unions of the most aggressive type, their only object being undoubtedly to obtain better conditions of employment and higher pay, an object which they have already largely accomplished by incessant agitation and, attempts were made to crush them.... Now they have reached the stage of being accorded generally a somewhat grudging recognition.[9]

This was an exaggerated assessment, but it gave an insight into the development of more confident, radical and well-organised civil service unions. It was also an insight into a new brand of union activist who, while steeped in the culture of civil service trade unionism, was also influenced by the ideas of socialism and independent working-class political representation. The rise of New Unionism in the latter part of the nineteenth century encouraged the most oppressed and marginalised within the unskilled sections of the working class to organise into new militant trade unions, recruited from a range of occupations and industries. This movement made a deep impression on the emerging leaders of civil service unionism.

The process of radicalisation deepened prior to the first world war, with further growth in both the workforce and in union membership. It was also set against the backdrop of the 1906 Liberal government, which expanded public services under pressure from the trade unions and the newly formed Labour Party.

It was symptomatic that W.J. Brown's Assistant Clerks' Association (ACA) grew from 554 members in 22 departments to 2,223 members in fifty-two departments between 1904–12.[10] Women typists also organised in protest at pay discrimination and achieved 90 per cent membership. Political agitation continued in pursuit of a whole series of demands, including opposition to controlled patronage in higher grades and in favour of equal pay, the right to political activity and for collective bargaining. The formation of a Civil Service Federation by nine unions in 1911 was a major step in inter-union cooperation. Links with the wider movement were further strengthened as other groups followed the example of the Association of Tax Clerks in affiliating to the Trades Union Congress (TUC); in 1916, the ACA leadership also organised a successful referendum to affiliate to the Labour Party.

Grievances were not entirely held in check during the first world war, and civil service unions agitated on issues such as the cost of living. When the government tried to extend working hours, joint campaigning by the unions, including a mass meeting in London, forced them to abandon their plans. Civil service workers were caught up in the wave of industrial militancy at the end of the war and civil service union membership increased as did union membership generally. In 1917, clerks at Woolwich Arsenal launched strike action over bonus payments, with female temporary postal workers striking a year later. In 1920, calls by the Irish TUC and Labour Party to protest the treatment of Irish political prisoners resulted in the formation of the Association of Irish Post Office Clerks, with Irish members of the Union of Postal Workers taking 24 hour strike action.

Reformism and bureaucratism

Since it had become increasingly clear that the trade union movement was not a temporary phenomenon but an industrial and political force to be reckoned with, the British ruling class, with self-regarding pride in its realistic, no-nonsense pragmatism, sought to engage those leaders whom they calculated could be brought under their influence. They aimed to incorporate them as unwanted but tolerated functionaries within a respectable and conforming political establishment. Many willing partners were to be found mainly, if not exclusively, among leaders of the more skilled sections of the working class. These were workers who had established a certain degree of security and status in society and who were more than willing to collaborate with the exploiters in the 'national interest'. Lenin commented in characteristically blunt terms: 'The leaders of this labour aristocracy constantly deserted to the bourgeoisie and were directly or indirectly in its pay. Marx earned the honour of incurring the hatred of these scoundrels by openly branding them as traitors.'[11] However, this approach was only one side of the ruling class's twin strategy. When strikes did occur, and specifically during periods of heightened class struggle, the old methods of legal and physical repression were ruthlessly employed.

The ideological justification underpinning class collaboration is reformism, the idea that the working class can, on an industrial, societal and political basis, secure concessions or reforms on a long-term or even permanent basis under capitalism. Conflict was to be resolved reasonably through negotiation and partnership, establishing a generally peaceful co-existence between worker and employer, and even between the classes. It is in this respect that reformism carries within itself the seeds of betrayal of working-class interests.

Reformism implies that the worker and employer, and on a wider level the working class and the capitalists, share the same ultimate interests and that progress can be achieved on a gradual basis, even to the point that class antagonisms disappear or are reduced to an insignificant level. Reformists, and even many of the left who would describe themselves as socialists, reject the fundamental insight of Marxism that class antagonisms are irreconcilable and that only a socialist transformation of society can end exploitation and secure stable, fulfilling lives for all.

Reformism had a basis in the experience of the working class; employers were often compelled to give concessions on wages and conditions. They did so based on cold calculation about the overall impact on their profits. It was often more cost-effective to settle disputes, especially when they were unable to break or defeat strikes.

Similarly, wider societal reforms by the government and state were conceded from above to prevent the threat of revolution from below. The resources that allowed this element of flexibility for the British ruling class were obtained through its super-exploitation of the colonial masses in a worldwide Empire, stretching from India to Ireland. This did not mean that the ruling class had any intention of voluntarily sharing its plunder with its own exploited workers. Concessions and reforms were won through struggle, not by moral appeals or supplication.

The labour and trade union movement, despite ebbs and flows in the balance of forces and shifts in consciousness and militancy, was growing in power and influence. The impression that accommodation could be reached, and the desire for mutually beneficial co-existence in preference to industrial and political strife, was crystallised in reformist ideology.

Reformism was also the ideological bedrock on which collaborationist union bureaucracies were built and developed. The rise of the 'professional' union negotiator became more prominent in the industrial unions during the first half of the twentieth century. Right-wing bureaucracies were being established around status-driven careerist full-time officials who, by dint of higher wages and a lifestyle removed from the membership, increasingly saw themselves as a 'diplomatic corps', or interlocutors, between workers and management, and effectively between the classes. They regarded their primary role as resolving grievances rather than organising workers to fight for concessions through militant struggle; managing expectations and policing activists became part of their job description.

The class war is not one battle but a series of conflicts, industrial and political, over extended periods of time, spanning many generations. At some junctures, temporary settlements and concessions may be won by individual sections or groups of workers, or indeed by the wider working class itself. The fact that these advances are possible tends to instil the idea that progress is permanently achievable – an illusion shattered in times of economic downturn and reaction. The employer and government always attempt to take back what was ceded under pressure, as they seek to maintain and accumulate profit, the imperative by which they seek to exercise control in the face of the capitalist system's own internal contradictions.

Unions are not revolutionary organisations, although given certain circumstances they can conduct struggles of a revolutionary nature. In industrial disputes their role is to negotiate settlements in their members' interests. Whether such outcomes meet workers' demands depends on a whole variety of factors in any given struggle. Ultimately, the balance of forces is decisive; strike action must be deliverable, sustainable, and effective to force concessions, or to stop attacks on wages and conditions. The level of combativity and militancy among the workforce, activists and leaderships in pursuit of demands which have the support of members is also critical, as is the effectiveness of specific strategies and tactics employed in a campaign or strike.

For the right-wing union bureaucrat or activist, these questions are rarely seriously considered; for them, the employer is almost always too strong and strikes never deliver. Nor does the ultra-leftist. For them a strike must deliver every single dot and comma of the union's demands, whatever the reality of the balance of forces; every settlement, whether or not supported by most members, is a sell-out. Both approaches appear to be opposites, but are two sides of the same coin, both rooted in opportunism and in an inability, or deliberate refusal, to understand the nature of class struggle. As already noted, this does not move in straight lines but in ebbs and flows, with advances and setbacks, often even in the same specific struggle.

This does not mean that socialists and communists are opposed to reforms, or regard such concessions as insignificant, or entirely illusory. On the contrary, those arguing for a revolutionary transformation of society and the abolition of capitalism are always the most consistent and determined fighters for concessions in industrial and political conflict. They are also the most consistent and articulate advocates of independent working-class representation. Nevertheless, it was the deeply rooted idea of reformism that became by far the dominant ideological force in the formation of the political wing of the trade union movement – the Labour Party.

Trade union bureaucratism and its interconnection with reformist ideology were also reflected in the distinctive development of the civil service trade unions, characterised by their specific relationship to their employer – the government and state. The result was the emergence of the Whitley System as the principal structure for collective bargaining.

The immediate background to 'Whitleyism' was the wave of militancy and strike action across Britain that followed in the wake of the Russian Revolution and the end of the first world war, even mobilising previously 'reliable' sections like the police. The ruling class was shocked by these developments and viewed the threat of strike action by civil servants – their own employees – with trepidation. They were also concerned by the expansion and growing organisational capability of the civil service unions, as joint campaigns were conducted throughout the service; attempts by some unions to build closer links with the TUC and with the Labour Party presented a further worrying development.

As masters of compromise under pressure, the British establishment demonstrates an impressive ingenuity in attempting to stall in the face of every problem by establishing a review or commission. In this case, the Liberal peer John Whitley was charged to look at the problem of industrial relations and come up with a solution. His 1918 report advocated joint work councils as a forum in which management and workers might settle grievances and advance cooperation without resorting to industrial action.[12] The government had not intended this system to be available to their own employees, but to serve as a template for the industrial sector, where it failed to take root in any real sense.

Some union left activists and leaders advocated the establishment of strike policies, but they were still very much aware of the major imbalance of power between unions and the state. They also grasped the difficulty of coordinating effective widespread action across a variety of associations and grades, with wide disparities in class composition. Nevertheless, the tempestuous revolutionary currents in wider society, coupled with the increasingly obvious discontent of its own workforce, led the government to concede union demands for the introduction of Whitleyism, as the system became known, into the civil service.

Whitleyism did deliver some benefits over the years, but it also tied the unions to a collaborative form of industrial relations that provided the government and its various departments with a relatively stable negotiating medium. This ensured that they could deliver their strategic priorities for the civil service within the parameters of broader economic and political policy. This was especially so in terms of expenditure, which had a direct bearing on pay rates and other related issues. Above all, the Whitley system of 'negotiated compromise' was designed to operate within boundaries marked out by the government.

Collectively and individually, the unions relied on developing existing methods of public, political and parliamentary campaigning to advance grievances on the core issues affecting their members. This tended to channel anger and militancy, while eschewing the strike weapon became a strong brake on the development of genuine collective bargaining. The competing concerns of different unions representing the full gamut of the workforce, from the highly paid, more conservative, higher grades, to the lower paid, also allowed the employer considerable room to divide and rule, leaving the more militant unions pursuing independent but often isolated activity. Tensions were particularly evident between unions representing clerical workers and those composed of industrial civil servants and postal workers, the latter employed in a revenue-making enterprise more closely resembling the relationship between industrial unions and private employers.

This highly structured form of institutionalised collaborationism encouraged the development of a bureaucratic culture in civil service trade unionism that was evident not only in activists and leaders of a conservative bent but also among the left, even those who considered themselves as militants. While some leaders sometimes threatened strike action, they still believed that the balance of forces, both organisationally and industrially, rested in the government's favour and that the Whitley system provided the better strategy for advancing members' interests.

Whitleyism was an alternative that suited both union leaders and the government, despite the latter's initial reluctance to concede to its introduction to its own workforce. Over the years, the system also provided fertile soil for the development of a particular stratum within the unions that strengthened the basis for collaborationism – lay bureaucratism. The stereotype of the bureaucrat as one employed by the union and elevated above the rank-and-file membership has considerable basis in fact, but it is only part of the story. The question of bureaucracy within the unions is wider than the role and nature of full-time officials.

As unions developed, the role of shop stewards, or elected union representatives, became increasingly significant. While many were committed, even militant, advocates for their members' demands and interests, others acted in the same collaborationist manner as the full-time right-wing bureaucrats. In the more extreme cases such lay representatives could become almost as completely detached from the workforce they represented. They were cheaply bought with time away from the workplace and integration into the negotiating officialdom. This, in turn, engendered a shared ambition to 'succeed', in other words to make deals that fell short of what members deserved. Lay activists could also police and manage workplace anger, militancy and expectations more effectively than full-timers, in some cases even acting as allies to right-wing bureaucracies in silencing socialist or communist activists.

Even in a union led by the left, the conservative lay bureaucrat is often a real obstacle to the development of militant struggle. In right-wing unions, such lay bureaucracies are meticulously constructed by the right wing, with the strategic purpose of developing a bulwark against militancy and genuine democratic expression. The Whitley system was a structure almost deliberately designed to produce such a lay bureaucracy.

Left and right

Formed in 1921, the Civil Service Clerical Association (CSCA) under its socialist general secretary W.J. Brown was at the forefront of campaigning and support for the Labour Party and cooperation with other TUC-affiliated unions.[13] It established a political fund that was the legal foundation for political campaigning, including standing or supporting parliamentary candidates; members who did not wish to pay the levy could do so by not paying their subscription for one month of the year.

Parliamentary activity had been a central feature of union campaign work and the CSCA developed considerable expertise in targeting and lobbying MPs of various parties on individual issues. In 1923, the union responded to a government refusal to concede in a pay rights case by supporting the Labour candidate in the Liverpool Edge Hill constituency, a highly effective campaign credited with unseating the Unionist candidate, John Waller Hills, who was financial secretary to the Treasury. W.J. Brown himself stood unsuccessfully for parliament in Uxbridge in 1922 and Wolverhampton West in 1923 and 1924.

During the 1926 General Strike, the CSCA and other central government and local government unions were in the TUC's 'Third Line', remaining at work and contributing the maximum financial and other practical support to the strikers. Brown moved an amendment calling for a series of 24-hour general strikes at the TUC's planning meeting in London. He gave full support to the miners who had been locked out by their employers but said that, 'two kinds of general strike were possible': the first, a 24-hour one which, 'was not a revolutionary act', and an indefinite one, which was. He stated the latter should not be embarked on unless, 'the ultimate upshot was revolution' and that, 'the use of a weapon which by its very nature was revolutionary, with no intention of making a revolution... 'could only lead to harm.' Correct as his analysis was, he did not even get the support of his own CSCA for his amendment.[14]

Brown bitterly lamented afterwards that, 'the half-hearted strike which none of the leaders except Cook [the miners' leader] was prepared to take to its logical conclusion... left the miners high and dry'. The TUC leaders, he argued, 'achieved a final debasement... by way of self-justification, the slogan, "Never again!" If, "never again" then why at all? And if at all, why, "never again."'[15]

The government was merciless in taking vengeance on the trade union movement following the defeat of the General Strike. The Trade Disputes and Trade Union Act (1927) outlawed secondary action and criminalised participation in incitement to take unlawful action. It also allowed the sequestration of union funds in such circumstances and outlawed mass picketing and enforced contracting-in to political levies. The civil service unions were specifically targeted; they were barred from operating political funds and prohibited from affiliating to the Labour Party and TUC, as well as from professional and international civil service organisations.

This deliberate attempt to further sever civil service trade unionism from the wider movement had a deep impact, but did not go without a response. A Parliamentary Fund was established for W.J. Brown by 'active individuals' who collected money from 'voluntary subscribers' and in the 1929 general election he stood for Wolverhampton West and won the seat for Labour.[16]

Nor did legal restrictions prevent civil service unions from campaigning for their demands, including during the period of the National Government in the early 1930s. Calls for public expenditure reduction to deal with the economic slump led to cuts in civil service workers' pay. Despite the industrial weakness of the unions, fightbacks against attacks on pay and conditions were launched, which included demonstrations in major cities, notably a 100,000 turn-out in London in October 1931.[17]

The influence of socialism and of individuals like W.J. Brown played a significant part in the development of civil service trade unionism. Brown was from the London working class, a union activist from his teens. A committed socialist and a member of the Independent Labour Party, he was greatly influenced by the New Unionism and the October Revolution.

Yet, he was an idiosyncratic figure who made no real attempt to build an organised left presence even within his own union; he even clashed with fellow socialists in the CSCA when he left the governing Labour Party in 1931 in protest at its failure to advance workers' interests. He initially aimed to set up a new workers' party, but split from Oswald Mosley, one of his fellow rebels, over Mosley's nascent fascism. The union conference overturned an executive recommendation to end his political candidature, but he still lost his Wolverhampton seat, standing on an Independent Labour ticket in 1931.[18]

During the second world war, he stood again for parliament, winning Rugby from the Tories as an independent in 1942; he was re-elected three years later, but lost the seat in 1950. Disillusioned by party politics and by the Soviet Union, where he had spent six months during the mid-1920s, he moved to the right. Brown made attacks on the TUC and the Communist Party, consorted with press baron Beaverbrook and went so far as to argue against CSCA's re-affiliation to the TUC and Labour Party, when restrictions were removed by the Attlee-led Labour government in 1946. Brown's insistence on a right to complete freedom of expression as an MP, whilst remaining parliamentary secretary of CSCA, led to repeated clashes with the left-dominated National Executive Committee (NEC). He was grudgingly allowed to remain in his paid position until his retirement in 1948, but after his departure, delegates at the annual conference the next year angrily protested the generosity of his severance arrangements.[19]

While socialists from the Labour Party left had played a key role in the leadership of the CSCA from the 1920s, by the 1940s, the NEC was reported to be, 'dominated by Communists and their allies'.[20] Len White, who had succeeded Brown as general secretary, was a member of the editorial board of the *Daily Worker* newspaper (predecessor to the *Morning Star*), but denied being a member of the Communist Party.

Industrial unions had witnessed the development of rank-and-file socialist groupings – 'broad lefts' – in reaction to double-dealing by right-wing trade union leaders. The most significant betrayal was Black Friday in 1921, when locked-out mineworkers resisting deep pay cuts were betrayed by leaders of the Triple Alliance of miners, railway and transport workers. This emboldened Lloyd George's government to launch a full-scale assault on pay, terms and conditions. Following this defeat and that of the General Strike, socialists like the miners' leader, A.J. Cook, a founding member of the Communist Party, led efforts to organise the left both industrially and politically against the right wing, resulting in the formation of the National Minority Movement, a template for the establishment of future militant broad left groupings.

Socialists and communists in civil service unions were also organised, as is attested by their consistent presence in the CSCA leadership, not as open, broad left-type formations but as 'secret' lefts. The fragility of such an approach was exposed when the right wing, who had always organised in secret, adopted a more open organisational form. Battles between socialists and the right wing within the trade union movement are in themselves a critical and concentrated form of the wider class war in society. While these antagonisms existed from the beginning of civil service trade unionism, as Brown's case demonstrates, they would develop in a far sharper form under the post-war Labour government.

Post-war developments

The 1945 election led to major advances for working people. These included the nationalisation of major industries and the creation of the welfare state, with its twin pillars of the National Health Service (NHS) and an expanded social security system. Efforts were made to tackle endemic social problems like disease, poverty and unemployment which were still familiar to a population which had lived through the 1930s, conditions that they were no longer willing to tolerate, especially after the enormous sacrifice involved in defeating fascism in the second world war.

The decline of Britain as an imperial power and the emergence of the United States as a hegemonic force in the world order saw Britain mortgage its interests, economic and political, to US capital. The Marshall Plan was ostensibly a massive investment intended to rebuild the European economies devastated by war, but its central purpose was to stop the spread of communism and create markets for American goods and services. The main condition for aid set by the United States was an austerity programme, limiting the Labour government's freedom of action in introducing the reforms demanded by the working class. There was also a political price to pay. America demanded full and unconditional support for the Cold War through Britain's active participation in the newly established North Atlantic Treaty Organisation (NATO). On the home front, pressure was applied on the government to curb the rise of militant trade unionism and the increasingly influential shop steward movement.

With press backing, anti-communist witch-hunts were initiated by the Labour government and right-wing trade union leaders. They were assisted by employers who sacked and black-listed workers, while the judiciary delivered its legal backing to the wave of victimisation and reaction. Left-wing Labour MPs were expelled and various communist-led organisations banned. In early 1949, the TUC's right wing published anti-communist pamphlets such as *Defending Democracy: Communist Activities Examined* and *The Tactics of Disruption,* which were distributed to affiliated unions.

Labour Party chairman, Morgan Phillips, had already prepared the ground:

> We can expect a campaign of sabotage against the Labour government and all it stands for by communists and their fellow travellers, with communist-inspired attempts to foment discontent in the factories and workshops, which may result in slowing down and hampering the production drive, on which our national prosperity and recovery depends... We can also expect intensified attempts to continue their efforts to undermine and destroy the Labour movement from within, particularly the activities within the trade union movement in the interests of the Communist Party... Now is the time for all Labour people to go out on a great campaign against communist intrigue and infiltration in the Labour movement.[21]

There followed bans on communists from holding union office in the Transport and General Workers Union (TGWU) among others, a policy driven by right-wing general secretary Arthur Deakin, and enacted in July 1949. Meanwhile, the TUC General Council urged working people to, 'open [their] eyes to the dangerous subversive activities which are being engineered' against, 'the declared policy of the trade union movement.' Communist dockers' leader Jack Dash would later describe this time of 'Deakinism' as 'McCarthyism'.

Socialist trade unionists and Communist Party activists, who had built a strong base in the civil service unions, opposed the US-inspired austerity measures. As a result, they were labelled as 'abject and slavish agents of forces working incessantly to increase social misery'. CSCA general secretary Len White opposed the TUC position, stating:

> The TUC document *Defending Democracy*, in which it called for action against communists in trade unions, was an attempt by the general council to incite political discrimination in a union which had no political ties...

We are quite capable of dealing with any people of the left, right or centre who abuse their position. The time has come for the TUC to mind its own business and let us mind ours.[22]

The CSCA NEC backed White, but the TUC stance set the ground for right-wingers to attack the union leadership. As one London branch secretary wrote:

...our general secretary and deputy secretary are believed to be communists – or near-communists – and some 13 members of our present national executive committee support the communist "line" even if they may not be members of the party. That is the problem we have to face and the battle we have to fight.[23]

Union witch-hunts are almost always predicated on the need to deal with workers' industrial opposition. During the late 1940s, strikes were met with the full force of the state, including the prosecution of London dockers and the use of the Emergency Powers Act.

Civil service trade unions were also placed under intense scrutiny by prime minister Attlee, resulting in purges of communists from the civil service, albeit on a small scale. During the second world war when Britain and the Soviet Union were allies, the CSCA's communist-led NEC had appointed several communists or supporters to key full-time posts. But as early as 1945, Len White, questioning a tendency to 'to engage in propaganda', said that he doubted their views represented those of the general membership. As the Cold War intensified, an open right wing formed in the CSCA. As is often the case with such groupings, they described themselves as 'moderates', openly challenging the union leadership, under the name of the Conference Campaign Committee (CCC).

The CCC opposed the Executive's proposal to re-affiliate to the Labour Party as they claimed it was an attempt to use it to attack the party leadership's Cold War stance, most noticeably its pro-

American foreign policy and its austerity programme. They found willing allies among the union's full-time officers and Labour Party moderates, including future TUC general secretary and anti-communist witch-hunter, Vic Feather. The wider establishment, particularly the press and media, gave widespread publicity to the group's Red Scare tactics.

The CCC demonstrated an organisational efficiency and determination that shook the NEC and the wider left. They communicated directly with branches, published propaganda attacking the executive which they claimed had placed politics above members' concerns.

When the Executive fought back and published a record of the union's achievements and the work it had done to advance members' interests, the CCC published electoral slates listing their candidates prior to NEC elections, which were held at the national conference based on branch nominations. At the 1948 conference, the first time such slates were published, the CCC made considerable electoral gains and in the next few years achieved a working majority.[24]

Events in the CSCA were linked to the government's determination to channel civil service activists away from political activity. The 1949 Masterman Committee, although drawing a distinction for industrial civil servants for whom it recommended political freedom, tightened the rules for clerical workers, even for the lower grades. Anyone who wished to stand for parliament had to resign.[25]

Although right-wing factions claimed that their non-political stance allowed a concentration on serving members' interests, the exact opposite was true. The union's 1950 annual conference censured CCC Executive members who had opposed conference policy on pay. This feature of their leadership would be at the core of the battles between left and right in the 1970s through to the 1990s, when they repeatedly ignored conference policy.

Witch-hunting drives in the civil service unions were remarkably enduring. In 1961, the Tory government came under pressure over a series of spy scandals. Prime minister Harold Macmillan established an inquiry under Lord Radcliffe, which offered an opportunity to target communists in civil service trade unions who, it was argued, were a danger to national security. Radcliffe expressed serious concern about the presence and influence of communists, among both full-time and lay officials, particularly those on union national executive committees.[26] A ban on any suspected communist union officials entering government premises or negotiating on behalf of civil service workers resulted in half a dozen full-time union officials losing their jobs. The Labour Party's right-wing leader, Hugh Gaitskill, backed Radcliffe. The report provided ammunition to Gaitskill in his campaign to extirpate socialist policies and ideas from the party itself. He encouraged and assisted moderate union leaders, intent on rooting out militancy, to impose their own internal bans on communists holding union positions and to try to neuter the powerful shop steward movement.

The civil service was also undergoing significant change during these decades. The continuing development of the welfare state meant another phase of expansion, accompanied by a growth in union membership and a drive for union mergers. Another feature of the post-war period was the dispersal of civil service work and workers away from London; in 1931, 72.5 per cent of the civil service was based in London, but by 1977, the figure was just 26 per cent. Accompanied by a marked proletarianisation of the civil service workforce, this geographical shift helped in building effective trade unionism.

However, gains won by the British working class in the post-war period did not mean a truce in the class war. They were instead the product of ruling class caution at the potential strength of a trade union movement which by the 1970s was thirteen million strong. But the end of the economic upswing during these decades also signalled the intention of the capitalist class on an international basis to take back those gains which had been achieved over generations of struggle. This was a project long in the planning. In Britain it meant the long-term dismantling of the welfare state, including social security and the NHS, along with other governmental and local authority services like council housing. The public sector cuts by the James Callaghan-led Labour government in the late 1970s would result in the so-called 'Winter of Discontent'. Unions representing workers from both the private and public sectors took industrial action. Many public sector workers engaged in large-scale activity for the first time, including civil servants. This marked a qualitative development in workers' resistance to attacks on their conditions and in defence of public services.

Ruling-class reformers had once created a civil service capable of administering the most powerful capitalist nation on earth. However, by the late 1970s, public sector workers and service users alike were faced by the consequences of a system and a country in economic and political decline. In the future, every government from Callaghan onwards would place cuts and privatisation at the centre of their programmes. These were implemented with varying degrees of intensity and savagery, according to the level of resistance met from the unions and other campaigning social movements. Margaret Thatcher's comment that 'there is no such thing as society' was more than the provocative goading of the left by a neoliberal philistine. It was an ideological statement of intent to which the subsequent decades of attacks on public services have borne witness – a race to the bottom in the interests of corporate power and profiteering.

Even prior to the economic downturn, the adoption of a strike policy in 1969 by the newly renamed Civil and Public Services Association already indicated the development of a more militant consciousness among the union's largely working-class membership. This set the conditions for the development of a cadre of militant socialist activists, who would later organise themselves formally as Broad Left. Meanwhile, the right wing had coalesced in ideological and organisational form within the rebranded National Moderate Group, representing big business and state interests and acting as a surrogate for Conservative and right-wing Labour opinion within the union. Against the backdrop of the neoliberal reaction, a relentless struggle would continue over the next two decades to defeat collaborationist methods and build a fighting union capable of defending and representing members' interests.

....

Notes & References

1. V.I. Lenin, 'On Strikes', *Collected Works*, vol.4, Progress Publishers, Moscow, 1964, pp.310-319. First published in *Proletarskaya Revolyutsiya*, No. 8–9, 1924.

2. *Report of the Organisation of the Permanent Civil Service*, Northcote–Trevelyan Report, 1854.

3. B.V. Humphreys, *Clerical Unions in the Civil Service*, Blackwell & Mott, London, 1958, p.7.

4. *The Independent*, 13 July 2004.

5. *Establishment matters; First Report of the Civil Service Inquiry Commission*, Playfair Commission, 1875.

6. Humphreys, *Clerical Unions*, p.18.

7. E. Wigham, *From Humble Petition to Militant Action: A History of the Civil and Public Services Association, 1903–1978*, Civil and Public Services Association, London, 1980, p.8.

8. Humphreys, *Clerical Unions*, p.32.

9. Humphreys, *Clerical Unions*, pp.36–7.

10. B. Newman, *Yours for Action*, McCorquodale, London, 1953.

11. V.I. Lenin, '"Left-wing" Communism: an Infantile Disorder', *Selected Works*, Progress Publishers, Moscow, 1968, pp.512–585.

12. Great Britain. Ministry of Reconstruction. Commission on Relations between Employers and Employed. Final Report, Cd, 9153, London, 1918.

13. The new union was formed by the merger of the Civil Service Clerical Union and the Clerical Officers' Association. It was renamed the Civil and Public Services Association (CPSA) in 1969.

14. *London Daily Chronicle*, 30 April 1926.

15. W.J. Brown, *So Far…*, George Allen & Unwin, London, 1943.

16. *Western Morning News*, 1 June 1929.

17. *Reynold's Illustrated Newspaper*, 13 October 1931.

18. *Leicester Evening Mail*, 28 October 1931.

19. *Western Morning News*, 25 May 1949.

20. *Daily Herald*, 22 December 1947.

21. *Daily Herald*, 22 December 1947.

22. *Newcastle Journal*, 27 May 1949.

23. M. Gerth, *Anti-Communism in Britain During the Cold War: A Very British Witch-Hunt*, University of London Press, London, 2023.

24. *Evening News*, 18 May 1948.

25. *Report of the Masterman Committee on the political activities of Civil Servants*, Cmd. 7718, 1949.

26. *Committee of Enquiry into Civil Service Security Procedure (Radcliffe Committee) Report*, 1961–62.

Daily Mail
COMMENT

A threat to democracy

THE election of John Macreadie as leader of the Civil Service union the CPSA has for the first time hoisted a member of the Militant Tendency into power in a major union and given him a seat on the general council of the TUC.

His opponents say that he won through a variety of malpractices including the giving of inadequate notice of the ballot and holding it at awkward times in inconvenient places.

Even so he only won by a wafer-thin majority, so that skulduggery in just one large branch could have swung the vote his way.

It is to the credit of the union that it is undertaking an inquiry into the election which may lead to Mr Macreadie's being ousted.

Its members though have little else to be proud of in that their apathy, reflected in a low poll, allowed a member of a subversive organisation to grab the reigns of power.

Mr Peter Bruinvels, MP, wants the Government to purge the Civil Service of supporters of Militant. He has a point. The Militants create mayhem wherever they settle.

Positioned in the heart of our Civil Service they are a threat to our democracy.

■ The Daily Mail, 09/03/86

Quelling riots

IN the Tottenham riots last October
--- 300 police injuries and p c

2. The struggle against the Moderates

Battlelines

Post-war civil service growth and decentralisation brought mainly women and young workers into the civil service, a process replicated in other areas of the public services. In previous generations, they would have found employment in industry. Class loyalty to the labour and trade union movement was based on an understanding of the gains by their forebears – the NHS, the welfare state, advances in living standards, education and workers' rights. The period was also one of enormous political upheaval; French workers in 1968 came close to toppling the established order with a ten-million-strong General Strike, and a mass Vietnam anti-war movement developed internationally.

Whenever the government, Labour or Tory, set an incomes policy, public sector workers, and particularly civil servants, were first in line for an attack on their living standards. The need for a strike policy was a recognition that the Whitley system alone was no longer sustainable. Motions to the CSCA conference in 1969 called on the NEC to 'formulate a strike policy' and create a new name for the union.[1] Following the conference, the union's name was changed to the Civil and Public Services Association (CPSA) and the new strike policy was drawn up by the general secretary, Bill Kendall, a former communist who had embraced Catholicism. It made use of traditional public, political and mass protest campaigning methods such as work-to-rule and overtime bans. The key principle was selective action with relatively small groups of workers acting on behalf of other members involved in the dispute. Selective strikes in the revenue-gathering services, for example, would have an immediate impact on the finances of the government.

For an entire section of the trade union movement that had never taken industrial action, the introduction of a strike policy was a huge step forward. CPSA members were to take their first action in 1973 against the Heath government's pay freeze, and again in 1979, during the Winter of Discontent, in pursuit of a twenty per cent pay claim from Callaghan's Labour government. On both occasions some gains were secured for members. Selective action also had an impact in departmental disputes like the Air Traffic Control assistant's strike in 1977 led by John Macreadie, Frank Bonner and Alistair Nicholson. However, the limitations of an industrial action strategy based almost exclusively on this specific tactic would become clear in the 1981 pay strike.

The new policy heralded the entry of an important section of workers, however tentatively at first, into the arena of industrial struggle. Although the right-wing bureaucracy sought to downplay its significance, this marked a clean break with the self-imposed limitations of the past, enabling civil service workers to fight back. It was a step from which there would be no return. Its adoption was also a major setback for the right-wing, and for the government and the state; it signified a loss of the control with which they had previously contained civil service workers' campaigning options. Only 'political' campaigning, lobbying, or negotiating within the Whitley system had been permissible – never strike action. No matter how much they tried to downplay the importance of the policy, it seriously diminished the prestige and authority of the establishment, reflecting as it did, the proletarianisation of the government's own workforce, and a widening political and social gulf developing along class lines.

The National Moderate Group, which had tried to resist the strike policy, brought together various right-wing elements in the CPSA. It was financed and supported by reactionary front organisations linked to the government and intelligence agencies of the United States and Britain. The Group also formed part of a network of pro-NATO Atlanticist Labour MPs and trade union leaders, such as Frank Chapple of the electricians' union EETPU. Their aim was to drive out socialist ideas, activists and organisations from the labour and trade union movement.

CPSA activists and campaigning journalists like Paul Foot, Seumas Milne and Paul Osler exposed the real relationships and interests that the Moderates represented.[2] The Jim Conway Foundation, for example, was a CIA front organisation that received funding from various sources, including an £80,000 donation from a Tory Party-managed trust fund in 1994. Meanwhile, the Trade Union Committee for European and Transatlantic Understanding (TUCETU) had close links to the American Embassy and was run for 40 years by an individual later revealed as a CIA asset. The Movement for True Industrial Democracy (TRUMID) was the brainchild of SAS founder, Colonel David Stirling, who had planned paramilitary action against strikers in the 1970s. Adding much-needed spiritual heft was Catholic Action, an international lay crusade against the spread of communism. Support for the Moderates also came from some rather nefarious individuals, such as Roger Windsor, whom MI5 attempted to place in a CPSA full-time position, a move blocked by activist Ray Alderson, a Communist Party member, who challenged his references. Windsor went on to secure a position in the National Union of Mineworkers (NUM) where he played a controversial role in the Miners' Strike of 1984–5.

The election of the Thatcher government in 1979 was a key event in a worldwide reactionary assault by capital aimed at clawing back reforms won by the working class. The public services were a major target. The method was systematic disinvestment, cuts, and privatisation, along with the abandonment of class cooperation and 'social contracts'. But beyond that was also an attempt to smash the labour and trade union movement, politically and industrially, and in particular its left wing.

Thatcher revived the well-tested theme that public spending was a wasteful extravagance. Tory propaganda portrayed the civil service as bloated and unaccountable to democratically elected governments. Their strategic aim was to cut jobs and services, drive down conditions and hand over assets, including the civil service estate. The Tories understood that their economic policies would provoke resistance from the working class. Accordingly, 'reforms' aimed at purging the civil service of its public service ethos, which they regarded as a form of 'socialism', thus ensuring a politically reliable state vehicle delivering for profit, not people.

The Tories were concerned about the threat of an activist base in the civil service unions, strengthening resistance among members whose pay, terms and conditions would now be under consistent and unrelenting assault. These processes were underway in all the civil service unions representing manual and specialist grades: the Civil Service Union (CSU); the Inland Revenue Staff Federation (IRSF); the professional and technical specialist union, Institution of Professionals, Managers and Specialists (ISPMS); and the executive grades union, the Society of Civil and Public Servants (SCPS).

It was in this context that the National Moderate Group in CPSA operated as the Tories' 'quislings'. During Thatcher's premiership, Tory ministers met weekly with senior civil servants and union officials to discuss developments in the civil service and to finesse the most effective methods to break the workplace influence of union representatives. The political orientation of leaders like Kate Losinska, presented by the media as 'a London housewife', who held the union's presidency at various times, was wholly in step with free-market advocates.[3] Indeed, the Moderates became key advisers to Tory minister Norman Tebbit as he drew up the government's anti-union legislation.

The Moderates' main political function was to prosecute the class war within the labour movement in the interests of the capitalist class. The Tory government under prime minister Edward Heath had been brought down by the NUM's militant action in 1974, and attempts by both Labour and Tory governments to impose anti-union legislation had floundered in the face of mass opposition. The collective strength of the trade union movement in this period was a major factor influencing the outcome of the unfolding battle between the classes, which by no means was a settled question. It could have meant a fundamental return of power and wealth for the ruling class, or the prospect of an alternative to the profit system and the building of a socialist society.

Like other right-wing groupings in the trade union movement, the Moderates presented themselves as 'non-political' and 'non-factional'. Their sole aim was supposedly to represent ordinary workers while exposing militants, subversives and strike-happy activists whose hidden aim was to overthrow capitalist society. In this they had the full support of the press who were happy as always to run Red Scare exposés. Moderate leaders also had full access to establishment figures, including anti-socialist and anti-communist Labour MPs like Brian Walden, TUC bureaucrats and fixers, as well as the intelligence services and Tory politicians. The foundations for this 'collaborative' approach had been set out publicly in 1975 by Kate Losinska in a *Reader's Digest* article, 'The Marxist Battle for Britain', which called for action to prevent a left-wing takeover.[4] She got straight to the point: 'With their massive and covert recruitment of public sector employees – nearly ten per cent of the active membership of my union now supports the militant-left – Marxists are simply following a blueprint that helped bring control in Eastern Europe'.

She went on to identify public sector strikes, a relatively recent phenomenon, as a warning sign: 'With local and central government paralysed, extremists could conceivably take over the whole country'. The biggest casualty of Marxist militancy, she explained, 'has been the tradition that public servants would, whatever their grievances, carry on with their duties'. She concluded: 'Our hard-pressed security forces now face many new tasks. At one time they were mainly concerned in catching traitors passing State secrets to Soviet bloc countries. Today they must also check the subtler sabotage of Trotskyists prepared to do anything to discredit the State'.

Losinska was crystal clear on the pro-capitalist politics of the Moderates. They would strenuously oppose the idea that public sector workers should take strike action to defend themselves and rejected any concept of unity with other trade unionists in fighting for the interests of the wider working class. She also gave an equally explicit warning that socialists and communists were to be treated as enemies of the state and that all methods were permissible in suppressing militancy, including dehumanising activists: 'In the first place most militants are loners. They don't get their satisfaction or make their mark down avenues that most people tread... their politics are a product of a serious personality defect'.

The anger of activists at her widely publicised comments led to a motion of censure against her at the union conference. A censure motion is usually a mechanism of democratic accountability that allows the conference – the parliament and ruling body of the union – to demonstrate its disapproval of the actions of the executive or elected union officials. On this occasion, the president characteristically took legal action to stop it from being debated.[5]

The Moderates would continuously hold office, with just a few short periods of left leadership, from the late 1970s until 1998, when the new Public and Commercial Services Union (PCS) was created by a merger of CPSA and the Public, Tax and Commerce Services Union – which itself had brought together the IRSF, the CSU and the SCPS. During their decades of power, the Moderates' primary role was to aid the government in reshaping the civil service through cuts, privatisation, decentralisation and marketisation. In order to achieve this, they would appeal to the more conservative elements in the union's membership, while policing the union's activist base. As well as smearing the left, they consciously sought to dampen members' expectations and subvert union democracy through their refusal to implement conference policy. These methods became increasingly crude and ineffectual over the years, but from the cold, calculating viewpoint of the ruling class, the Moderates served their interests very well. Kate Losinska was awarded an OBE in 1985.

Offering an alternative: a fighting left

From their early days, trade unions have witnessed struggles between left and right, and between the forces of left reformism and Marxism. This is a concrete manifestation of the wider class struggle which finds its most continuous and sharpest form in the workplace.

Like other sections of their class, low-paid civil service workers, mainly in clerical grades, looked to their unions to combat attacks on living standards and conditions of service. Communist Party and Labour Party left-wingers had for decades been most prominent in organising the left within civil service unions. However, as indicated in Losinska's *Reader's Digest* comments, the state and right-wing were becoming increasingly concerned with the growing influence of Trotskyist groupings like the International Socialists who became the Socialist Workers Party (SWP) in 1977 and the Militant Tendency, which formed the Socialist Party in 1997.

The Communist Party still held considerable influence within industrial and general unions in the 1970s, particularly through the extensive shop steward movement and party branches in factories, shipyards, mines and depots.[6] In the civil service it operated as a more discreet 'secret left', a consequence of the anti-communist Cold War witch-hunts. Despite the self-evident limitations of this form of organisation, communists in unions like CPSA played a role in blocking right-wing forces from winning complete control of the civil service trade union movement.

Standing in distinction to this 'secret' form of organising was the open 'broad left'. This can be defined as a democratic rank-and-file body of socialist activists within a trade union who are committed to building a united front to defend and promote members' interests. It aims to grow union strength in the workplace, promote socialist ideas among activists and members, and build links with socialists in other unions and progressive organisations through joint activity, unity and solidarity.

In the 1970s, the Communist Party took a strategic decision to organise within emerging broad left alliances. In the CPSA, pressure from organisations such as Militant, the SWP, Labour lefts and independents encouraged the Communist Party to play a significant role in establishing the union's Broad Left grouping. Pressure for this development had come particularly from Militant activists like Kevin Roddy and Doreen Purvis, who were from the lower-paid clerical grades of the Department of Health and Social

Security (DHSS), who along with Department of Employment workers, were at the sharp end of direct government assaults on pay and conditions. They also faced pressure due to the growing attacks on the welfare services that they provided to the most disadvantaged section of their own class. Others included Chris Baugh from the Land Registry, a major figure in CPSA and PCS Militant and later Socialist Party group, who served one year as national vice-president in a Moderate-led NEC and who was later elected assistant general secretary of PCS. Also prominent was Tony Conway, a Communist Party member, who served as National Broad Left organiser. A leading figure in Unity, a Communist Party-inspired inter-union grouping, he was elected to the PCS NEC in 2006, before becoming a full-time officer in 2011.

The CPSA Broad Left was formed on two key principles: to advance and defend the interests of CPSA members, and to advocate socialist ideas and fight for a socialist society. These principles captured the profound ideological difference between socialists and the right-wing. Within Broad Left there was common agreement that promoting the interests of their members was both a political and an industrial question. Attacks on members came from the same source – the government, which represented the interests of the capitalist class and the profit system. If workers were to achieve a stable and secure existence, it could only be based on the socialist transformation of society.

The CPSA Broad Left's organisational structure broadly reflected that of the union itself, it was a national organisation with elected national, departmental and regional committees. Where there were sufficient members, town and city groups were also formed with a key organising focus in the branches and workplaces. It adopted a united front strategy which, in simple terms, meant that different socialist groups and independents from a range of viewpoints were pledged to work and campaign together while retaining their separate identities.

Militant and other Trotskyist groupings argued for the 'right to tendency'. This meant the right to disagree and campaign against agreed Broad Left policy whilst adhering to the minimal but critical requirement for groups and individuals to retain membership. In practice, this meant supporting Broad Left candidates and not standing in union elections in opposition to them.

The united front approach contained difficulties and dangers within a union broad left organisation. The narrow self-interest of individual groups could become elevated above that of the wider organisation. On the other hand, the impetus to maintain unity could also bring pressure to accept compromises that diluted or abandoned programmes, policies and even methods. The danger lay in adopting aspects of opportunism, class conciliation and bureaucratism in which the pursuit of electoral power could override the socialist principles on which the organisation was formed. These issues aside, the formation of the Broad Left in the CPSA represented a major advance in leading resistance to the Moderates and the government. It became the foundation upon which one of the strongest and most effective rank-and-file socialist organisations in British trade union history was built.

Broad Left's aim was to develop socialist policies for the union, which meant addressing the bread-and-butter pay, terms and conditions, issues affecting members in the workplace and developing policies and strategies to deliver them. Internal issues of union democracy were also openly and fiercely debated. One example was the formation of a Campaign for Union Democracy to win support to replace the branch workplace block vote with 'one-member-one vote', a position that prevailed on the left despite strong opposition from Militant at the time. Yet, issues affecting the working class more generally were not neglected. Political campaigning covered housing, anti-racism, women's rights, and international issues, including international solidarity with the anti-apartheid struggle in South Africa and opposing sectarian divisions in Northern Ireland.

Quite hypocritically given Losinksa's own posturing, the Moderates sought to label Broad Left attempts to discuss such wider issues within the democratic structures of the union as 'political' and of no relevance to members' terms and conditions, claiming it was evidence of the left's 'nefarious and subversive' and 'extremist' socialist agenda. But contrary to the Moderates' narrow 'business unionism', such issues did concern members and appeared as legitimate areas for policy and campaigning, as they affected workers in their day-to-day lives. Discussions on issues such as Apartheid and Northern Ireland, for example, were often the most animated and participatory at workplace and annual general meetings.

The right-wing caricature of 'non-political' ordinary workers, prey to communist or Trotskyist agitators, was repeatedly employed to smear Broad Left activists. The 'agitator' stereotype, usually portrayed as arriving from 'outside', or 'parachuted' into unions or working-class communities to stir up discontent, remains a favourite trope in right-wing politics and popular culture. One example is *The Angry Silence* (1960), a crude anti-communist and anti-trade union film, directed by Guy Green and starring Richard Attenborough as a lone 'hero' working through an industrial dispute.

Despite such cartoonish portrayals, the establishment was fully aware that workers could not be convinced to stand up against the status quo, and certainly not take strike action, simply through the prompting of manipulative 'agitators'. Workers will consider action when they have no other choice but to defend their conditions, or when they sense a real opportunity to advance their terms and conditions. In the period from the mid-1970s almost all struggles were defensive struggles. The political orientation of the activist base of any union was therefore an issue of critical importance, as it largely determined whether employers would have a free hand or meet resistance. However, union representatives will only succeed if what they are saying relates to workers' own experiences. They must present a realistic strategy to address grievances and ambitions. While a union bureaucrat dampens enthusiasm by telling workers how difficult it is to fight back, the activist explains the need for struggle but honestly admits that victory is possible but not guaranteed.

The role of socialists and communists in the workplace and in the union is to explain why conditions are under attack and to show what must be done. Based on the principles of democratic participation and decision-making, they aim to organise their fellow workers, building confidence and solidarity. No socialist has ever gone into a workplace and conjured up a strike where there was no grievance – that is fantasy. The conditions must exist for struggle to occur. When civil service workers in the early 1980s entered a period of unrelenting struggle, it was because of unrelenting attacks on conditions, jobs and pay.

1981 pay strike

The Tories saw the trade union movement as a major obstacle to be confronted and neutralised. Provoking confrontation with the unions was a necessity if they were to advance their strategy of achieving a fundamental shift in favour of capital, but they had been badly stung by the forced retreats of the early 1970s. Under Margaret Thatcher, however, they hoped that civil service unions would prove an easier touch. They were encouraged in this view when the CPSA's Moderate-dominated NEC acquiesced to a new technology programme which, if fully implemented, would mean tens of thousands of job losses. Accordingly in early 1981, the government suspended a national pay agreement and withheld a pay comparability report. Despite inflation running at fifteen per cent, a six per cent pay award was imposed.

The founding of an open Broad Left had led to the emergence of a cadre of socialist activists whose influence had steadily increased. They now demanded 'effective action' and a coordinated response from all nine civil service trade unions under the Council of Civil Service Unions (CCSU). This included civil servants working in defence, unemployment benefit offices, Jobcentres, skill centres, social security, passports, taxation, revenue and customs, courts, immigration, and other services and departments.

In January 1981, a CPSA special pay conference agreed on a fifteen per cent pay demand. It also backed this with a strategy to achieve it. This set out that no section of the membership should be excluded, but that selective strike action should be taken in the most effective areas – customs, immigration and the Civil Aviation Authority. [7] Other components included a one-day strike of all members; consultation with other civil service unions to set up 'all unions' campaign committees; a strike levy; and regular information bulletins. Industrial action was to be escalated as and when circumstances required.

The dispute began with a one-day civil service-wide strike followed by long-term selective action, involving as few as 5,000 workers in key areas. This was accompanied by short-term guerrilla action – such as walkouts, work-to-rules and go-slows. Such tactics had been successfully applied in previous campaigns, such as the Air Traffic Control and British Telecom computer centre disputes. Unfortunately, the Tories had prepared and were determined to stand firm against the CCSU strategy of relying on small groups of workers supported by strike pay and members' levies to win disputes. For their part, the CPSA Broad Left argued that selective action of itself would be insufficient to move the government. Leaders like Broad Left's Kevin Roddy argued that members must be prepared for an escalation towards all-out action if necessary. To demonstrate that all other routes and methods had been tried, it was necessary that a 'strategy of intensification' be adopted.

The government was immediately shaken by the first wave of national one-day strikes in March 1981, which paralysed central government services across the country, including ports and airports.[8] Downing Street itself was picketed. The strikes were solidly supported, particularly in large workplaces like the Longbenton and Washington child benefit centres. Over 600 members walked out at the army pay unit, disrupting contract payments for the British Army. In Southampton, holidaymakers walked through empty customs stands, manual workers were sent home from the Portsmouth Naval Dockyard when supervisors struck, driving tests were cancelled, Gatwick and Heathrow airports were shut, and in Manchester air traffic engineers took their first ever strike action, organising joint picket lines with other civil servants. A walkout at the health physics departments at Devonport and Rosyth seriously impaired the re-fitting of new nuclear submarines in dry dock, while silent protests brought workers' discontent and anger to the door of the 'brass-hats'.[9]

Selective action was also taken by workers at the Government Communications Headquarters (GCHQ) in Cheltenham – a key element of US and UK intelligence gathering. This 'threat to national security' directly contributed to the subsequent union ban there.[10] Threats to bring in military personnel to break the strike led to pledges of solidarity from the TGWU, which represented many civil service industrial workers. Action in supposedly no-go areas like the Ministry of Defence and the courts shook the Tories and provoked hysterical rage from the media. Strikers were accused of 'putting personal gain before the defence of the realm' and being 'parasitical and without public conscience'.[11] But anachronistic press stereotypes of the 'pen-pusher, brolly brigade' were belied by the social composition of the civil service workforce, now predominantly working class, proud and committed union members who were prepared to fight for their pay, terms and conditions.

By April, government income was halved due to selective strike action in the Inland Revenue and VAT computer centres and it was reported that £5.5 billion had been withheld from the Treasury. Government borrowing went up threefold and chancellor Geoffrey Howe conceded, 'action was doing substantial damage to government finances'.[12] Pay increases were due on 1 April, but the Moderate leadership failed to coordinate action nationally, leaving the organisation of protests to the local strike committees. They also refused to circulate details of protests to members, even urging them to stay at work and advising them to restrict activity to making financial contributions. Local strike committees responded by coordinating protests and unofficial walkouts.

'What will it take to win?' was the question being asked by the membership. The CPSA conference in May 1981 overwhelmingly supported a strategy involving the closure of ports and airports, indefinite action by passport office staff, the continuation of selective action and an increased strike fund levy. It was also agreed to launch a five-day strike as a stepping-stone to all-out action if all other measures failed.

While the level of action required to win a dispute can never be specified with absolute accuracy, it is certain that if unions are not prepared to fully mobilise their memberships and apply the strongest possible pressure and leverage, then any employer will dig in until the mood dissipates. While it is a matter of speculation whether the escalation of selective action or a five-day strike would have moved the government in 1981, there is no doubt that the Tories were under growing pressure. Their anti-working-class strategy, still in its experimental stages, was deeply unpopular. They also faced opposition on the streets and in working-class communities and would have struggled to stand firm in the face of such pressure. However, despite demands for escalation, the CCSU leadership persisted with selective action.

Sensing hesitation and weakness, the Tories waited. Little wonder. It turned out that behind the members' backs, union leaders had begun to sue for peace in secret talks; even union executives were unaware of the negotiations.[13] Those leaders engaged in the talks capitulated in the face of a Tory precondition that any new offer, no matter how poor, must be put to a membership ballot. In accepting such terms, the leadership was handing the initiative to the government, easing union pressure and signalling to the membership that the strike could not be won other than by accepting a settlement on government terms. In television interviews, these same leaders talked about an 'inevitable return to work'.

The Tories offered a 'take it or leave it' seven per cent. But members rejected this as an insult. The IRSF and CPSA both voted for all-out action. This was a watershed development in civil service trade unionism. But CCSU persisted with their limited tactics.

CPSA full-timer John Macreadie's demand at the NEC to take unilateral all-out action was ruled out of order by the acting president, who insisted that the power to call action had been 'handed over to CCSU'. Having demoralised members by refusing to build for an achievable victory, Moderates then blamed them for not supporting the strike. Instead, they engineered a return to work.

Although ending in defeat, the 26-week strike, the longest national dispute since the 1920s, had mobilised civil service workers to strike on their own behalf for the first time, an experience that irreversibly radicalised them. It was a major milestone in transforming CPSA from a 'staff association' into a fighting trade union – with one of the most militant rank-and-file socialist broad lefts in the movement. The Tories had won the dispute, but for most civil servants, once regarded as among the least combative sections of the organised working class, the strike would not be their last. It was not so much the end of a dispute as the first major battle in the continuing war between workers and a series of governments to defend pay, conditions, and services. It was these conditions that shaped the CPSA Broad Left into one of the most militant and effective in the trade union movement.

When workers take strike action, it challenges the idea that all power lies with the employer and instead reveals in the starkest terms their own collective power. The question of solidarity becomes not just an idea but a practical necessity. It becomes clear who is in control and who really keeps essential services going. Strikes politicise workers, leading them to question assumptions about society and who runs it. They also reveal the talents of many who would previously never have dreamt of making a speech or organising a picket line.

Debates on industrial and political strategy were not just restricted to activists. 80,000 workers from the Departments of Employment and the DHSS had been left out of selective action at the beginning of the strike. These workers were at the sharp end of service delivery to some of the poorest and most marginalised sections of society and were among the most militant in the civil service. Activists had forged strong links with unemployed workers' organisations and unemployed workers' centres. The same press and media that regularly denounced benefit claimants as 'scroungers' attempted to stoke division between workers and benefit claimants by raising concerns over the impact of strikes.[14] The aim was to keep these workers on the sidelines of the dispute to prevent an intensification of the political pressure on the government.

Debates centred on whether members should issue emergency benefit payments to claimants – a tactic designed to obviate accusations that the union was hurting vulnerable sections of its own class. This tactic would have strengthened solidarity as unemployed workers generally supported the union campaign. In administering benefits, the union would be implementing a time-honoured principle of the trade union movement that striking workers alone should determine what services should operate under union control. Others argued this would be 'scabbing on our own dispute' and no consensus was reached. Action did take place in some Department of Employment and DHSS offices, but it was not generalised and was more in response to suspensions of workers refusing to carry out duties or over the targeting of union representatives.

While there could be no glossing over the fact that the government had frustrated the union's pay campaign, its initial effect was to strengthen the Broad Left and the left generally. Local, regional and workplace groups had grown stronger, and membership had increased, with a new layer of activists coming forward, determined to fight back. Kevin Roddy was elected as CPSA president alongside a majority on the CPSA NEC, which was however lost a year later.

The severe drawbacks of selective action were also exposed during the strike. Whatever role it may once have played in accustoming workers to industrial action, it had quickly become a brake on the development of more ambitious strategies. The government understood that such action could be defeated by waiting until union finances evaporated. The tactic also reduced those not on strike to mere spectators, sowing the illusion that easy and pain-free 'struggle' was possible. Finally, the tactic was ruthlessly exposed by the introduction of increasingly sophisticated technology that enabled work to be switched away from strike-bound workplaces, giving the employer control over the tempo and dynamic of the dispute. The right wing used all this as proof that industrial action could not deliver.

No dispute is ever simply industrial in its nature. Not surprisingly, the 1981 pay dispute had important political effects on the civil service unions. Internal debates around union democracy were sharpened, and the CPSA leadership's failure to implement policies and strategies agreed by the union conference led to demands for democratic oversight and for annual pay conferences. The strike also directly raised the question of working-class political representation in members' minds, with most Broad Left members calling for affiliation of the union to the Labour Party.

Thatcher's attacks intensified, but trade unionists continued to fight back. Less than a year after the national pay strike, industrial action again broke out, supported by the left-wing NEC, over staffing in the DHSS. Centring mainly in Oxford and Birmingham, it involved hundreds of offices and thousands of workers, but again finished inconclusively.

New Realism: division and splits

During the early 1980s, the trade union movement suffered major setbacks, the most significant being the defeat of the NUM in the 1984–85 strike. This exposed the vicious nature of class society with the destruction of mining communities across the country. The NUM met the full force of the state. This included police violence and security services infiltration and full-scale propaganda campaigns in the media, painting the miners as the 'enemy within'. Yet, the government came very close to losing the dispute. It was the failure of the Labour Party and TUC to give the miners their fullest support that was the decisive factor in their defeat.[15]

In response to the Thatcherite assault, leading figures in the movement began to develop the concept of New Realism. There is always a new name for defeatism, betrayal, and class collaboration. CPSA general secretary Alistair Graham was regarded as the intellectual architect of this 'dented shield' strategy. It was argued that the defeat of the miners proved that the Tories and the ruling class were too strong and that the unions had to come to an accommodation with them. In practice, this meant accepting cuts, privatisation and concession bargaining, including acquiescence to legal restrictions on union activity.

The ruling class also expected that 'reasonable, moderate' leaders in the labour and trade union movement would root out 'troublemakers' and 'subversives' – and some were more than willing to oblige. Like all such capitulations that deny the capacity and the right to fight back, New Realism stoked division and disorientation. This cleared the way for witch-hunts and the gradual organisational collapse of the trade union movement from a peak of thirteen million members to around six million in the space of a decade and a half. It was also the foundation upon which the neoliberal consensus emerged, and which led to New Labour, hailed by Thatcher as her greatest achievement.

The CPSA 1981 pay strike accelerated a process of change already evident within the left in the union. This involved a shift in Broad Left's political balance with a rise in the influence of Trotskyist groups, principally Militant. These attracted many younger activists who had been drawn to socialist ideas by the Tory attacks. The SWP too, was influential, but demonstrated a certain lack of political confidence over the potential to defeat the Moderates, encouraging its CPSA activists to find work in the local authorities, as coming areas of struggle where they might build more influence.

In seeking to reach the most combative class fighters, particularly among young workers, and win them to Marxist ideas, the tactic of 'entryism' led to Militant winning the leadership of the Labour Party Young Socialists. This resulted in a witch-hunt by the Labour Party apparatus, ostensibly because it was an 'organisation within an organisation', but more accurately because of its growing influence.

Earlier attempts to drive out Militant in the 1970s had stalled, but in the wake of Thatcherite reaction, Neil Kinnock's Labour Party sought to make itself 'electable' by purging socialists. As the most organised left grouping, Militant became the main target. Its leading role on Liverpool City Council in standing up to Tory cuts enraged both the establishment and Labour's right wing. Councillors were removed from office and subjected to financial penalties, while the Liverpool District Labour Party was suspended. Bans, proscriptions, and expulsions followed in a major campaign that extended through much of the 1980s.

Militant's origins in CPSA lay in the 1970s when full-time officer Terry Adams recruited fellow full-timer John Macreadie and went on to build a caucus of lay activists. Militant had some support among activists in other unions, but nowhere else did it attain the type of influence it had in CPSA. It was by no means the only group involved in growing the left in the union, but it increasingly assumed the dominant position within Broad Left, which had formerly been held by the Communist Party. Other organisations, most noticeably the SWP, Labour lefts and independents, continued to operate within Broad Left.

Several factors define how a socialist grouping can operate effectively in building a union rank and file. Foremost is its attitude to the united front strategy. Any grouping intent on placing its own narrow interests above that of the unity of the left will never hold influence for long, as such opportunism will inevitably result in sectarian division and demoralisation. Macreadie was a leader of exceptional ability whose confidence in socialist ideas and his non-sectarian instincts were a strong influence in shaping the methods of the Militant grouping in CPSA. He was consistent in advocating that activists should listen to members' concerns before attempting to formulate the union's demands, whether it be in a local office dispute or in relation to wider national issues. 'A good ear first, then a good voice' summed up Macreadie's approach.

In formulating strategy and organising campaigns, he believed that a direct relationship must exist between the wider perspectives of a socialist organisation and the concrete conditions faced by workers. However, his oft-repeated view that activists should never run ahead of the members did not mean proceeding at the pace of the slowest or most conservative worker. Instead, demands should be framed which members would see as both necessary and achievable and worth fighting for. Socialist activists may have the strongest theoretical understanding, argued Macreadie, but they must be capable of learning from fellow workers, sharing their everyday experience, and understanding their priorities.

Militant's dominance in Broad Left was the result of a clear socialist political perspective. This informed its methods of work in the union and helped it recruit many of the most combative union campaigners. Typical was Danny Williamson, who successfully built a cadre of young activists at the Department of National Savings offices in Glasgow. In assessing the priorities and concerns of members and activists, the Militant union caucus in CPSA, through internal debate and consultation with the wider left, developed an approach towards policies, strategy and tactics, based on a careful analysis of the balance of forces at any given time. In rejecting both ultra-leftism and opportunism, they won the support of the broad mass of independents within Broad Left.

The Communist Party's influence on the left in CPSA and its predecessors had waned due to a series of factors, not least the rise of Eurocommunism. This claimed to replace 'Stalinism' with attempts to achieve socialism essentially through the methods of social democracy. It was a gradualist stance that left little appetite for confrontation with the ruling class. Indeed, some former Communist Party members became partially or fully integrated into the right-wing union bureaucracy, giving the defeatism of New Realism some degree of 'left' cover.

Amid the Miners' Strike in 1984, elements within Broad Left broke away to form a so-called 'left rank-and-file' organisation called BL84. The Communist Party drove the split, but not without internal disagreement. The fears of those who regarded it as a strategic error were vindicated by the subsequent development of the new grouping. The main issue appeared to be organisational – whether Broad Left's decision-making conference should move from full membership participation to a regionally delegated form – but this masked the real political differences that surrounded the embrace of New Realism.

The Communist Party's influence in BL84 dissipated very quickly as the grouping itself moved closer to the Moderates. Some of the more opportunistic were rewarded with full-time positions, often becoming enthusiastic and savage witch-hunters, while others simply fell out of activity altogether. In contrast, Tony Conway, initially BL84's secretary, would go on to play a major role in reuniting the left and in building and maintaining left unity after the merger to form PCS.

'Subversives cannot be tolerated'

CPSA general secretary and prime mover of New Realism, Alistair Graham, decided not to seek re-election in 1986. His record had been a miserable one, refusing to lead the fight against attacks on pay and jobs, while embracing new technology on the government's terms. He was also a self-declared enemy of Militant and the Broad Left, actively initiating investigations.[16] Viewed as a rising star of the trade union movement, it was even hinted that he might become the general secretary of the TUC. His failure to control the left in his own union ended that ambition and led him towards a career in a series of establishment and governmental positions.

Broad Left members elected John Macreadie and Eddie Spence to stand for the general secretary and national treasurer respectively, but the left was split when the BL84 group stood Geoff Lewtas and Christine Kirk for the same positions. This division in the left and the Moderates' recent victory in the NEC elections led them to assume they were home and dry. Indeed, their general secretary candidate, John Ellis, was so relaxed about the result that he went on holiday during the election.

In a shock result, Macreadie won the general secretaryship, while Kirk, the only woman standing in a majority female union, defeated both Spence and the Moderate candidate to be national treasurer. Macreadie's victory did not occur because of membership apathy, as the press would later claim, but because of the loss of 150,000 civil service jobs and attacks on union rights, such as the union ban at GCHQ.

The Moderate leadership refused to accept the result. The narrowness of Macreadie's victory, 121 above Ellis's vote, was used to challenge the result and call for a re-run. This resulted in a frenzied Red-Scare campaign, with full involvement from the press, the government and the security services, and Tory and right-wing Labour politicians.

The election of a committed Marxist as leader of the largest civil service union had sent shockwaves throughout the establishment. A general election was due within a year and despite the defeat of the miners, fierce industrial disputes were taking place across a range of industries and services. While the patriotic fervour of the Falklands War had not entirely abated, it was receding as the scale of the Tories' assault on the working class bred deep resentment and resistance, including in the civil service where, despite attempts by the Moderates to avoid it, membership pressure forced the NEC to support a major pay campaign.

Broad Left had mobilised for the election and had presented large sections of the membership with a genuine alternative. Graham was so knocked off balance by the result that he expressed his disbelief that the election of a Moderate NEC could be followed by members going on to back a 'key figure from the revolutionary left'. Wild warnings of the consequences of the result were made by the new Moderate president, Marion Chambers, who openly pleaded for members to make complaints about the conduct of the election.

Anticipating the tide of reaction that was to be unleashed, Macreadie and Broad Left launched a nationwide campaign to underline the need for socialist leadership and a genuine fight-back. Macreadie pledged that he would work to defend members' interests and mobilise to resist government attacks. He also renewed the Broad Left pledge to fight for affiliation to the Labour

Party, arguing it was no good just waiting for the return of a Labour government, but that unions must unite in opposition to Thatcher. But perhaps most disturbingly for the establishment, he openly advocated the need for a socialist transformation of society.

With a new job as chief executive of the Industrial Society lined up, Alistair Graham used his last days as general secretary to help coordinate the attack on Macreadie. Uncritically regurgitating Moderate propaganda, the press launched a campaign to overturn the election and, under the heading 'A threat to democracy', the *Daily Mail* proclaimed: 'The election of John Macreadie as leader of the Civil Service union CPSA has for the first time hoisted a member of the Militant Tendency into power in a major union and given him a seat on the General Council of the TUC'.[17] It went on to claim that the election was won, 'through a variety of malpractices' and commended the Moderate NEC for launching an inquiry that, 'may lead to Mr Macreadie being ousted'. The *Mail on Sunday* went further, screaming: 'LOCK HIM OUT'. It described an 'astonishing plan' by the Moderates to physically prevent Macreadie taking up post by blocking entry to his new office, cutting off his phone and ordering bailiffs to evict him.[18]

In response to the NEC's refusal to endorse his election, Macreadie applied to the High Court for an injunction to stop them from indefinitely holding up his appointment. The union leadership had also given Marion Chambers and the Electoral Reform Society a remit to investigate the so-called ballot irregularities. These actions were in blatant breach of union rules. There was no precedent for a candidate who had been democratically elected to office being debarred from taking up a position.

A few activists argued that there was no point in socialists appealing to the 'bourgeois courts' as a matter of principle. But this dogmatic view did not take into account that many members saw Macreadie's approach as a reasonable way to seek a remedy. After all, they would expect their elected representatives to exhaust every avenue to defend, not only the right of an elected candidate to assume office, but also union democracy itself. Above all, Macreadie and his left supporters were acting to allow CPSA members to elect whatever candidate they saw fit, without political or factional interference from inside or outside the union.

Claiming he had no interest in the politics of the situation, Mr Justice Vinelott saw things differently. Union rules stated that it was mandatory to present the elected candidate with a contract. Since Macreadie had not yet been given a contract of employment, the judge ruled that he was not general secretary and therefore the union executive was entitled to defer his appointment until their investigation was completed.[19] The point of law used by the judge to back the Moderates was a legal sleight of hand, but the ruling was essentially political. The establishment simply could not 'uphold democracy' in this case because the risks of allowing a Marxist to become general secretary of a union representing state employees were far too serious to contemplate. Not only might Macreadie galvanise CPSA members, but his leadership might also provide a focal point for resistance across the broader trade union movement where workers were fighting fierce, if isolated, battles, despite the deadening effects of New Realism.

In response, Broad Left campaigned against the Moderates' usurpation of union democracy and demanded a special conference. The NEC pressed ahead with the investigation, installing the defeated candidate, John Ellis, as interim general secretary. He immediately made it clear that he would pursue a policy of cooperation with the Tories, signalling that he was open to their idea of introducing divisive regional pay rates. The Electoral Reform Society's two-month investigation found no 'hard evidence' of ballot-rigging, but recommended a rerun anyway, purportedly because of 'human failing' in breaching regulations – ironically the major irregularity identified in the report was that of a right-wing branch that had supported Ellis.[20]

Although Broad Left candidate Eddie Spence, who had marginally lost to Christine Kirk, stood down in order not to divide the 'left', BL84 again stood in the re-run for general secretary, splitting the left vote. Contrary to the rules, the Moderates, who had themselves introduced workplace balloting rather than the previous method of branch block votes, changed the voting system in the rerun to one of desktop balloting, a system that was far more open to abuse and interference from management. Against the backdrop of a strident press campaign and right-wing support in the labour and trade union movement, Ellis was elected. Peter Bruinvels MP, a longstanding and vocal supporter of political purges of civil servants, welcomed his victory in the House of Commons: 'Is this not the way that democracy can be seen to be at work, and does it not show that, in true and fair elections, the right people can be elected?'.[21]

The level of state interference in CPSA during this episode was only fully revealed in 2016 with the release of Cabinet Office papers under the 30-year rule. These indicated how concerned Thatcher and her senior ministers were at the development of industrial and political militancy in their own state apparatus, planning how to combat the Militant Tendency, Broad Left and socialists like Macreadie.[22]

Although union activists at the time knew how closely the right wing was working with the Tory government, the detail provided in the state papers is remarkable. It presents clear evidence of state interference in the internal union affairs, including the democratic right of members to choose their own leaders. If the 'wrong' leaders were elected, the tactic was not to engage with them but to isolate them, branding them as 'subversives' and as threats to national security. Activists who raised concerns about government interference would be accused of 'paranoia' and 'spreading conspiracy theories'.

In 1986, cabinet secretary and head of the civil service, Sir Robert Armstrong's lengthy analysis marked 'Secret and Personal' stated that Macreadie won the general secretaryship on a 'wafer-thin majority' and that: 'There are moves afoot in the CPSA to challenge, and try to reverse this election, and secure the election of Mr John Ellis, a more moderate candidate who had been generally expected to win'. He went on to describe how internal union complaints against Macreadie could be registered, but drew the conclusion that, '...it is not possible to prevent Mr Macreadie from taking up office... and to pursue the aim of MT [Militant Tendency] within the CPSA...' However, an established procedure did exist, 'to deny access to a secret establishment to a union official who is, or has recently been, a member of a... subversive group, acknowledged as such by the Minister, whose aims are to undermine or overthrow Parliamentary democracy... by political, violent or industrial means'. This involved issuing 'a notice of refusal to negotiate or denial of access to Mr Macreadie'. He added: 'I do not think that there should be any real problem about that... we can make the charge stick':

> There would certainly be no difficulty about issuing such notices in respect of the Ministry of Defence and Home Office. But it is doubtful that would go far enough. The object of the exercise would be to exclude Mr. Macreadie from central negotiations as well as departmental negotiations.

A later memo from Armstrong's junior, N.L. Wicks to prime minister Thatcher read: 'The principle needs to be established – subversives (if it can be proved Mr. Macreadie is a subversive) cannot be tolerated in such jobs'.

The release of these papers prompted PCS general secretary Mark Serwotka, with NEC backing, to write to the Cabinet Office regarding revelations that the state security service MI5 had, during Thatcher's period as prime minister, identified 1,420 civil servants to be kept under surveillance and barred from certain roles. A total of 700 were identified as Trotskyists, 607 as communists, 45 as fascists, 35 as Welsh or Scottish nationalists; a number of 'black or Asian racial extremists', as well as 'anarchists' were also named.

In the wake of the 1981 national pay strike, which had cost the government over £1 billion, and which they were determined never to repeat, Tory ministers and Moderate leaders forged even deeper bonds, including joint working to draw up anti-trade union legislation. Meetings between Moderates and other civil service union leaders discussed the causes of growing militancy and the measures needed to combat it. These included reviving, developing and implementing anti-communist measures from the 1950s and 60s, such as the use of disciplinary action and summary dismissal, the withholding of pay and denying promotion. Also raised was the casualisation of the workforce and the privatisation of vulnerable areas, such as computer services, as well as removing the check-off system whereby union subscriptions were deducted at source.[23]

The events surrounding Macreadie's election were a harsh education in class politics for activists and members alike. When their interests were threatened, the establishment encouraged and supported their surrogates in the union to take ruthless action to stop the appointment without regard for the rules and constitution. In short, all regard was cast aside for the supposedly sacrosanct 'standards of democracy'.

1987 pay campaign

The Moderates may have stopped Macreadie from becoming general secretary, but members demanded action against falling living standards. A Special Pay Conference in November 1986 pressed the NEC to launch a campaign which led to nationwide action alongside the executive grades' union SCPS. At the conference it was argued that if the union's pay demands were to be achieved, including stopping Treasury proposals for regional and merit pay, preparations for all-out action were required.

A rolling regional programme of action was launched during 1987, as was selective action, but the long timeline for regional action led to a loss of momentum. All-out action, as in 1981, was the only sure way of applying enough pressure to win the dispute, but this was not an option that the right wing would countenance. Yet again, weak leadership allowed the Tories an advantage. They used it by launching a propaganda offensive against civil service workers, particularly those in the militant sections of the DHSS and Department of Employment, whom they again accused of hurting benefit claimants by their actions.

Broad Left's demand for a second ballot for an all-out strike following a short period of action was not supported at the union's 1987 annual conference. Instead, a further period of extended action was agreed upon before moving to an all-out ballot. In a surprise for the right-wing, Broad Left won a majority on the NEC, although Moderate leader Marion Chambers retained the presidency. In a further blow to the right wing, John Macreadie won the deputy general secretary election. Members voted for further regional strikes and selective action, and a two-day national strike. Industrial action, as in 1981, showed the potential industrial power of civil service workers, but during the dispute itself the Tories won a general election, a demoralising setback that had an impact across the labour movement.

Predictably, weeks of selective action did not exert sufficient impetus to move the new Tory government, and the Broad Left-majority NEC voted for all-out action. However, the 'secret left' leadership of SCPS responded by ending their campaign, leaving CPSA to fight on its own. Coupled with the impact of the Tories' re-election and yet another Red Scare campaign in the press, this led to the call for all-out action being defeated by 53,251 to 19,468 in a membership ballot.[24] This setback had allowed the right wing to frustrate the left-led NEC in carrying out its wider programme. With defeat comes demoralisation. Holding the president and general secretary positions, the Moderates were now able to use every disruptive method in their arsenal against the left and were returned to power in the subsequent annual election.

A key lesson was learned. If the left hoped to carry out its programme, they must win the three main positions of power – the president, the general secretary and the NEC.

Notes & References

1. *Nottingham Guardian,* 15 May 1969.

2. *The Guardian,* 9 September 1995; see also, R. Ramsay, 'The Clandestine Caucus: Anti-socialist campaigns and operations in the British Labour Movement since the war', Lobster, Hull, 1998.

3. *The Independent,* 26 December 2013.

4. *Reader's Digest,* February 1975.

5. Lord Denning, GB Court of Appeal: Losinska v. Civil and Public Services Union, 1975.

6. R. Seifert and T. Sibley, *Revolutionary Communist at Work: A Political Biography of Bert Ramelson,* Lawrence and Wishart, London, 2012; K. Halpin, *Memoirs of a Militant: Sharply and to the point,* Praxis Press, Glasgow, 2012.

7. *The Scotsman,* 30 January 1981.

8. *Liverpool Echo,* 5 March 1981; *Cumbernauld News,* 12 March 1981; *Birmingham Mail,* 6 March 1981.

9. *Western Daily Press,* 11 March 1981.

10. H. Lanning and R. Norton, *A Conflict of Loyalties: GCHQ 1984–1991,* New Clarion Press, Cheltenham, 1994.

11. *The Scotsman,* 24 March 1981.

12. *Daily Mirror,* 8 April 1981.

13. Kevin Roddy, 'Lessons for the Future', *Militant,* 14 August 1981.

14. *Belfast Telegraph,* 25 March 1981.

15. S. Milne, *The Enemy Within: The Secret War Against the Miners,* Verso, London, 2004.

16. *Newcastle Journal,* 21 January 1986.

17. *Daily Mail,* 9 March 1986.

18. *Mail on Sunday,* 6 July 1986.

19. *Daily Express,* 16 July 1986.

20. *Aberdeen Press and Journal,* 9 October 1986.

21. House of Commons Debates, 26 January 1987, vol.109.

22. *Morning Star,* 13 March 2017.

23. *Morning Star,* 13 March 2017.

24. See, *Daily Express,* 27 April 1987.

or replaced by British Nuclear Fuels.

Health Service.

Union Reds routed

VICTORY: John Ellis

THE Civil Service's biggest Trotskyist hotbed has been purged by moderate union boss John Ellis.

Clerks employed at the DHSS at Newcastle Upon Tyne voted 10-1 to back their leadership against Militant-dominated extremists who have ruled the branch for years.

Newcastle Central branch of the white-collar CPSA is the biggest in the union and its 4,000 block vote has had a major bearing on policy decisions.

Triumph

Voting on a new constitution for the branch was 1,702 in favour with 187 against.

Triumphant Mr Ellis, CPSA general secretary, said: "After years of making up their own rules and making members' lives a misery we now discover the extent of their support, a pathetic 187.

"We can now go forward and flush them out for good."

Poll tax pledge

LABOUR leader Neil Kinnock vowed yesterday that a Labour Government would scrap the poll tax. He told a Scottish TUC rally at Westminster that the community charge — due to be introduced in Scotland in April, followed by England and Wales next year — was "inefficient, expensive and crushing." He spoke after a 300,000-signature petition opposing the poll tax was delivered to Downing Street.

Mirror 2.2.89

3. Witch-hunts

'Newcastle Eight–NEC Nil'

Witch-hunting in the civil service had a long pedigree. In the late 1970s, Ministry of Defence union members in Gibraltar were suspended and locked out during a work-to-rule. When the union bureaucracy attempted to force the workers into a Commission of Inquiry against their wishes, Terry Adams, a newly appointed union full-timer and Militant supporter, backed their position. The Moderates tried to sack him but a campaign by members forced a retreat. Despite such early setbacks, the Moderates would continue in the next decade to attack branches and individuals, even colluding with management in the sacking of selected activists.

Following the electoral defeat of the Broad Left majority NEC in 1988, the Moderates were determined to consolidate their position and break the power of the left. It was well known that general secretary John Ellis had written to the Head of the Civil Service to say the union was under new management, reassuring him that a compliant leadership would keep the militants in line. The socialist leadership of the Newcastle Central Office (NCO) branch provided one obvious target.

With over 5,000 members the Newcastle branch was the biggest in Britain. The branch had risen to prominence following the bitterly fought, eight-month-long Newcastle shift workers dispute of 1983–84. This had been provoked by government plans to save £700,000 by cutting the wages of computer workers, but ended up costing the government at least £170 million. One member of the Committee of Public Accounts which produced a report on the strike commented that, '...on any sane analysis it cannot be justified', but DHSS second permanent secretary Sir Geoffrey Otten explained:

> I would like to record that one of the reasons it was intractable was that we were dealing with the Militant

Tendency at the Longbenton site in Newcastle and it was clear from one stage to another of this dispute that there was a sizable faction among the strikers who did not want a settlement.[1]

The implication was that these workers were manipulated into taking or persisting with strike action even though there was little prospect of a fair settlement. This reflects the politicisation of a terms and conditions dispute by the government.

Prior to the NCO branch annual general meeting in 1988, disaffected former Broad Left members formed a Campaign to Defeat Militant Tendency (CDMT). Their leader, Kevin Oliver, who had been elected treasurer on a left slate of candidates, wrote to branch secretary Barry Fuge, copying in Moderate national president Marion Chambers, implying that there had been financial irregularities and a misuse of materials, including postage and paper, during the previous year. The branch executive called for an inquiry, but Oliver refused to present his case or take any part in the process.

Oliver wrote again to Chambers, claiming that the branch was 'like Prontaprint'.[2] He produced sample left material as evidence and made non-specific claims of 'threats and intimidation'. He also demanded that CPSA headquarters should investigate, as otherwise the account books and vouchers might disappear if elected branch representatives got their hands on them. On Chamber's instruction, he sent all the material dating from 1985 onwards to union headquarters. Branch accounts were suspended, in Chambers' phrase, to 'protect the innocent'.

In this febrile atmosphere the left were defeated at the local annual general meeting, which coincided with the defeat of the left in national elections. Oliver was elected branch secretary, but he resigned shortly afterwards with two other recently elected officers, again citing threats of intimidation and violence. Such allegations, made without evidence, had been used in the past to justify witch-hunts and establish 'cause' to suspend branches.

The NEC then made several charges, individually and collectively, against branch activists: Sandy Donnachie, Barry Fuge, Steve

McNeaney, Peter Mahony, Terry Martin, Alan Maughan, Doreen Purvis, Pat Rivers and Dave Robson. The charges made against the Newcastle activists included using CPSA branch funds to produce Broad Left material; defying a presidential ruling by recommending one candidate (John Macreadie) in the 1986 re-run general secretary election; taking a share of two conference delegates' expenses payments for the 1986 pay conference; and taking money for use of the union's photocopier.[3]

The charges were a bureaucratic attempt to decapitate the branch leadership. Purvis, the Broad Left candidate for national president, was not even on the branch executive. Nevertheless, she was targeted for the dual purpose of removing a highly popular electoral rival and opening up wider attacks on Broad Left and Militant at group and national levels.

DHSS section lay officials and full-timers were brought in to run the branch and the union journal *Red Tape,* edited by press officer Barry Reamsbottom, gave a highly partial and distorted account of events with no right of reply. The normal democratic life of the branch was crushed. No meetings were convened to explain the situation, effectively disenfranchising members, while 50 democratically elected representatives were removed. Unable to tolerate the risk of the left being re-elected, the Moderates were determined that what could not be secured democratically would be imposed bureaucratically.

A 'Trounce the Trots' circular, produced by CDMT and authored by Reamsbottom, offered a glimpse of the personal vitriol directed at activists:

> You may be aware that for several years our branch of CPSA has been controlled by the Militant Tendency... You may not know that their activities are highly political, as opposed to trade union activities, or that their need for absolute control at NCO is essential to their objectives of vote gathering to elect and appoint Militant supporters to influential positions in CPSA. Their prime objective is disruption...

Our general comment is to marvel at the hysterical approach, smile at the distorted analysis and underline the puerility of Militant's approach to debate...THE QUESTION IS, ARE OUR BRANCH FUNDS BEING USED TO SUPPORT MILITANT'S ACTIVITIES?

...We are family people, not political activists...WE WANT TO DISENTANGLE THIS BRANCH FROM POLITICAL FACTIONALISM'.

Even under this reputational assault the former branch officers continued to meet, albeit 'in exile', to assist and, wherever possible, give representation to members. They also advised on issues facing members in their day-to-day work and even issued circulars.

Meanwhile, the press continued to repeat the Moderate narrative. Red-baiting headlines such as: 'Whitehall Union Bosses to Probe Lefties Cash Con' (*The Sun*); 'Militant Facing Backlash in Union' (*The Times*); 'Union Reds routed' (*Daily Mirror*); 'branch was a Trotskyite Print Plant' (*Evening Standard*). In this atmosphere of anti-socialist hysteria, it was hardly surprising that the DHSS Section Executive Committee fell to a right-wing/BL84 majority.

The tribunal appointed by Ellis was chaired by former union general secretary, Bill Kendall, and others with ties to the Moderates or with a record of anti-left activity. Chambers decreed the tribunal to be *sub judice*, offering a quasi-legal veneer of gravitas to an otherwise disreputable process. The intention was to silence debate within CPSA branches, although many ignored this and put motions to AGMs and special meetings, which were ruled out of order by the national union with threats of dire consequences.

Had the defendants not participated in the tribunal, they would have been accused of running away from proper scrutiny. This could leave them open to accusations of political posturing at the expense of defending their reputations in the eyes of their members. For them, non-attendance was not an option, facing their accusers was a political duty and strategic imperative. When Ellis rejected their demands for legal representation and for the accounts to be made available and entered in evidence, the Newcastle activists responded with a letter from their lawyers stating: 'As the rules of natural justice prevail over the rule book, I would suggest that discretion was exercised so as to ensure that the persons against whom allegations are made have every opportunity of making an informed response'. The letter was ignored by the Moderates, who were prepared to abandon even elementary notions of natural justice to pursue their political vendetta.

The Newcastle activists made a formal statement that the tribunal was unconstitutional, as no initial investigation had been made and there was no explanation of how charges had been arrived at, let alone how they were apportioned to individuals. The activists were eventually allowed to see branch accounts, but Ellis insisted this must be under 'supervision'. This was undertaken by some individuals who had written the original letters of accusation, which formed part of the evidence against the defendants. Their requests to call up to thirty-one witnesses from the branch were also rejected, with only five allowed from outside the branch. The right to have the branch accounts entered in evidence was similarly denied, as was the right to know how the charges had been specified. 'Supplementary evidence' was included, consisting of thousands of leaflets supposedly produced by the Newcastle activists for a range of organisations, but the accused were given no opportunity to assess it. The purpose of the tribunal was clearly to allow the accusers to prove guilt, rather than for the accused to prove their innocence.

Citing ill-health, Kendall resigned, although it was widely rumoured he could not stomach the process. He was replaced by Charlie Turnock, formerly of the National Union of Railwaymen, a hardened witch-hunter fresh from the investigation of Liverpool Labour Party. When Tribunal member, Len Moody, also resigned, Turnock suggested the tribunal could 'pick up someone later' who could listen to tapes of proceedings. The NCO representatives walked out, but Chambers backed the Chair, and they eventually returned in a final bid to clear themselves.

Fuge had produced a fourteen-page document in 1986, outlining the use of paper in the 5,000-member branch. It forensically explained the use of 23,700 pieces of paper that had been produced in circulars and correspondence, showing that the evidence against him was at best, circumstantial, and at worst, fabricated. The five witnesses from outside the branch allowed by the tribunal also rebutted many of the allegations, confirming that they were in fact responsible for some of the material that NCOs was accused of producing. The NCO representatives described the witnesses as 'magnificent'.

Nevertheless, the tribunal upheld the complaints and the NEC voted to expel the accused, now widely known as the Newcastle Eight. The *Newcastle Journal* triumphantly reported that the activists had been found guilty of 'using the union's resources to publish propaganda material.'[4] It went on to state that the executive also voted by 21–1 that Chambers and Ellis should conduct an enquiry into John Macreadie, 'another Militant supporter'. For his part, Fuge responded that, 'the tribunal was set up to victimise us politically as part of the Left-Right struggle in the union', while Macreadie pledged that 'he would continue to carry out the decisions of CPSA members and work to improve their conditions' and 'would not be diverted by further attacks'.

The Moderates tried unsuccessfully to stop any right of appeal. As a result, the 1990 national conference became a showdown between them and the expelled members. Amid further press attacks, they sought to create an atmosphere of intimidation by hiring security guards and demanding that observers be removed from the hall during the appeal debate. The expelled members were also isolated in a room outside the main conference hall, guarded by CPSA full-time staff. They could not hear the discussions and were led in, in alphabetical order, one by one, to make their appeals before being taken back immediately to the room. Waiting to make their appeals, the Eight felt the accumulated pressure of years of attacks, slander and smears. As a national left leader, Purvis, reflected: 'I felt if I crumbled, everyone would'.[5] They all later commented that the atmosphere was 'very strange'; their appeals were heard in absolute silence, but all spoke with clarity and dignity under the most stressful circumstances.

Broad Left and its allies approached the debate in a very disciplined manner. Chambers had made clear that a limited number of speakers would be allowed for either side of the debate. Broad Left nominated Steve Cawkwell, Dawn Castle and John McInally among others, but Chambers refused to call prominent left-winger Mark Serwotka. One BL84 leader suggested an alternative ten-year suspension, while another broke ranks and spoke against the expulsions.

To the fury of the NEC and their small group of supporters in the conference hall, the appeal was upheld by a clear and convincing majority. In the wake of this stunning defeat for the Moderates, celebrations began straightaway. The Eight returned to the conference that afternoon with t-shirts bearing the legend 'Newcastle Eight–NEC Nil'. The Moderates' response was unrestrained and emotional. They were clearly shocked, and for the rest of the conference, NEC speakers, whatever the subject of subsequent debates, spat out abuse at delegates, accusing them of allowing the guilty to go free.

The scale of the Moderates' defeat was echoed in the press, which had denounced the Newcastle reps and extolled the NEC's action. The *Financial Times* barely managed four short paragraphs announcing the result, ending its report with 'Security guards had been hired... but the appeal passed off peacefully'.[6]

The Moderates' defeat had wider industrial and political consequences. Before the appeal debate, Ellis made a speech at conference attacking the record of the recently defeated Broad Left-led NEC. The press reported his comment that the union would reject the 'potty lunacies' of the left who wanted to take industrial action against the government's strategy of breaking up departmental services in preparation for privatisation.[7] However, many members had been revolted by the undemocratic methods of the right wing, including the misuse of union resources and publications, as well as the downright malice underpinning their attack. Had the Newcastle Eight been defeated, this would have dented confidence in building workplace resistance, but victory produced the opposite effect, empowering activists.

The Moderates controlled the main levers of power within the union, including support from a loyal bureaucracy and even assistance from sections of the 'left'. However, their failures over the Newcastle witch-hunt demonstrated that there were serious limitations to their dominance. The campaign against the witch-hunt suggested that, even under the most vicious assault, the left would not meekly capitulate but fight back and even win.

Meeting witch-hunts with such resolve is not just a matter of individual character but political understanding and conviction. They can never be fought and defeated by seeking accommodation and compromise. Instead, the key tactic in the Newcastle case was to reach out to activists and workers, building solidarity and giving the witch-hunters no opportunity to exploit and press home the attack. As Purvis later commented: 'The experience of being attacked in this way, by your own union leadership, was a difficult one. We knew they were out to destroy us, politically and personally. The witch-hunt put enormous strain on all of us, and our families. But we never thought at any stage we should back down or give up.'[8]

It did not escape the notice of many members that the Newcastle activists had led their members in strike action and had opposed the union leadership's accommodation with government attacks on civil service workers. Some in BL84, not least those in or around the Communist Party and Labour left, became increasingly estranged from those who had collaborated with the Moderates, starting a process that would lead to a realignment on the left.

But this was not the end of the witch-hunts. The Moderates were under siege and were determined to hold on to power at all costs. This would lead to an intensification of their destructive and divisive methods. In the wake of their humiliation over the Newcastle campaign, they soon demonstrated that they would even collude in the sacking of their own members.

The Bedminster sackings

In April 1993, after several years of pay cuts and freezes, Graphical, Paper and Media Union (GPMU) members at the J.W. Arrowsmith print company in Ashton, Bristol voted to work-to-rule and for an overtime ban in support of their union's national pay claim of £6.50 a week. The company threatened to dismiss these workers unless they each signed a letter disassociating themselves from the union's action. As no one did, all of them were sacked an hour after the deadline expired. Among the 120 who lost their jobs were employees off sick or on leave, women on maternity leave, and one member who was due to retire the next day with 43 years' service. A lockout was then enforced, and a week later all received a letter with individual contracts which imposed a two-year pay freeze, a cut in overtime and shift rates and derecognition of the union. The company anticipated the workforce would be so intimidated by their shock tactics that they would sign up, but they miscalculated; only six people returned to work, and the union mounted daily pickets from 5.45 am to 9 pm.

The company decided to advertise the jobs belonging to the sacked workers in the Bedminster Jobcentre as 'vacancies'. Employment Service (ES) guidelines were clear that in trade disputes, management should take account of a whole range of factors. These included: the nature of the dispute itself; trade union attitudes; the strength of picketing; the attitude of the general public; media reporting; and the amount of business normally taken from the employer. The Arrowsmith vacancies should have been suspended on any one of these factors.

When news about the proposed vacancies broke, it seemed that CPSA members at the Jobcentre had exerted sufficient pressure for their branch officers to reach a negotiated settlement with departmental area managers, who had themselves argued that the vacancies should be refused on the grounds of 'community feeling' in South Bristol. The branch immediately alerted CPSA headquarters and kept it informed of events daily. Additionally, the controversial decision to refuse to pay unemployment benefits to the sacked workers, as they were 'involved in a trade dispute', meant that any assistance given by the company, like advertising, would show evident bias in their favour. CPSA members at Bedminster were rightly concerned that any such partisan behaviour would destroy the reputation of their Jobcentre and the department more generally. It would also place them under intolerable strain, even presenting a danger to their safety, as feelings were running high in the local community.

It initially seemed that area managers were prepared to suspend all action on the vacancies pending the outcome of national negotiations, as requested by the branch. However, under pressure from the hardliners in senior management, they suddenly changed their minds and insisted that the vacancies should be displayed the next day. Members were aghast at this decision and urged management to stick to their own guidelines and remain neutral.

Had the Bedminster workers quietly published the Arrowsmith vacancies, this would have been regarded by many as open collaboration in the recruitment of scab labour. It would also have been a clear message that the department would allow its services to be used by companies sacking their employees to enforce reduced terms and conditions. Subsequent events, like the GMPU lobby of the Jobcentre and hostile local press coverage, would soon confirm that CPSA members were correct to disassociate themselves from the recruitment decision.[9]

On 6 July, CPSA members at Bedminster voted in a secret ballot to walk out for one day in protest at the advertisement of the print workers' jobs. In a show of solidarity, they joined the Arrowsmith picket line. Management refused to accept that it had made a mistake in advertising these jobs, but did not hesitate to lash out at its own staff. Steve Goldfinch, a Bedminster striker and ES probationer, and Amanda Lane, the Avon West branch secretary, were sacked. Lane, who was not employed at Bedminster but who had led the negotiations and directed the ballot and walkout, was now accused of damaging the 'impartiality and neutrality' of the ES. Other strikers and branch officers were financially penalised.

Enraged by the Bedminster action, management had over-reacted, but there was a wider context. The Tory government wished to neuter union solidarity in order to push forward its privatisation agenda through a policy of market testing. The ES had been chosen by the Tory government as a testing ground for private sector methods, including attacks on terms and conditions and the undermining of union rights. This was highlighted by 'Anderson of P&O and advisor on market testing who told the government that white collar trade unions in Whitehall are a major deterrent to potential bidders'.[10]

The spotlight also fell on ES because its CPSA members were among the most militant in the union. Along with activists in the DHSS section, they had built up strong connections with unemployed workers' groups over many years and had been at the forefront of opposition to the attacks launched on unemployed people since the election of the Tories in 1979.

Other significant disputes in the ES and DHSS during this period were marked by the bitter intensity and determination of workers to defend their jobs and fight back against victimisation. Management, for example, had been stung by a year-long campaign by the CPSA Sheffield and Rotherham branch. Activists Sally Pearse and Martin Godfrey had been demoted, and fourteen others disciplined following a successful campaign against the employment of a National Front organiser with undisclosed criminal convictions in the Sheffield Jobcentre. Partway through an industrial tribunal, ES management agreed to reinstate Pearse and Godfrey within six months and set aside all the disciplinary letters.

The ES management clearly intended to set an example and deal with the strikers as harshly as possible to discourage others. For the Moderate leadership of the CPSA, the strikers' main offence was that they had acted in solidarity with fellow workers. The fact that not all the strikers were sacked was due to a tactical consideration that a powerful enough message had been sent within the boundaries of proportionality. As soon as negotiations broke down, the branch contacted CPSA headquarters. The submission arrived in advance of the walkout and a report was faxed the next day after it had taken place, but when the union's national disputes committee refused to give official backing to the branch on the grounds it was not a 'trade dispute', it claimed that the submission for action had arrived too late. It also argued that the dispute could not be endorsed as it would leave the union open to legal challenge and sequestration of funds.

Both management and the CPSA leadership had a strong vested interest in making an example of Amanda Lane, who was a prominent Militant and Broad Left activist. She had served on the union's national executive committee in 1987–8 and on the ES group executive committee; she had also run as a presidential candidate for both the national and group executives. Above all, the Moderates had never forgiven her for her role in giving 'highly effective evidence' in the Newcastle tribunal.

The fight for reinstatement got off to a tremendous start with a three hundred-plus rally in Bristol, with speakers including GPMU's Mike Griffiths.[11] There was real outrage at the Bedminster sackings, arising as they did from an act of solidarity of the type that defines the very best of the trade union movement. Practical support was received from the neighbouring Avon West CPSA branch, which also developed strong links with the GPMU branch, jointly campaigning against the victimisation and demanding the reinstatement of Lane and Goldfinch. Magnificent solidarity also came from further afield, with messages of support and donations from a range of union organisations including the convenors at Swan Hunters Shipyards on the Tyne, Strathclyde Fire Brigades Union, the Second Severn Crossing's Joint Shop Stewards Committee and from trades councils and branches of UNISON, MSF, UCATT, NCU, NUT, IRSF and TGWU. Typical was the statement from Jim Friel, the GPMU father of the Press Room chapel at the *Daily Record* in Glasgow: 'It is good to know that despite the draconian anti working-class laws of the present government there are still trade unionists willing to stand up and be counted on an important matter of principle.'[12]

The anger of Bristol members led to demands for joint industrial action with the Bedminster ES strikers from DHSS members in the city, but the Moderates refused permission to ballot on the grounds that action by 'separate departments' would be 'illegal'. They also attempted to deny Jobcentre workers the right to run their own ballot and only relented in the face of members' anger. However, they unilaterally cut the demand for a three-day strike down to two and agreed to ballot only a limited number of offices. Despite this and a campaign of intimidation and disinformation by management, members voted by 2:1 for strike action. The Moderate leadership had only allowed a single day to carry out the ballot and then purposely delayed announcing the result. Members in one office only knew they were given authority to strike at 4.30 pm on the day before the action; five other offices that had voted for action were told at the last minute that they had to go into work. In September, ten offices came out on strike and received wide support from other trade unionists and the public, with the local press reflecting city-wide anger at the way both Arrowsmith and CPSA members had been treated.[13] The Moderates ignored this show of support, sinking to a new low by using management's doctored strike figures to discredit the action.

Members at Bedminster demanded an all-out strike, but this was refused by the national leadership. A very serious discussion was held about embarking on unofficial all-out action, but since the national union had already signalled that it would not back this, the only outcome would almost certainly have been the sacking of the strikers. The Moderates' actions came under intense scrutiny from members, who were genuinely shocked at the betrayal of the Bedminster strikers. Indeed, the methods that they employed also caused revulsion beyond the union itself.

Chambers and Reamsbottom, who had succeeded Ellis as general secretary in 1992, said the decision not to endorse was based on 'legal advice', but when the branch pressed for a copy of this advice, it was refused. It transpired that no written advice existed and the decision not to support Bristol members was based solely on a brief phone call between the union's deputy general secretary, Alan Churchard and the union's solicitors.[14]

At an Interim Relief Hearing held shortly after the sackings, a letter from the deputy general secretary to the Bedminster CPSA union representative Louise McGirr was produced, which highlighted the union leadership's refusal to back the dispute as it was not a trade dispute.[15] This was presented as evidence by the management. It was subsequently revealed that they had advised CPSA full-time officials that Lane and Goldfinch were to be sacked, but they were not told this by the union. All this amounted to a repudiation of the dispute by the leadership, which left the strikers at the mercy of the most vicious management in the civil service. By this act of revenge against their political opponents, they were supporting the victimisation of their own members.

Not content with this betrayal, the Moderates repeatedly accused Amanda Lane of organising illegal solidarity action, stating that she and other 'militant' activists in the branch bore sole responsibility for leading members into action which the union 'could not support'. In other words, they only had themselves to blame for their sackings. In contrast, the branch argued that it was a legitimate trade dispute, which involved the safety and well-being of members, as well as breaches of procedure by management, a view widely understood across the CPSA membership.

Reamsbottom began the NEC debate on the sackings by launching an attack on the strikers' action with a vicious verbal assault on Amanda Lane. This prompted the Moderates to contribute one by one in an orgy of lies, smears and insults. The debate was the antithesis of the trade union movement's principles of solidarity and unity. Vice-president Tony Rouse snarled: 'She got what she deserved'.[16]

Rather than working with their victimised Bedminster members to develop a strategy to win reinstatement, the Moderate leadership proceeded to frustrate and sabotage the campaign. Had the strategy of the Avon West branch been pursued by the national union, including an escalation of industrial action, it would have offered a fighting chance of winning. The Moderate position, however, simply gave the management confidence that the union leadership would not seriously press for reinstatement. Ignoring the wider implications of the sackings, the NEC agreed with the recommendation that the sackings should be treated as 'personal cases'.

Reamsbottom took over a month to make any comment on the dispute, and even that was an inclusion on page two of his 'News from the General Secretary' circular, which reported that a barrister had been appointed for the industrial tribunal hearing and mentioned providing funds for a national petition. Neither of these, nor the parliamentary pressure happened, except that generated by the strikers themselves. He later complained:

> It was deeply saddening...to see an unofficial bulletin being distributed in the union and elsewhere which tells a number of lies about our efforts. The NEC was appalled by this and agreed I should write to the authors of this divisive and damaging document asking them to put out an apology and a retraction of the lies. If they won't do so I will be forced, reluctantly, to publicly set the record straight.[17]

Unsurprisingly, management included the circular in their submission to the Civil Service Appeals Board hearing and the industrial tribunal.

Despite repeated requests, the national union leaders refused financial assistance for their sacked members. This contrasted with the policy later developed by PCS. The Moderate leadership also ignored the precedent set at the previous year's CPSA national conference, when delegates had overwhelmingly voted to support Sally Pearse and Martin Godfrey. A series of petty measures were also designed to frustrate the campaign, including a refusal to circulate the details of the Bristol Trades Council march and rally and the refusal of credentials for Lane to attend the TUC Women's Conference as an observer.

As in the Newcastle Eight case, the Bedminster sackings were used by the Moderates in a ruthless internal war against their left opponents. They believed that after an initial burst of anger, the whole issue would subside, but they had miscalculated. The campaign launched by the Bristol strikers continued over the next few years with the full support and solidarity of left activists, including those from other unions such as GPMU. Again, they had picked on the wrong people – activists who were prepared to fight back. Extensive protest activity followed during which Lane individually addressed meetings in thirty towns and cities, with over 200 meetings held the length and breadth of Britain.[18]

A 'Defend your Union' campaign was set up, which demanded that the national union campaign for reinstatement be implemented, following the precedent set in 1993 by the RMT, which had secured the reinstatement of sacked London Underground shop steward, Pat Sikorski. A motion to the union conference demanded that Reamsbottom issue an all-members circular supporting the sacked members. It also pressed him to request wider TUC publicity for the campaign and to pay the victimised workers' wages for as long as the campaign lasted. But the leadership had no intention of putting effort or resources into any 'official' campaign. At the 1994 union conference, president Chambers removed no fewer than 62 motions on the Bedminster sackings from the agenda. The NEC also refused point-blank to implement the terms of motions supporting the campaign and calling for financial support for the sacked members.

The 'Defend your Union' campaign received a significant boost when the Civil Service Arbitration Board ruled that Amanda Lane had been unfairly dismissed, a decision reported on local television under the headline 'Vindicated'; but the Moderates refused to build on this and persisted in their attempts to treat the sacking as a personal case. When the industrial tribunal in the autumn of 1994 eventually found that Lane had been unfairly dismissed, but had contributed to her sacking, they were jubilant as they thought it drew a line under the entire matter.[19] This was far from the case.

Although the prospect of reinstatement had been removed, the case inflicted deep reputational damage on the Moderates and on Reamsbottom in particular. The refusal to implement conference policy and financially support Lane and Goldfinch was viewed with disgust. When the leadership refused for a second year to implement a democratically agreed conference decision to support the sacked members, a leaflet was distributed throughout the union by the Bristol strikers entitled 'Reamsbottom Accused'. The leaflet stated:

> From the very first day of the sackings Reamsbottom conducted a vicious smear campaign against the strikers and Amanda Lane in particular. He used the sackings as a weapon in the ruthless internal war he has conducted against his left opponents in CPSA since the day he narrowly won the position of general secretary. His first comment on becoming General Secretary was that he intended to 'harry the alien influence of Militant from CPSA', a comment that told management left activists were legitimate targets for them to victimise and even sack.

It concluded that:

> Neither Reamsbottom nor his Moderate faction showed a scrap of goodwill, support or solidarity for the sacked members. They obstructed and sabotaged the campaign for reinstatement at every opportunity... [and]... hoped that after an initial burst of anger the sacked members would simply walk away from the struggle. They did not and the Moderates made sure they would suffer for it... Amanda Lane spent two years fighting against the sackings. This was because her commitment to CPSA and its members was such that she believed management should never get away lightly with victimising trade unionists. As a result of that sacrifice and commitment and the widespread

support built against the behaviour of Employment Service management, activists and members are safer than they otherwise would be.

The campaign was a stark warning to the Moderates that if they worked with management to victimise activists, they would be held to account. Reamsbottom's failure to understand or credit the commitment of Amanda Lane, Steve Goldfinch and the other victimised Bristol members exposed him as a caricature of what a trade union leader should be.

While the Newcastle witch-hunt and the Bedminster sackings were the most notable examples of hostile Moderate activity, these were not isolated events. Some union activists were subjected to investigation, and others to low-level harassment – the process itself was the punishment, whatever the outcome. Similarly, branches that were deemed to be a threat were suspended or had funds withdrawn.

As in the Newcastle campaign, the left in CPSA and in the wider movement gave unstinting support to the Bristol strikers. In both these cases they organised opposition to Moderate betrayals, fighting back in the branches and departmental groups. They coordinated speaking tours, distributed literature, organised motions to conferences and forged links with activists from other unions and campaigns. This political work, together with the personal sacrifices of the Newcastle and Bristol activists, had a tremendous impact, inspiring a hardened core of workers who understood the class nature of these battles. Far from intimidating and silencing their opponents, the Moderates' attacks on their own members during the late 1980s and early 1990s built the type of solidarity that set the conditions for their eventual defeat and the election of a socialist union leadership.

Notes & References

1. *Militant,* 27 June 1986.

2. Prontaprint was a well-known high street print shop chain in the 1980s. It is still in business.

3. McNeaney was later released from the charge of photocopier misuse.

4. *Newcastle Journal,* 13 March 1990.

5. Doreen Purvis, interview with author, 2017.

6. *Financial Times,* 18 May 1990.

7. *Liverpool Daily Post,* 15 May 1990.

8. Doreen Purvis, interview with author, 2017.

9. See, *Bristol Evening Post,* 21 June 1993.

10. 'Striking Against Market Madness', Militant Labour leaflet, October 1993.

11. *Bristol Evening Post,* 26 August 1993.

12. 'Defend Your Union' leaflet, August 1993.

13. *Bristol Evening Post,* 2 September 1993.

14. 'Defend Your Union' leaflet, May 1994.

15. This was a preliminary hearing to a full industrial tribunal in which union representatives can appeal and seek remedy on the basis that their sacking was due to trade union activity.

16. 'Defend Your Union' leaflet, September 1993. Based on a report to Broad Left's national committee by Chris Baugh, then union national vice-president, and John McInally, NEC corporate trustee.

17. 'News from the General Secretary', October 1993.

18. See, for example, *Leicester Daily Mercury,* 16 February 1994.

19. Goldfinch had not been employed long enough to reach the legal time limit to appeal to a tribunal.

PERSONAL TO YOU
THE ORDINARY CPSA MEMBER,
ONLY YOU CAN:

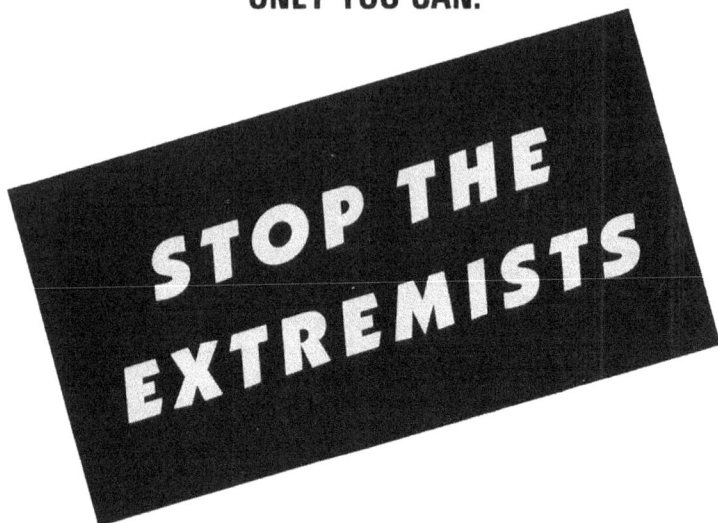

1. SHOW THIS LEAFLET TO OTHER CPSA MEMBERS.
2. CAST YOUR VOTES ON THE PINK VOTING PAPER.
3. POST IT OFF WITHOUT DELAY IN THE POSTAGE-PAID ENVELOPE PROVIDED

Issued and Published by the National Moderate Group in the CPSA

Contact: Mrs M Chambers, 2 Strangeways, Watford, Herts. Mr J Billouin, 3 Broad Street, Swindon, Wilts.
Mrs M Kaye, Newlyn, 17 Meadow Close, Houghton-Le-Spring, Tyne & Wear

■ The Moderates' Red Scare tactics at play, 1990.

4. Towards unity

Democracy and decision making

The Moderates' period in office until 1999 was maintained by bureaucratic methods that had become all too familiar. Lacking a clear class perspective, they sought to 'mitigate' the government's cost-cutting and privatisation agenda while dampening any real resistance from their membership. This meant continuing to wage a war of attrition against union activists, the majority of whom were either members of Broad Left (reconstituted as Left Unity in 1992) or those generally supportive of left policies. Treating the union as a personal fiefdom, they showed utter disdain for its representative democracy. As opposition to their business unionism grew, they risked even more desperate measures to retain power.

Union democracy was not, as the Moderates attempted to frame it, an abstract issue for 'politically minded activists'. Instead, it became the main battleground over how the union should stand up for members' interests. In refusing to carry out policies decided at the annual delegate conference, the leadership effectively limited resistance to government attacks and weakened coordination with other public sector unions on national campaigns.

Broad Left had won an unexpected victory in the 1987 national elections. As discussed in Chapter Two, this was largely due to the leadership's lamentable record in responding to Thatcherism, combined with their cynical efforts to overturn the election of John Macreadie. The left NEC held office for one year only, frustrated by the rejection of their call for all-out action. The Tories' general election victory that year was also a low point for morale. If that was not enough, they faced a further determined rearguard action from Chambers, Ellis and their remaining Moderate supporters on the NEC to prevent the left majority from carrying out the militant programme on which it had been elected.

With bureaucratic delays, threats of legal action, presidential rulings and misuse of communications, not least the union's journal *Red Tape*, the right wing fought to oppose the will of the NEC's majority. In a serious setback, they also successfully blocked the appointment of Kevin Roddy to the key position of national organiser, although two Broad Left activists, Frank Bonner and former general treasurer candidate Eddie Spence, were appointed to full-time positions. If the left had learned the lesson of taking and holding key positions of power, so too had the Moderates. The unpredictable balance of power that resulted from their loss of NEC control held many dangers for them and their establishment backers. They were now determined never again to allow the left to win at national level.

Besides government and media backing, they drew some support from sections of the union membership. Unions are not socialist political parties, but broad workers' organisations with memberships that reflect the range of political opinions found in wider society. The right wing's propaganda formula was reducible to a simple message: 'Campaigning and strikes don't work; the government, with a democratic mandate for its programme, is too strong for us'. This found an echo with more conservative members, not least among those who were more concerned with personal career advancement than a struggle against the government.

All factions produced material for the union's national elections in the early 1990s. Broad Left and later Left Unity, with its hundreds of activists, leafleted workplaces across the country. On the other hand, the right wing, with few activists, seldom carried out such activity. Mailshots containing election material were sent to workplaces, but while the left had to painstakingly compile address lists, the Moderates simply plundered official union records in clear breach of electoral regulations.

The Moderates' election material followed a familiar Red Scare template that had barely altered over the years. Their 1990 election leaflet was a typical example. There were exaggerated claims about their 'achievements', comparing their record with, 'the year when the Trotskyist Militant Tendency/Broad Left last controlled the NEC, you got 12 months of strikes and strife with nothing gained'. Members were urged: 'DON'T LET IT HAPPEN AGAIN ONLY YOU CAN STOP IT, FIGHT BACK AGAINST THE EXTREMISTS – VOTE MODERATE'. And in case the message had not sunk in: 'DON'T BLOW IT BY ELECTING A HARD LEFT NEC' and 'STOP THE EXTREMISTS'. The leaflet also helpfully reproduced Broad Left and BL84 lists with the battle cry: 'HERE ARE THE LEFT-WING EXTREMISTS'.

The Moderates were perfectly entitled to produce their material. However, they crossed a line by producing an insert in the official election ballot pack which set out the three lists of candidates using the same designations as in their unofficial material. This went beyond legitimate electioneering and constituted direct political interference in the ballot. Had any government or organisational ruling body branded its electoral opponents in such a way, it would be rightly regarded as ballot-rigging.

These efforts were underpinned by consistent press support. The newspapers gleefully described CPSA as the 'Beirut of the trade union movement', a phrase attributed to Barry Reamsbottom.[1] The intention was to portray a union in constant turmoil with an embattled moderate leadership, beset by left-wing extremists operating in the bowels of Whitehall. This was irresistible copy for right-wing journalists like Woodrow Wyatt, another former socialist who pursued the left with concentrated malice. His *News of the World* column 'The Voice of Reason', regularly spewed out lurid warnings about how the 'Reds' or 'Trots' planned to win power in the union as part of a wider conspiracy to install a Soviet-style dictatorship in Britain. According to Wyatt, they were only prevented from doing so by a small band of heroic Moderates, representing the 'silent majority'.

In the 1992 general secretary election, John Macreadie opposed Reamsbottom for the union's most senior position. The left ran a very strong campaign, and confidence was high given the repeated leadership betrayals of members' interests. When he announced the result at the NEC, outgoing general secretary John Ellis let it slip that a delay in making the result public was due to the last-minute arrival of about 3,000 ballot papers. As Reamsbottom glared at Ellis, a voice rang out: 'That'll be the MI5 vote then!'. Uncannily, Reamsbottom had won the election by just over 3,000 votes. Whether Ellis's slip was by accident or design is a matter of speculation. Although he was a convinced right-winger, he made it clear on more than one occasion his contempt for Reamsbottom's personal hatred toward his political enemies. Suspected electoral irregularities were often raised by the few left members on the NEC, but they were difficult to pursue without categorical evidence and unbiased investigation, and they were dismissed as 'speculation'.

Echoing Thatcher's attack on the miners' union, a triumphant Reamsbottom stated unequivocally in his first public communication as general secretary that his main objective was to, 'harry the alien influence of the Militant Tendency from the union', as the 'real danger came not from the employer or the Tories, but from the enemy within'.[2]

The annual delegate conference, to which branches submitted motions decided upon at their AGMs, was regarded by activists as the 'parliament' of the union. At conferences, policy was debated and decided upon, which the NEC was obliged to implement. Yet the Moderates did not accept the legitimacy of conferences nor the idea of representative democracy in any real sense. They had few branch delegates, although the formation of BL84 provided some additional weight for them on the conference floor. Nor had they any interest in serious conference debate, preferring to discredit delegates by accusing them of 'outside political interests' and 'not representing their members'. For the Moderates, the annual delegate conference was an ordeal to be endured for one week each year before returning to the safety of their bunker at union headquarters, from where they could ignore the terms of conference resolutions with impunity.

They opposed virtually anything put forward at conference by the left, almost as a matter of principle. Even a conference vote to affiliate to the Campaign Against Domestic Violence was opposed by Reamsbottom with NEC backing, followed by a series of distractions, smears and 'investigations'. Similarly, motions on issues such as housing, abortion and women's rights, South African apartheid and British policy in Northern Ireland were regarded as irrelevant. In seeking to impose such strict parameters, the leadership sought to prevent the union from becoming a wider campaigning body. Sometimes they failed to sideline debates on such issues and were forced to give official union backing to causes like the anti-apartheid struggle, albeit grudgingly.

During the early 1990s, the NEC as a body seriously declined in prestige. Usually, a handful of left activists were elected, but they were frustrated in initiating genuine debate on conference decisions, issues of union democracy, or the development of campaigning tactics. Reamsbottom set the tone; whatever the subject under discussion, his routine was unchanging. His 20 minute reports swiftly descended into rants about 'Trot' infiltration, peppered with highly personal attacks. His affectation of a sophisticated intellectualism for the benefit of his Moderate audience consisted largely of contributions laced with pre-prepared witticisms, culled from the *Oxford Book of Quotations,* with little or no regard to their appropriateness or relevance. Many contributions from NEC right-wingers in debates were read from scripts prepared for them by full-time officers in a similar tone to Reamsbottom. Typical was one intervention from the aggressive vice-president Tony Rouse, who said, 'these Trotskyites should be taken from this room, tied to a lamp post and whipped until the skin is flayed from their backs'.[3] It was to the credit of the socialists who served on the NEC throughout this period that they stuck to their principles, exposing the right-wing and refusing to be demoralised or intimidated.

As president and general secretary, Chambers and Reamsbottom personally spearheaded these cynical tactics. Other employed officials fell in behind them. These figures tended to be either former socialists or communists who had capitulated to New Realism and who justified their unprincipled loyalty by claiming they were merely carrying out management instructions; others were former BL84 lay activists who had been rewarded with full-time jobs in the union bureaucracy. This latter group's offensive behaviour was distasteful to many members. Their role was essentially to police the left activist layer, through internal enquiries and setting up disciplinary management sanctions, while also deliberately frustrating campaigns of left-led departmental groups.

But no right-wing grouping could maintain power or rely indefinitely on its full-time bureaucracy. Support among lay activists, such as branch secretaries and other local office bearers, was also necessary to achieve complete control. Again, this was the role into which some BL84 members readily inserted themselves, a symbiotic relationship in which these former socialists surrendered to the Moderates' reactionary agenda in return for prestige and preferment. Like their full-time counterparts, they became 'attack dogs' challenging the left politically and electorally, initiating complaints that resulted in the Moderate leadership undertaking investigations aimed at circumventing union democracy, and on more than one occasion, rerunning elections that had failed to produce the results that would mutually benefit BL84 and the right-wing leadership.

Beyond this, the narrow activist base of the Moderates consisted mainly of people who had little or no record of trade union activity even within their own workplaces. Indeed, they were often incapable of carrying out the most basic work expected of union representatives, let alone local leaders. Some were right-wing Labour adherents, others came from the centrist Social Democratic Party that had split from Labour in 1981 – some were even Tories. But most were simply the type of cautiously conservative members who provided the right wing's main electoral support. Often, they had been 'talent spotted' at union courses or had been advanced through personal recommendation. Manageable and malleable, they were trusted to be placed on Moderate candidate electoral lists and sometimes were catapulted into the highest level of lay leadership.

Unsurprisingly, the Moderates were able to control only a few branches, but these included two with substantial memberships: Newcastle Central Office, where the left leadership had been bureaucratically removed; and the Driver and Vehicle Licensing Agency in Swansea, where a combination of a ruthless right-wing and tepid left leadership saw them wield power for some years. In contrast, they had virtually no activist base in the union's largest departmental groups, the DHSS and DE, whose membership was the size of some unions. In effect, the union was now increasingly functioning as a tiny clique disconnected from the mass of workplaces and loyal only to their establishment backers.

'Bonfire of agreements'

The dominance of the Moderates challenged any concerted response against attacks on members and on public services. As such, they allowed a free hand to successive governments in targeting specific sections of the workforce, notably those administering benefits. In effect, they presided over what was appropriately described as a 'bonfire of agreements', diminishing terms and conditions that had been negotiated and won over many decades.

Arguably, the worst betrayal was the surrendering of national pay bargaining, a process which took place fitfully from the late 1980s onwards. This eventually led to a weakening of collective union power and negotiating strength on the most basic issue of wages. Previously, civil service grades across Britain and Northern Ireland had been paid the same rate, one of the historic achievements of civil service trade unionism. Now instead of bargaining with one central national employer, the new 'departmental' or 'agency' model involved negotiations with as many as 260 separate units. For the Tories, this was a cherished project. As they had intended, the fracturing of central bargaining led to the introduction of substantial variations in pay rates for the same work; the inevitable impact was lower wage rates across the entire civil service.

This development was to have unexpected consequences for the Moderates. Broad Left made an open appeal to those in the BL84 who had witnessed their comrades' integration with the Moderate group. The resulting rapprochement led to the establishment of a reconfigured socialist rank-and-file organisation under the name 'Left Unity'. Although a few could not forgive the role played by some BL84 members in the Newcastle witch-hunt, most activists enthusiastically welcomed the re-establishment of a united left. The main political force in Left Unity, as in Broad Left, remained Militant and the independents who generally supported it, but there was also a broadening of political support. Communist Party activist Tony Conway, for example, argued strongly for its activists to join Left Unity and played an important role in the realignment on the left.

The Tories sought to further exacerbate divisions among civil service workers by seeking to introduce more extreme measures, such as Merit and Regional Pay. The former was based on performance, while the latter offered higher rates in areas where recruitment was more challenging. Even the Moderates were unable to stop individual departmental union sections from fighting off these attacks. More generally, the betrayal over national pay bargaining deepened resentment among the workforce, laying the basis for future struggles.

Along with the abolition of national pay bargaining, the Moderates also presided over the breakup of the civil service into agencies and the introduction of 'business' methods, such as Market Testing. They were incapable of resisting these attacks, either actively supporting them, or at best offering no alternative but acquiescence.

Their refusal to initiate coordinated national action led workers in departmental groups, branches, and individual workplaces to organise their own fightbacks. The right wing tried to create barriers to such groups taking industrial action, but they were forced by members to give official sanction to a series of local and group strikes. Nevertheless, they invariably worked actively to undermine them and, in the case of the 1995–96 Employment Service pay dispute, even openly betrayed them. While frustrated at national level, the left worked upwards from the individual workplace to branch, city or town, and to departmental groups, with the intention of generalising common grievances and demands.

Although CPSA activists were fighting with one hand tied behind their backs, the level of struggle maintained by civil service workers, mainly in the lower-paid administrative grades, was remarkable. Mark Serwotka, future PCS general secretary, had led and won a six-month dispute in Caerphilly in early 1987 and another extended dispute in Aberdare.[4] Later that year, a three-month staffing dispute at Easterhouse Unemployment Benefit Office in Glasgow, involving workers on 50 per cent strike pay and an all-Glasgow one-day strike, won another decisive victory.[5] This was in the wake of Thatcher's re-election and the Moderates' return to national union leadership. In November 1987, workers also took successful action against the introduction of the Youth Training Scheme into the civil service, defending the wage rates of young workers and new entrants, whom the government intended to exploit on the cheap.[6]

The message from these disputes was that militancy pays. Enraging management and Moderates alike, they also created an experienced and hardened cadre of strike leaders and a militant membership in many sections of the union. They were particularly dangerous for the right wing, who were forced to concede demands for action they would have preferred not to authorise.

If it had not been for the development of an organised socialist presence within the union, membership anger would have been of a more episodic and fractured nature and more easily dissipated. Broad Left and its successor Left Unity played a decisive role in channelling this anger into effective campaigns and industrial action. The new grouping was the key subjective factor in transforming members' desire to resist into a fighting force. In a relatively short period, it rebuilt a sense of combativity and solidarity, despite the balance of power being tilted in favour of the government. It also helped launch a coordinated fight against the Moderates, which otherwise would have been impossible. Its organising role included publicising grievances, problems and disputes through a highly developed communications strategy, including leafleting, town, regional and branch meetings. It also trained new activists and fostered political education through debating ideas, strategies and policies. Equally vital was the type of organisation that had been painstakingly developed over the years by activists in workplaces like the Easterhouse benefits office, where there had been seven Broad Left activists, including three members of Militant, out of 47 strikers. This became the foundation upon which the left's influence at branch, regional, departmental and national levels was built and maintained.

If the influence of Left Unity was critical in the fight against the Moderates, that of Militant was the key subjective factor within the wider left. The effectiveness of socialist groupings or organisations is not measured by the plaudits of friends but by the attacks of the enemy. Reamsbottom's boast that he would 'harry Militant' from the union was a recognition of the threat posed by it. During the 1980s, Militant was at the height of its influence and at the epicentre of resistance against the rightwards drift of the Labour Party. Its strong defence of socialist ideas and the right of Marxists to be in the party did not stop the expulsions, but did gain the grudging respect of many in the movement and drew towards it a number of committed class fighters, including within CPSA.

Militant's commitment to the United Front, along with its perspectives based on class struggle and demands that chimed with members' grievances and aspirations, made it a dangerous enemy for the right wing. John Macreadie played a highly significant role in instilling in Militant activists a simple but very important way of thinking; no matter how powerful the right wing appeared, they could and would be defeated. He emphasised: 'We will fight with other socialist activists and we will win the leadership of our union, not for narrow sectarian interests but to build it into one capable of defending its members' interests, and that of the working class, who rely upon the services they provide'.[7] This confident political attitude defined the best of the work of socialists and communists in CPSA. It militated against the resigned mentality that can develop even among 'militant' union activists when faced with entrenched right-wing leaderships. This often manifests in an erratic veering between despair and elation in response to events, inevitably descending into ultra-leftism and opportunism.

Civil servants work within the bureaucratic structure of the state. For them, government policy and strategy are not abstract issues but of direct consequence to their jobs, pay and conditions. They also have an impact on the future of the services they provide to their communities and their class. It is thus no coincidence that the struggles within the union were expressed in such an open and highly politicised form, with the most class-conscious members drawn to socialist ideas, some joining revolutionary organisations. The Moderates had hoped to create a model of business unionism, but instead had facilitated a highly effective broad left response in the shape of Left Unity.

The path to unity and a left-led PCS

As we have seen, trade union organisation in the civil service was traditionally organised on the basis of grades: the large mass of clerical and administrative workers in CPSA; technical and specialists in the Institute of Professional, Managers and Specialists (IPMS); manual staff and other specialists in the Civil Service Union (CSU); tax staff of all grades largely within the Inland Revenue Staff Federation (IRSF); and executive grades in the Society of Civil and Public Servants (SCPS). A cross-sector Council of Civil Service Unions also included the FDA, which represented senior civil servants.[8] Whilst this highly stratified structure reflected the different social positions of staff, the culture of the civil service allowed for a certain amount of inter-grade mobility. Some workers could enter the service within the administrative grades but then rose to senior management status.

The economic and political environment from the mid-1970s onwards had conditioned developments in all the civil service unions. There was growing openness towards more industrial action and political campaigning, with an attendant sharpening of internal left-right tensions. At the same time, there was also an increased awareness that these new conditions required greater industrial unity. This inevitably led to consideration of amalgamations between the unions.

In the past, there had been considerable apprehension as soon as merger talks appeared on the horizon. This was not unexpected given distinctions of class and status. Attachment to existing traditions of individual unions and concerns about political shifts and loss of influence also played their part. For example, opposition to a merger between CPSA and SCPS in May 1985 was common to both the right-wing leadership and the Militant-led left, and attempts to form a new union failed.[9] In this case, many Moderates, who split over the issue, had been fearful of losing their hegemonic position in any new formation, while the left opposed the diminution of union democracy contained in the proposed new Rules and Constitution. In addition, there existed a tenacious view advocated principally by Socialist Caucus that a merger would create a 'bosses union'. This was based on the idea that anyone in a position above that of the basic clerical grades was a 'manager'. This narrow view failed to consider that in some departments, such as the Department of Work and Pensions (DWP), not all executive officers had supervisory responsibilities – and indeed some were among the most loyal and militant union members. Far more importantly, all staff, save the most senior managers, faced cuts in living standards. Fortunately, by the mid-1990s when the merger to create PCS was being considered, the 'bosses union' argument had lost all credibility.

The general principle of merger with the CPSA also raised concerns among executive grades in other unions, largely on the grounds of the union's reputation for fractious internal struggles. Most had little time for the Moderates, but they were also uncomfortable with what they regarded as the 'hard left' organised in Left Unity. The antipathy to Militant and its campaigning methods was particularly pronounced among some who had been promoted from administrative grades.

Against this background, the first step on the road to the formation of PCS in 1998 was the bringing together of the CSU with the SCPS to form the National Union of Civil and Public Servants (NUCPS) ten years earlier. This was a largely successful undertaking in which the more proletarian CSU membership – manual workers and specialists like instructional officers, engineers, coastguards and communications staff – gave weight to the politics of the merged union, which featured a carefully constructed alliance of left-wing and centrist Labour and Communist elements and a less virulent and organised right wing.

New Labour elements in the NUCPS initially found common cause with the more markedly right-wing leading elements in the Inland Revenue Staff Federation (IRSF), where the internal political culture had something in common with the CPSA. But when in 1996 the NUCPS and IRSF merged to form the Public Services, Tax and Commerce Union (PTC), these distinctions lost some of their character, reflecting a sharpening industrial relations climate. The scene was set for the new PTC's merger with CPSA.

Irrespective of the iron grip of the Moderates on the main positions of power in CPSA, the union's rules and constitution were remarkably democratic by the standards of the movement. Many on the left had reasonable concerns about what form of political configuration would emerge in the new union. Previous mergers had been opposed by the left on the basis that such proposals reduced rather than expanded democratic accountability. There had also been fears that the political complexion of the other union's leadership would embed rather than challenge Moderate methods and practices.

There was particular disquiet that the proposals contained a backward move to biannual elections and conferences, leading some individuals on the left to vote against the merger. On the other hand, there was considerable confidence within Left Unity that democratic advances could be secured through votes at conference and in national membership ballots. Similarly, worries that PTC's senior full time and lay leaders, John Sheldon, Peter Lamb, Hugh Lanning, Peter Donnellan and James Undy might make common cause with Reamsbottom and Chambers against the 'hard left' were balanced by the calculation that when socialists and communists from PTC joined the ranks of Left Unity, new opportunities would open up to fight the Moderates.

Yet, the key factor underpinning the left's support for the formation of a new union remained an inescapable industrial and political logic. Whichever government was in power, its key objective would be to deliver a neoliberal agenda in the interests of the capitalist class, with the civil service their main target as part of the wider war on the public sector. In creating a union with a united workforce representing the vast majority of civil service workers, and by embedding militancy within the new formation, it was believed that the aim of building a democratic, fighting union could be realised.

The road to merger was protracted, but differences were at last overcome. By March 1998, the benefits of a single union covering most civil service grades were undeniable. Balloting among the various occupational groupings resulted in overwhelming votes in both CPSA and the PTC to merge to form the Public and Commercial Services Union (PCS).[10] This decisively changed the character of civil service trade unionism, intensifying the struggle to reorientate the new union to resist continuing government attacks.

The changed balance of forces produced by the merger soon proved detrimental to the Moderates, as discontent with their methods quickly spread to former PTC activists and full-timers. Political alignments within the new union would be further shaped by the anti-working-class policies of New Labour. Tony Blair's election the previous year had been welcomed by most workers after eighteen years of Tory rule, but it became increasingly clear that Thatcher's claim that New Labour was her 'greatest achievement' was no throwaway gibe. As detailed in the next chapter, Blair's government maintained the Tory cuts agenda for public services and ramped up outsourcing and privatisation. It also betrayed the trade unions by refusing to ameliorate, let alone abolish, the most repressive anti-union laws in the industrialised world. Imperialist adventures would soon follow in which the New Labour leadership stood four-square with profiteers and warmongers.

The transitional arrangements for the two unions' merger meant that their general secretaries, Barry Reamsbottom and PTC's John Sheldon, would jointly hold the position until 2004, or until one or the other retired; Sheldon was due to retire in 2001. Instead, the new union's annual delegate conference in May 2000 voted for an earlier general secretary election to take place, a decision endorsed by 62,296 votes to 2,766 in a membership ballot.[11]

An intense debate now opened up within Left Unity, and an election was held to choose the group's candidate for general secretary. Full-time officer Terry Adams stood as the candidate of the Socialist Party, narrowly defeating Mark Serwotka. The latter's strong showing was in large part due to rumours that the Socialist Party had in fact already made an internal decision to support Hugh Lanning, a PTC full-time officer. This proved to be true. It had agreed to give 'critical support' to Lanning on the basis that the anti-Moderate vote should not be split and following assurances regarding his programme. They argued that building on the alliance developed with activists and officers from the former PTC was the surest way of defeating Reamsbottom.

The Socialist Party now submitted an emergency motion to a Left Unity conference held in Manchester in the wake of the earlier election, calling on Adams to stand aside and for Left Unity to support Lanning's candidature. The motion was only narrowly passed, reflecting opposition to the Socialist Party's position, not only from the SWP and Socialist Caucus, but also those independent socialists who usually voted with them.

After the conference ended, those unhappy with the decision stayed behind to discuss their response. The general view was that a credible left candidate was essential in the new union's first election for general secretary. Mark Serwotka was pressed to stand but initially declined. As a clerical worker in the Sheffield DHSS office, he worked part-time due to caring responsibilities for his two young children. He finally agreed, so that members would have the opportunity to vote for a socialist rank-and-file activist, in contrast to the full-timer Lanning, who was regarded as a 'soft' left. While Serwotka's record of activity as a strike leader and workplace organiser made him the strongest candidate among activists, he had little expectation of winning.

There was now a dramatic development. Reamsbottom, who had been confident of success as the Moderate candidate, did not gather anywhere near the fifty branch nominations needed to stand. Under threat of legal action, he now secured a deal to stay in position until May 2002, working with whoever won the election to ensure a 'smooth transfer' of responsibilities. He also negotiated full payment of his salary up until 2004 and a £120,000 payout on leaving the union.

In response, the Socialist Party considered its options, including calling for the election nomination process to be rerun. Having won the Left Unity election, this would allow Terry Adams a chance to argue that, given changed circumstances, he was the 'legitimate' left candidate. For their part, Lanning's campaign made clear they would not support any reopening of the electoral process, ostensibly on 'democratic' grounds, but underlying this was a hard practical consideration – they were expecting to defeat Serwotka.

Having originally expected to have Reamsbottom as his challenger, Lanning now found himself fighting the 'wrong campaign' with a candidate to his left. Indeed, momentum for Serwotka's candidature was growing across the union. When the Socialist Party again raised rerunning the electoral process at a special Left Unity National Committee, the independents were still opposed. Isolated and with no other alternative, the Socialist Party finally decided to back Serwotka, as did Left Unity as a whole. This decision did cause some resentment among some in the Socialist Party who felt one of its members should have been the candidate, given its prominent role in building the left.

The Socialist Party's position in seeking an alliance to support Lanning had been a principled one. Moderate rule had been a disaster for members, and defeating Reamsbottom, an open reactionary now branding himself as a 'Blairite', was of paramount importance. But their approach did not convince the wider left. The tactic of Adams winning the Left Unity nomination, only to step down in Lanning's favour based on a very narrowly won emergency motion, lost the Socialist Party even more support. While Serwotka agreed to stand for general secretary in defiance of a democratic Left Unity election, it was the correct decision politically and one justified by the subsequent history of PCS. By any objective assessment, the Socialist Party made a miscalculation, an honest one, but a miscalculation, nevertheless.

The candidates' election addresses proved crucial in persuading members that Serwotka would transform the union into one robustly representing their interests. Lanning's address tended to emphasise service aspects of developing the new union, but Serwotka's was openly militant, demanding a return to national pay bargaining and stressing the need for all unions to stand up to the government, anticipating the coordinated approach that would become the hallmark of PCS policy in the years to come. Some of Lanning's supporters posed the question – can you trust running a multi-million pound organisation to a benefits clerk? The members' answer was clear – yes, we can!

The struggle against the Moderate bureaucracy in CPSA had created a highly politicised activist layer. They and many members took a very dim view of the idea that what the new union required was yet more 'professional' leadership. One telling incident caught the mood of members: a group of typists wrote to Serwotka to tell him he got their vote because they considered him 'one of us'.[12]

On 6 December 2000, Serwotka won by a margin of 40,740 to Hugh Lanning's 33,942 to become PCS's first elected general secretary.[13] The turnout of 30 per cent in a postal ballot conducted under the restrictive anti-union laws, constituted strong membership participation. The outcome was part of a bigger picture. Civil service workers had been some of the first to become disillusioned with the New Labour government, but this spread quickly through the wider trade union movement. Serwotka's victory was one of a number in that period that saw socialist leaders being elected to general secretary positions. Branded by the press as the 'Awkward Squad', those elected included: Bob Crow – RMT; Billy Hayes – CWU; Paul Mackney – NATFHE; Mick Rix – ASLEF; Tony Woodley – TGWU; Brian Caton – POA; and a few years later in 2005, Matt Wrack – FBU.[14]

His election was also a signal to the more combative sections of PCS, especially those from the former CPSA, that the days of inaction and collaboration were over. However, the Moderates were far from defeated, even forming their own alliance with the anti-left Membership First group from the former PTC. This was further reflected in the contradictory nature of the NEC elections, which saw Left Unity chair and Socialist Party member, Janice Godrich, elected as union president, while the Moderates secured a very narrow majority on the committee of 24 against 22.

Despite the NEC result, the union was moving more decisively leftwards. The annual delegate conference in May 2002 delivered a major setback for the right wing when a series of activist motions from branches were voted through. In an article in *The Guardian*, campaigning socialist journalist Paul Foot wrote:

> The final straw for the right was the 2002 PCS conference in early May. It was the most left-wing conference ever. A whole raft of motions was passed by an overwhelming majority – including a motion supporting Palestinians and calling for sanctions against Israel, a ban on arms sales, and a boycott of Israeli goods and for [Israeli leader] Sharon to stand trial as a war criminal. A motion supporting the Stop the War Coalition was also passed. The right meanwhile was humiliated on motion after motion. Policy agreed at the conference put PCS firmly on the

hard left of the union movement. Conference also voted virtually unanimously to call on Reamsbottom to retire on 31 May.[15]

For Reamsbottom, who had shared duties with Serwotka for almost eighteen months, the conference was a deep blow both politically and psychologically. He was clearly stung by the way delegates expressed open contempt for the record and methods of the Moderates and himself personally. The union he had helped to establish clearly had little further use for him, or his type.

Incapable of addressing Foot's political analysis, he fired off an immediate riposte to *The Guardian*, which began with his trademark tabloid polemic: 'I'm all for democracy and giving people the right to vote for Trotskyists, as long as they know what they are voting for'. He went on to make the bizarre claim that, 'in a more complex ballot than the general secretary election, there was a lower turnout, but the hard left polled much worse than the moderates.' He also claimed that: 'Mark Serwotka now has to accept that PCS members have voted to change the control of the NEC. His "election" eighteen months ago, in an unlawful ballot, cannot overturn or undermine that result'.[16] Misreading the narrow majority that his supporters had on the NEC as proof that his position was recoverable and no doubt confident of establishment backing, he had embarked on a course of reckless adventurism that would seal both his and the Moderates' fate.

Right-wing coup

By the time of his *Guardian* letter, Reamsbottom was already on the move. Openly usurping Janice Godrich's presidential powers, he had called an NEC meeting at short notice on 23 May 2002, without even informing her of its purpose. His supporters knew his plan well in advance. This was nothing less than an attempt to overturn Serwotka's democratic election as general secretary, in effect a coup to keep himself in power.

Just hours before the meeting, Reamsbottom informed Godrich that he had obtained legal advice which stated the general secretary election should never have taken place and should be ignored. Serwotka, who was due to take up sole control of the union on 1 June, was not the general secretary, and therefore he himself would remain in post until April 2004 after all. Godrich ruled the meeting unconstitutional, but Reamsbottom's supporters attempted to remove her from the chair and replace her with veteran right-winger and witch-hunter, Ted Euers. Left Unity and other left supporters on the NEC reacted furiously, forcing the Moderates to move to another room where they continued their meeting and proceeded to remove all Left Unity members from key NEC sub-committees.

While events were unfolding at the NEC, John Macreadie, whom Serwotka had appointed as his senior policy officer, issued a branch circular in Serwotka's name explaining that a major assault on the union's democracy was underway and that it would be resisted. This bold initiative, along with the defiance of the left on the NEC, set the tone for the fightback. Meanwhile, the Murdoch press had been well briefed on Reamsbottom's actions. *The Sun* speculated, 'Union lefties KO'd?', and claimed that, 'Tony Blair was said to be delighted when the news reached Downing Street'.[17] Reamsbottom himself declared that the union had been 'saved in the nick of time' from 'unrepresentative Trotskyists'.

Rage at Reamsbottom's actions unleashed an unprecedented level of protest throughout PCS and across the wider trade union movement. Above all, resistance to the coup was fired by the deepening realisation that New Labour would be little different from the Tories and that strong leadership would be needed to challenge Blair's government. Since Serwotka's election, the desire for change had already seen 27,000 new members recruited.[18]

Under the banner 'Democracy Alliance', meetings were held by PCS members throughout the country in workplaces and in various towns and cities. Petitions were circulated and union headquarters was flooded with letters and faxes of protest, many from members who, without prompting from Left Unity and other activists, expressed outrage and opposition to the right wing's actions. As Nigel Green, a Royal Parks member, commented, 'Barry

Reamsbottom is a civilian version of General Pinochet'.[19] Demands were also made for a special conference. The campaign was further boosted by messages of support from several union leaders and individual trade unionists. RMT's Bob Crow warned that if Reamsbottom appeared at TUC congress in the guise of PCS general secretary, he would personally challenge his right to be there.

Reamsbottom had badly miscalculated in assuming that Hugh Lanning would fall into line with the coup. He failed to grasp that whatever differences existed between him and Serwotka, they were dwarfed in comparison to their mutual contempt for Reamsbottom's devious methods. Lanning's role in the dispute was widely admired and appreciated, together with his consistent campaigning for the Palestinian cause and his major role in the struggle to restore union rights at GCHQ. He appeared at a mass rally on 19 July alongside Serwotka in the Friends Meeting House in London where he unequivocally stated that the manoeuvrings of the Reamsbottom faction were unjustifiable. He made no complaints about the electoral process and declared that Serwotka was fully entitled to assume office. Even more fundamental was Lanning's realisation that the Moderates had nothing to offer the PCS in resisting the challenges faced by civil service workers. He did not just oppose the coup in words but, to his considerable personal and political credit, played a major role in the campaign, helping to further isolate the increasingly desperate Moderates.

Reamsbottom had been convinced that Serwotka and Godrich lacked the financial resources to pursue a legal case. Instead, they put up their homes as security, which, along with donations from the membership and beyond, allowed them to contest his action. Had they lost the judgment, they would also have lost their homes. In a situation of 'dual power' in the union leadership, only bold, decisive action would shift the balance decisively in favour of the left. In a serious setback for Reamsbottom, the High Court awarded an interim judgement that kept both Godrich and Serwotka in post until a full hearing six weeks later.[20] Welcome as this was, it was by no means a settled matter that they would win at the full hearing. The final judgement in July, however, was a vindication of Serwotka's position. Sir Andrew Morritt confirmed that his election had been valid; that the purported NEC meeting of 23 May 2002 had not been properly constituted; and finally, that Reamsbottom could not backtrack on the previously agreed retirement deal.[21]

Legal judgments of this type – in this case, whether a major trade union should be led by a loyal functionary of the ruling class or a socialist committed to challenging it – are not based on some pristine principle of objective 'justice', but on a cold, calculated assessment of class interests. The changed balance of forces in the union and the wider movement, and the depth of feeling engendered by the coup were the most critical factors influencing the outcome. Reamsbottom's action reeked of desperation, not least in its blatant and egregious planning and execution. Giving it legal endorsement would have caused real damage to the credibility of the court. It was now evident to serious figures in the government and the judiciary that the Moderates were so politically and morally damaged that they could no longer be relied upon as reliable and effective allies. Reamsbottom had become an embarrassing anachronistic reminder of the brutal witch-hunting methods that had cleared a path for the neoliberalism of New Labour. If rising militancy was to be seen off among civil service workers in future, other methods would have to be found.

Serwotka and his supporters were determined to press home the advantage. The 2002 annual conference had voted for a special delegate conference to consider a return to annual elections, one of his election pledges. When the Moderate-controlled NEC refused to implement the vote, such an abuse of democracy had to be confronted. Godrich, Macreadie and Serwotka agreed to serve every Moderate NEC member with legal papers to enforce the conference decision. Completely shocked, one of them told Serwotka they never dreamt he would do such a thing, he replied, 'this is not a game'. It was a warning to the Moderate faction that they should never again flaunt the wishes of the union's members.

Reaction is often the chief motivating force in focusing the left on the need for unity in the face of the class enemy. 'Democracy Alliance' had brought together a very wide left coalition against the coup, with Left Unity as the politically dominant and most influential presence. Although the various left groupings continued to operate independently, the two key principles that defined the alliance were a democratic commitment to implement conference policy, and joint candidate lists for senior officer and NEC elections. With Serwotka as general secretary and Godrich as president, two of the key positions of power in the PCS had already been secured for the left; at the NEC elections in July 2003, Democracy Alliance won a resounding victory of 34 seats, compared with only 9 for the Moderates.[22]

The significance of the left's victory in PCS was commented upon in *The Socialist* in July 2003:

...members voted for the Democracy slate because they believed the union reps standing for election would stand up to management and New Labour with their business agenda, piling on the pressures [sic] and attacking working conditions. It was a damning verdict on the actions of the right-wing [Moderates]. Their leaders have paid the price – Reamsbottom, McGowan, Currie and Euers have gone.

It continued:

With general secretary Mark Serwotka, Janice Godrich has had to deal with the right-wing's attacks on union democracy over the past fourteen months, including their attempt to overthrow the results of the general secretary election and to curb the powers of the president. After fighting off the right-wing in the courts, a membership ballot supported an initiative from the left and voted to return to annual elections and annual conferences instead of biennial events. It must be the first time that a president of a major union has brought forward their own election by twelve months![23]

The task now facing the left was how to make the transition from opposition to effective leadership and how to use the power of the union to fight chancellor Gordon Brown's latest threats against civil service jobs, conditions and public services.

Notes & References

1. *The Scotsman*, 13 November 1990.
2. *Daily Express*, 20 May 1992.
3. Author's contemporaneous note.
4. *Merthyr Express*, 29 January 1987.
5. *Daily Record*, 16 April 1987.
6. *The Scotsman*, 11 November 1987.
7. Author's contemporaneous note.
8. The Association of First Division Civil Servants until 2000, now simply FDA.
9. *The Scotsman*, 3 May 1985.
10. *Birmingham Daily Post*, 11 March 1998.
11. *Morning Star*, 17 May 2002.
12. *The Guardian*, 29 May 2002.
13. *Morning Star*, 7 December 2000.
14. *The Guardian*, 18 February 2002.
15. *The Guardian*, 29 May 2002.
16. *The Guardian*, 30 May 2002.
17. *The Sun*, 24 May 2002.
18. *The Guardian*, 28 May 2002.
19. *Morning Star*, 17 July 2002.
20. *The Socialist*, 9 August 2002.
21. *The Scotsman*, 31 July 2002.
22. *Morning Star*, 5 July 2003.
23. *The Socialist*, 12 July 2003.

5. A fighting union

'Filthy rich'

The deadening embrace of neoliberalism by all major Westminster parties was the product of the country's specific crisis, which in turn reflected wider shifts in international capitalism. Once the world's greatest industrial and political power, Britain had become a largely rentier economy based on financial services and the money-laundering of the City of London. Within less than a generation, the centre of gravity within mainstream politics had moved to the right. One-Nation Toryism expressed through a cross-class social contract was effectively dead. Thatcher had viewed such a position with utter contempt and succeeded in creating a new consensus, based on the great lie that there was no alternative to the market, nor even to the extreme neoliberalism she championed.

Under Thatcher and John Major, the Tories had consistently targeted the civil service with considerable success. They cut pay and conditions, created standalone agencies, drove marketisation and business management methods, and privatised and outsourced services. Far from gaining a respite, this process had intensified under Blair and Brown's New Labour governments from 1997 onwards.

Nevertheless, the elections of Mark Serwotka and Janice Godrich, followed by the return of a left NEC in 2003, had created a strong mood of optimism among the union's activists and the wider membership.[1] The new leadership had few illusions about the challenges facing them but saw an opportunity to build an alternative to the class collaboration of the Moderates.

For socialists and communists active in their trade unions, being an oppositional force is one thing, but holding and exercising power is quite another. The Moderates had refused to fight back against government attacks and to build alliances with the wider trade union movement. Now the question was posed – was the new leadership capable of doing so?

It was not uncommon prior to the 1997 general election to hear workers express the hope that the rightwards drift of New Labour was simply a tactic to appease the Murdoch press, and that once in office they would undo the crimes of Thatcher. New Labour's victory saw workers, including most civil servants, welcome a new start with a 'progressive' government, pledged to rebalance power away from the profiteers, develop public services and treat workers with fairness and respect.

This was a false hope. Gordon Brown quickly abandoned any pretence that government should play a direct role in economic management when he handed over control of key aspects of monetary policy to the Bank of England, itself a form of privatisation. Despite being elected to represent the interests of millions of working-class voters, New Labour's message was clear – there is no alternative to the free market, or to cuts and privatisation.

New Labour architect, Peter Mandelson declared that he was, 'intensely relaxed about people getting filthy rich.'[2] Such hubris sprang from a cynical view that the working class had no other choice but to vote Labour. This error was to lead to the near destruction of the party in Scotland when workers moved, at first slowly and then in large numbers, to the Scottish National Party (SNP).

Labour's abandonment of the working class led to intense debate on the question of political representation among socialists and union activists, including within PCS. Blair's failure to substantially amend, still less repeal, the Tories' anti-union laws showed his contempt for the trade unions, including the affiliates who continued to bankroll his party. Home secretary Jack Straw even threatened to jail leaders of the Prison Officers' Association (POA) when they threatened industrial action. On the other hand, the party's corporate donors had merely to ask, and the government delivered.

In a lecture delivered at the University of Hertfordshire in 2007, Mark Serwotka declared that the election of New Labour meant a change 'in the singer, not the song' and highlighted the contrast between the promises of Labour politicians in opposition and what they delivered in government.[3] In opposition, Jack Straw had described privately-run prisons as immoral, but as home secretary, he renewed existing contracts and commissioned more. When the Tories said they would privatise air traffic control, Labour described it as 'privatising the skies', but, now in office, they continued with the same plans. Having claimed privatisation and outsourcing in central government was a 'waste of taxpayers' money', they went on to privatise more central government work than Thatcher and Major combined.

Serwotka set out the union leadership's opposing analysis. This rested on the simple fact that private companies cannot deliver cost-effective high quality public services to non-paying customers as this is not their business model. Any attempt to make these companies operate as if profit was not their main priority would require hugely increased public funding in compensation for, 'the additional resources and risks involved in serving people whose demand for services is not expressed in, or limited by, their willingness and ability to pay'. So, it was hardly surprising that these companies went on to ruthlessly exploit every conceivable contractual loophole to extract as much money as possible from public finances, as, 'any attempt to design contracts that anticipate every eventuality, and which potentially impose significant costs, penalties and risks on contractors, will be a powerful disincentive for companies to bid'.

He went on to describe how tremendous amounts of government time and energy were expended in artificially 'creating' public service markets by providing private companies with long-term contracts in which there was no real governance, with penalties for poor performance at best only partially enforced. To take just one example, the major contractor EDS secured an agreement from HMRC that it would only make payments for poor performance on condition it was awarded future contracts from the government.

Blair claimed that his government did not care whether services were delivered in the public or private sectors, as he did not base policy on 'ideology' but on 'what works'. This slick spin was intended to divert attention from his determination to deliver for profiteers, who correctly interpreted his soundbite as an open invitation to plunder the public services through the creation of artificial market conditions, with the government's role reduced to awarding contracts.

The Public Finance Initiative (PFI) had been introduced by John Major, but was supercharged by Gordon Brown to expand privatisation, a process he justified on the basis that it was required to conform to European Union policy. PFI enabled companies to systematically mine public finances by extracting risk-free profits from developments that the taxpayer would be paying back for decades. PFI was legalised theft on the most spectacular scale. One school in Belfast built under a PFI contract was due to close because of low pupil numbers, but as the Education Authority had signed a 25-year contract, it was still obliged to fulfil the contract at a cost of £400,000 a year.[4]

PCS publications and parliamentary briefings exposed the PFI scandal, as did other unions and the socialist press, but, with the notable exception of journalist George Monbiot, the mainstream media gave little attention to the greatest financial scandal since the mass privatisation of the country's utilities under Thatcher. The Tories and big business looked on in admiration at the sheer audacity of New Labour's scam; a Tory government would have struggled to pull off what Brown achieved. New Labour did more than emulate the Tories' robbery of public assets and finances, they exceeded it. The PFI scheme was terminated by Tory chancellor Philip Hammond in 2018, but an exposé in *The Guardian* in October 2022 reported that, based on an analysis of NHS Trust accounts, 101 of them owed about £50 billion in future PFI payments. It found that for a typical trust, over half of PFI payments were just for interest.[5]

Major's government had been undermined by allegations of sleaze, but this was also to be a factor in New Labour's eventual demise. Big corporations demonstrated their appreciation of the Labour government's role in representing their class interests by rewarding former ministers with consultancies and advisory posts – deferred backhanders for services rendered. The result was a revolving door between public duty and private profit.

Leading the way in this carnival of opportunism, Blair headed straight for the private sector, accepting consultancies from J.P. Morgan and similar. His net worth is now reckoned at over £50 million.[6] Months after stepping down as health minister, Patricia Hewitt was awarded consultancy with multi-national chemists Alliance Boots and a £55,000 per annum special adviser post with Cinven, a private equity company that had taken over the UK's BUPA hospitals; further lucrative appointments followed, including membership of NHS boards.[7] The lobbying activities of former defence minister, Geoff Hoon, offered at the premium rate of £3,000 a day, were exposed by *The Sunday Times* and Channel 4's *Dispatches* programme. He was quoted: 'I'm really looking forward to... translating my knowledge and contacts about the international scene into something that, bluntly, makes money'. Hoon's former ministerial colleague, Stephen Byers boasted of the influence he could exert for private companies at up to £5,000 a day, describing himself as a 'cab for hire'.[8]

Mandelson's 'getting filthy rich' comment had been embraced by New Labour politicians not simply as an endorsement of unrestrained capitalism but as a personal invitation. While Hewitt, Hoon, and Byers represented some of the more egregious examples of this culture, literally scores of New Labour MPs exploited the risibly weak regulations and powers of the Parliamentary Advisory Committee on Business Appointments and profited from their former ministerial positions. They readily took up consultancies and contracts with firms related to their previous areas of responsibility. Indeed, these were guaranteed as if covered by a promissory note. John Hutton, another former defence minister, walked into a top nuclear post with the US firm Hyperion Power Generation; when he was later asked by the Tory-Liberal coalition government to advise on public sector pensions, he did not need to be told that his job was to call for cuts.[9]

New Labour enjoyed relatively benign economic conditions until the 2008 financial crisis, which was inevitably followed by recession when Brown, who had by then replaced Blair as prime minister, implemented austerity policies to make the working class pay for the bankers' crisis. Working-class support for Labour would ebb away, resulting in the election of Cameron's Tory-Liberal Democrat Coalition government in 2010.

Fighting the cuts

New Labour ministers and their spin doctors liked to claim that one of the greatest obstacles they faced trying to change the civil service was 'producer power' – in other words, workers pursuing their own narrow interests over the public good. This cynical fabrication, borrowed from the Tories, denigrated public sector trade unionists and accused them of wasting taxpayers' money on protecting an allegedly inefficient workforce.

The scale of the struggle ahead became apparent on 12 July 2004 when, without consultation, chancellor Gordon Brown stated in his Comprehensive Spending Review that he would cut 104,500 civil service jobs and crack down on sickness absence. In the House of Commons Labour MPs bayed approval and waved their order papers, an obscene display that caused deep revulsion among civil servants and other public sector workers. Along with the job cuts, Brown intended to relocate 20,000 jobs from London and the south-east and sell off £30 billion worth of government estate and assets to the private sector. The government justified the cuts by claiming they would, 'concentrate investment in the front-line' to deliver better services to 'customers' and 'better value for taxpayers'.[10]

In conjunction with these attacks, departmental secretaries of state and managers imposed new private sector practices. These included aggressive attendance management techniques and a target culture that imposed unrealistic demands on staff and resulted in the use of distorted and manipulated data. Alongside this was the planned introduction of untested new technologies and methods. Notable among them was so-called 'lean working', a bastardisation of Taylorism that emphasised minimising 'waste' and maximising 'value'. Mainly applied in modern industrial settings like assembly lines, it appeared utterly unworkable for the type of public service being delivered. On top of this, Labour retained the decentralised pay arrangements imposed by the Tories that had resulted in the fragmentation of bargaining into multiple areas. The clear intention was to hold down civil service wages.

The essential background to Brown's onslaught on the civil service was the long run-up to the 2005 general election. It was a crude act of political opportunism to pre-empt calls from the Tories and Liberal Democrats for deeper public sector cuts. Predictably, his cuts did not satisfy the profiteers and privatisers who were waiting in the wings. The Tories would go on to demand 235,000 job cuts and the Liberal Democrats called for 'savage' reductions, but neither the government nor the opposition parties gave any detail as to where all these cuts would fall and what the implications would be for the public.[11]

New Labour's attacks on the civil service were more fundamental than anything attempted by the Tories. They had direct consequences for almost all civil servants, including those in areas that even under Thatcher and Major had maintained relative stability. Civil service staff – the majority low-paid clerical and administrative workers – were outraged by this betrayal.

Brown sought to divide public sector workers by suggesting that the civil service cuts would be used to fund those areas that he calculated the public would feel more sympathetic towards, like health and education. But other trade unionists and many of the wider public rejected this blatant attempt at political manipulation. They had voted Labour in the expectation that the vandalism of Thatcher and Major would end, but the proposed job cuts would not only have severe implications for the workers directly affected but also for the range and quality of public services. In justifying his cuts, Brown also regurgitated the old dogma that public sector spending was wasteful and inefficient. By claiming only backroom functions would be affected, he implied that these workers were mere 'lazy pen-pushers'.

He could hardly fail to understand that the front-line services he claimed to be prioritising were dependent on 'backroom' support. His cuts would mean increases in staff workloads and backlogs that would damage frontline operations and weaken service delivery. Claims that new technology, like the introduction of call centres and electronic communication, would compensate for staff losses were disingenuous and reckless. PCS predicted that cutting staff, while introducing untested new technology, would result in service delivery failures, which is exactly what happened. An even more concerning effect was the increased marginalisation of those affected by cuts to services, notably those without access to email or the internet.

An effective trade union response required a campaign that reached beyond industrial concerns like redundancies and office closures. Blair and Brown had no mandate for cuts and privatisation, as they had promised the electorate that they would defend and improve public services. Nevertheless, the cuts agenda was being driven by an elected government, with the corporate media encouraging them to step up their attacks on the public sector.

In order to build the strongest possible resistance to the cuts, the new Left Unity leadership of the PCS worked out a coordinated campaign across the industrial, political and public arenas, aimed at galvanising members on terms and conditions issues while reaching outwards for political and public support in defence of public services. This approach was encapsulated in the statement that: 'PCS members are campaigning to defend services they deliver into the communities in which they live and work'.[12]

Although the union faced many challenges, morale among activists had improved, and the atmosphere of internal division engendered by the Moderates was rapidly transformed to one of purposeful unity. There was also a growing mood of confidence among many members as they saw that their union at national level was now entirely focused on the issues affecting them in their workplaces. Grassroots organisation was a priority, and workplace activity saw membership grow by 30,000 during 2004. Departmental groups were now able to take effective action in their own sectors free from Moderate bureaucratic obstruction and, crucially, were even encouraged by the national leadership to coordinate such action, which they oversaw and monitored, and to which they allocated resources, including speakers. By the beginning of the year, some departmental groups, including the DWP and Driving Standards Agency, had already taken 'coordinated action' action on pay.[13]

Prior to Brown's cuts announcement, PCS had prepared members for the broad assault it believed was imminent. Activists and members were made aware of disputes in various groups, including the long-running campaign against 'modernisation' in the DWP, considered below. Turnouts at branch annual general meetings in the run-up to the annual delegate conference in May were exceptionally high. Members were becoming increasingly convinced that their union represented their first line of defence.

The 2004 conference was the first with a majority socialist leadership at national level. Mark Serwotka set the tone on the threat of job cuts: 'If the government says there will be 20,000 jobs cut in this or that department regardless, we will vigorously protect those services and jobs... including the very last resort of industrial action'.[14] Treasury pay caps were bearing down on civil servants. The PCS leadership had already authorised action across the civil service in the months before the conference, focusing public attention on the expensive madness of 229 different sets of pay negotiations. Conference now instructed the NEC to seek legal advice to ascertain whether a legal dispute involving the whole membership in the civil service could be held, and to ballot members for industrial action if pay limits were imposed for 2004–5. The union's campaigning approach pressured the government to signal that it might be prepared to open talks at a national level.

Conference also pledged to fight for the retention of retiral at 60 with full pension rights, with the NEC taking a major role in pushing for a joint TUC and National Pensioners' Convention march in June 2004. Other debates included motions exposing the corrupt use of private sector consultants, who were paid obscene amounts of public money, in some cases ten times more than civil servants, and who contributed little to the efficiency of the service. It was estimated that British taxpayers, so beloved of right-wing tabloids, were being swindled to the tune of £1 billion a year. Delegates gave examples of advice from these so-called corporate experts, including suggestions of placing potted plants in offices to improve staff morale and the exhortation given to Bristol Jobcentre managers that they should motivate workers by leaving a mint on desks as a 'thank you for your effort'.

The conference also demanded that the days of paying lip service to equality issues, as under the Moderates, were to end. The NEC was charged with developing a plan to involve more black members and other underrepresented groups in union activity, including active monitoring and reviews of progress. One of their first acts had been to reconstitute the union's youth work and revive the Youth Committee, which had been shut down by the Moderates as a potential centre of opposition. Delegates congratulated the NEC on prioritising this work, which included setting up a database of 25,000 young members and the appointment of a National Youth Organiser.

Conference reiterated its opposition to Blair's invasion of Iraq in 2003, which went ahead despite massive public opposition. An active anti-racist and fascist stance was also promoted, including a vote to affiliate to Unite Against Fascism (UAF). This affiliation put into sharper focus the necessity of establishing a political fund to extend the union's capacity to campaign beyond bread-and-butter issues and build alliances with other unions and social movements. The lack of such a fund was a consequence of the state's attempts from the 1920s onwards to isolate civil service trade unionists from the wider movement through legislation and restrictions on political activity. A membership ballot in November 2005, which resulted in an 80 per cent majority, reversed this position and began a new chapter in the union's political activity, which is discussed in Chapter Nine.[15]

Following the conference, the campaign began in earnest to prepare members for the first national ballot since the union's formation. A national circular from Mark Serwotka and Janice Godrich set out the scale of the challenge and identified the industrial and political tasks ahead. They made it clear that the union would resist job cuts, compulsory redundancies and relocations, as well as attacks on sick leave and pension rights.

They then set out the key elements of the campaign. First: taking the union's message to parliament and the public, 'in the most positive and professional manner possible', to inform them of the impact that these proposals would have on jobs and services. Second: urging senior government and departmental officials to 'constructively engage' with the union to improve service delivery. PCS would make representations to ministers, the Cabinet Office, Treasury officials and to senior officials in all bargaining areas and would build joint campaigns with other civil service and public sector unions around 'issues of common concern, ensuring maximum public sector unity', and providing members with the fullest information about where and how the cuts and relocations were threatened.

Members in the civil service and related public sector bodies were to be balloted in October for a one-day strike and were urged to play a 'crucial role' in what was to be a major campaign involving the branches, groups, and regions of the union; they were asked to attend branch and public meetings and actively ask non-members to join PCS.

Few activists or members had any illusions that opposing Brown's assault on jobs would be a one-off battle resulting in either a cut-and-dried victory or defeat. They knew it was a continuation and deepening phase of a long war which had been waged against the public sector and the wider working class since the dying days of the Callaghan government in the late 1970s. The make-or-break test for the union's socialist leadership would be how well they delivered an effective campaign to defend members' interests.

At the core of PCS's strategy was the call for a coordinated, united response from across the entire public sector union movement. Although the civil service was the specific target, no part of the public sector was free from government attacks. PCS took its campaign to the TUC congress, where the union made a strong impact in debates, also holding a fringe meeting with the general secretaries of twelve unions offering solidarity.

The national ballot was a referendum on whether membership would support the union leadership's strategy for the fight ahead, including supporting a one-day national strike on 5 November 2004. PCS demanded the following assurances from government:

- A national discussion on the proposed job cuts and relocation plans.
- No detriment to pensions and sick pay.
- No compulsory redundancies.
- Any relocation to be voluntary not compulsory.
- Equality proofing for all pay and pensions procedures.
- Moves toward a fairer national pay system.

Members were also aware of potential cuts in the Civil Service Compensation Scheme (CSCS), meaning that the full value of payments would be reduced if they were to lose their jobs. Left Unity, which had maintained an independent organising role among members, also fully mobilised and supplemented official union literature. It urged activists to hold branch meetings and involve active members in taking responsibility for tasks, ensuring that every member was individually informed of the need to support the campaign and vote in the ballot. They also strongly encouraged branches to hold all-members meetings; issue local circulars highlighting local as well as national issues; organise inter-departmental meetings and local rallies; leaflet every office; prepare hardship funds; issue press releases; lobby MPs; win over members unconvinced about supporting the campaign; arrange pickets and hold a major rally on the day of the proposed national action.

The ballot was won by a majority of 74,780 votes (64.5 per cent) to 40,142 (35.5 per cent) on a 42 per cent turnout.[16] This was a clear mandate for action and a major step toward building a fighting, campaigning union. All efforts now concentrated on delivering on the day. Expectations of membership support were high, but in the event were greatly exceeded.

As is common in industrial disputes, particularly under the restrictions imposed by anti-union legislation, far more workers took strike action than actually voted for it: 113,000 workers supported action in the ballot, but over 200,000 joined the strike. Turnout is indeed a far more accurate gauge of militancy and determination than ballot voting. At least 8,000 new members had joined the union in the run-up to the strike, some on the picket line itself. Describing the action as 'A Day to Remember', Serwotka and Godrich assured members that they had delivered a 'fantastic show of strength' with solid support from the public – a result of PCS's strategic decision to place the future of public services at the forefront of its wider campaigning.[17]

The strike forced the closure of museums, disrupted driving tests, job centres, benefit offices and customs, with around 160 government departments and agencies affected.[18] Many workplaces reported 100 per cent strike turnouts; seventy picket lines in London were visited by the PCS battle bus, while over 800 members marched to a Westminster rally, joined by other trade unionists and several union general secretaries. Rallies were held throughout the country: 800 attended in Glasgow, 250 in Manchester, 300 in Nottingham, 250 in Cardiff; in Belfast 2,500 members of PCS and the Northern Ireland Public Service Alliance (NIPSA) from a range of departments congregated at a demonstration outside the city's Transport House.[19]

The union's media campaign highlighted the disastrous impact of so many potential job losses, both for workers and for the communities that would bear the brunt of cuts and closures. One million leaflets were distributed explaining the services that civil service workers delivered and exposing the wider impact of cuts. This outward-looking approach gained strong popular sympathy for the strike. It also forced a reluctant media to report this aspect of the union campaign which, along with the lobbying of MPs and other campaigning, focused on the false claims being made by a government that was rapidly losing trust and support in the working class.

Taking on the hardliners – the PDS dispute

The one-day strike in November 2004 had been the first national response to Brown's cuts announcement, but union groups were already busy organising resistance against attempts to introduce 'modernisation' programmes in their various departments. During 2003, a major dispute had begun in the DWP that came to define the ability of members to fight back. It also provided a template for the coordination and interconnectedness of national and departmental strategies, illustrating the need for industrial action capable of inflicting real damage to the employer's operations, as well as to their reputation and credibility.

'Modernisation' was a euphemism for job losses and wage cuts. In the DWP its destructive impact was felt by workers and service users alike. Here ministers and management had grossly oversold their capacity to deliver their 'modernisation agenda', resulting in serious service delivery problems, including IT failures and call centre breakdowns. Unsurprisingly, the loss of 30,000 jobs across the department had also led to spiralling workloads. With assaults on staff rising by over 60 per cent nationally, the patience of members and activists was at breaking point; industrial action was becoming unavoidable.[20]

As part of their modernisation drive, the DWP's hard-line Executive Team (ET) attempted to impose a discriminatory pay and appraisal system, the Performance and Development System (PDS). Members and activists who felt that they were already being pushed to the limit reacted with anger. It was not enough that the government was attacking wage levels by exploiting the divisive nature of delegated pay, with PDS they now also had a system that would institutionalise low pay by linking it to hostile attendance and appraisal systems. PDS was also an attempt to go beyond departmental pay bargaining and introduce individual pay agreements. This would have meant an end to collective bargaining, with the unspoken aim of breaking union power.

The DWP was becoming something of a symbolic battleground. Delivering and administering benefits, it was in the very frontline of government attempts to break up the existing social security system, one of the main pillars of the welfare state. For their part, employers regarded DWP as one of the union's most militant and best-organised sections. They calculated that if PDS could be established there, it could be implemented throughout the civil service.

In 2001–2, during the transitional joint general secretaryship of Reamsbottom and Serwotka, a long-running dispute over safety concerns around the DWP's 'Pathfinder' initiative ended largely in management's favour. Reamsbottom had played his usual destructive role, advocating a selective action strategy where small groups of workers took strike action, while others played little more than a supportive role. It was the same strategy that had allowed the Tories to weather the 1981 pay dispute, and it inevitably brought a similar response from DWP management, who imported strike-breakers – mainly higher management grades – into the relatively small number of affected workplaces.

Industrial action tactics are not cherry-picked from an unchanging menu but must be deliverable, effective and sustainable. If they have been shown to be unequal to the task of applying sufficient pressure, they need to be revised. Along with assessing the level of action required, it is also necessary to calculate what level of disruption management was prepared to endure and what type of repressive and intimidatory measures they might employ. Given the inevitable media reaction, an effective public campaigning strategy is also essential.

Unfortunately, a small group around the Socialist Caucus grouping within Left Unity insisted, contrary to experience, that the same selective action strategy that failed in the past could now be successful in the PDS dispute. In contrast, the great majority of the members agreed that PDS could not be defeated by such tactics. There was no prospect of an easy route to defeat management's plans, and certainly no prospect of a quick victory. On this assessment, the Left Unity-led DWP group executive committee prepared members for a long-term, grinding struggle – a 'slugging match' as it was described.

Ministers and the senior managers had badly misread the mood of DWP members on the PDS issue. They calculated that the Pathfinder dispute had knocked the fight out of the union for a time and thought they had a good prospect of destroying collective bargaining and breaking their most rebellious workforce.

Whilst members needed little convincing that PDS would institutionalise low pay, they were more concerned about whether their union could organise effectively to defeat the scheme outright. The DWP group leadership, with the full backing and practical assistance of the national union, prepared the ground for the battle that lay ahead through members' meetings at all levels. Optimism grew with the realisation that their union was 'on the case', as one member said at a workplace meeting.

DWP workers were outraged by the injustice of PDS and equally contemptuous of its self-evident contradictions and irrationality. This was not restricted to the lower-paid grades; middle-managers too were appalled by the contempt shown to them by their superiors in the ET. Leaked documents revealed that the senior operations manager had claimed women workers 'lack ambition' and that middle managers themselves were an 'obstacle to change'. Such discriminatory thinking and disregard for their own staff also lost them the support of non-members whom they had previously relied upon to keep working during strike action. During the campaign, PCS recruited thousands of workers in the DWP and other areas, bringing the total national membership up to 300,000.

Brown's announcement of his planned 104,000 job cuts in the middle of the dispute only strengthened the resolve of DWP members. It also raised awareness of what lay ahead for all civil servants, and support for the campaign grew throughout the wider union. In thanking members for their solid support during group-wide strikes in February and in April 2004, PCS DWP group president Stella Dennis commented: 'Preliminary negotiations with senior management make it clear they don't have a clue about how this can be done without it having appalling consequences for both staff and the service we provide.[21]

The union strategy consisted of national days of action, non-cooperation, overtime bans, and press and parliamentary campaigning. Again, PCS's public work focused on how government policy was damaging public services. At workplace meetings throughout the country, members participated in debates about the union's campaign and were convinced of the necessity to focus public campaigning on the service issue.

Members' participation was not limited to supporting strike action but featured lobbying of their MPs for whom they outlined the background to the dispute. They also emphasised the consequences of the government cuts and privatisation for their constituents. This produced genuine pressure on ministers, not only from left Labour MPs but even from Tory, Liberal Democrats and those Labour MPs in marginal seats.

The union's strategy of national days of action and continuous disruption, involving the whole DWP membership, was aimed at steadily building maximum pressure. Alongside political campaigning, it was hoped that this would bring the ET to negotiation. National strikes in blocks of two days were not simply protest or political action, they had damaging consequences for the DWP's operations, in conjunction with other forms of disruptive action. Senior management belatedly realised that they had little control over the pace of the dispute as the union had prepared for a long struggle and had the means to sustain it. In an attempt to regain control and momentum, they began suspending line managers who were following union instructions not to complete staff reports, but these plans badly backfired when members responded with unofficial strike action, causing further disruption.

Senior management and ministers began to appreciate that the union's industrial strategy was deliverable, with members showing little sign of demoralisation when negotiations had not been quickly conceded. Further pressure was applied as the union highlighted the government's bid to transform the social security system into a punitive benefits regime. Various claimants' organisations backed the campaign, offering practical support and solidarity by joining picket lines, parliamentary lobbying and holding public meetings.

PCS conducted a 'Vote of No Confidence' in the DWP's ET among union members.[22] This provoked a furious and panicked reaction that caused great amusement among workers, including the alienated middle managers. This highly novel tactic had a more damaging consequence for the ET – it exposed its complete lack of authority, let alone respect, among staff. Their spluttering denunciations of PCS in challenging their status in this way revealed the blow to their collective ego.

Negotiations were conceded in the face of the union's threat of escalation to a five-day DWP-wide strike. Management made an insufficient initial offer which was rejected by the DWP group leadership. At this point, Mark Serwotka intervened with DWP minister Alan Johnson, a former general secretary of the postal workers' union, CWU. This resulted in a new and improved offer, endorsed by the union nationally. A meeting of branch representatives supported the deal by 80 to 16, followed by a membership ballot, resulting in an overwhelming vote in favour.

The settlement ensured that the worst aspects of PDS were withdrawn and included a joint commitment to continue negotiations, which yielded further concessions. The system itself would eventually be discarded. The settlement also involved a three-year pay deal that broke the Treasury's 3.5 per cent pay limit, with 4.6 per cent and 4.1 per cent increases in the first and second year. While this did not greatly reduce the gaps that had opened up in pay with other civil and public sector groups, it did, alongside other elements of the deal, provide some gains for members, particularly the lower paid with increases of 15 per cent over three years. While recognising that the deal did not go far enough on pay and appraisal, it represented a very serious defeat for ministers and senior management, not least in their attempt to disable the union.

The impact of the successful PDS struggle had wider consequences. Similar plans were dropped in other departments as ministers grasped that the days of dealing with a supine national PCS leadership were gone. The NEC, which had in its ranks some of the leading union activists in DWP, played a fully supportive role in the dispute, helping to build trust with the wider membership. This would prove a significant factor in the campaign to protect public sector pensions, in which PCS was to play their next critical role.

Attack on pensions – the call for coordinated action

Not satisfied with attacking the civil service, Blair and Brown opened another front by waging war on public sector pension schemes. Now it was not just civil servants, but millions of council and health workers, including teachers and firefighters, who feared having to pay more to fund their pensions or lose benefits if they retired due to ill health. In 2002, the government had chosen Adair Turner, Vice Chairman of Merril Lynch (Europe), to head the Pensions Commission. His previous career in British Petroleum, Chase Manhattan Bank and as director general of the Confederation of British Industry (CBI) guaranteed he would produce a report that claimed public sector pensions were unaffordable, with solutions that protected the profiteering elite at the expense of the working class.

The commission's first report in October 2004 merely confirmed the government in its intention to raise the pension age from 60 to 65 in 2006 for all new staff and in 2013 for existing staff. It was leaked to the press that the pension age might even rise to 70.[23] They hoped to implement these changes and a whole series of other detrimental measures without negotiation. New Labour ministers even contacted Labour-affiliated general secretaries, pleading with them not to respond with industrial action.

The predictable message from politicians and the media was that 'gold-plated' public sector pensions meant that reductions in pension rights were necessary and justified. In fact, as most public sector workers were relatively low paid, their pensions were modest; the average civil servant's pension was estimated at £4,800 a year.[24] New Labour's attack on these workers prompted such widespread anger that even the most moderate union leaders could not ignore the mood of resistance among their members.

The government also sought to divide and rule by contrasting the pensions of public and private sector workers. Taking advantage of the dramatic fall in private sector trade unionism, the government had allowed pensions in the sector to be systematically plundered by nearly £19 billion between 1987 and 2001, with companies allowed to take a contributions 'holiday' when stock prices were high. In 1991, nearly six million workers had final salary schemes, but this number had halved by 2004.[25] Demands for fair pensions for all, including private sector workers, were highlighted by PCS and were part of the wider TUC campaign.

Despite being the fourth richest country in the world, the UK spent only five per cent of its GDP on pensions, while eleven per cent was the average in the European Union as a whole. One in five pensioners lived in poverty, solely dependent on an inadequate state pension. 70 per cent of women had no private pension of their own. In 1979, the basic state pension had been 23 per cent of average earnings, but by 2004, it was less than 16 per cent. But it was not bad news for everyone, MPs had voted only a few years before to increase their salaries by 26 per cent and enhance their already generous pensions by increasing their rate to 1/50th from 1/40th of salary for each year of service.[26]

Chief executives of the major private sector companies were

also amassing handsome pension pots. Sir Christopher Gent of Vodafone, for example, had retired in 2003 on an annual pension of £702,000, while British Petroleum's Lord Browne's pension fund had accrued a cool £19.1 million. Inconveniently for the government, the Office for National Statistics revealed in 2004 that the super-rich had doubled their wealth since New Labour had come to power, increasing their share of national wealth from 20 to 23 per cent.[27]

With his plans for pension 'reform' taking shape, Blair attempted to soften up opposition at the September 2003 TUC by saying there would never be another Labour government of the left. Brown was given a hostile reception from delegates when he similarly taunted his audience by claiming that campaigning for pension rights would not work.[28] It was now that PCS played a critical role by insisting on an amendment calling for a national pensions demonstration, followed by a national day of action and subsequent industrial action. TUC leaders placed enormous pressure on Mark Serwotka as the union's representative on the General Council to drop the motion but, with the full support of the PCS delegation and left union leaders like the RMT's Bob Crow, he stood firm, and the amended motion was eventually carried. This militant response to the government's theft of pension rights set out a clear strategy for a coordinated campaign that would prove capable of forcing a government retreat.

On 18 February 2004, a TUC-led Day of Action was widely supported across the public sector with marches, rallies and lobbying that also drew support from private sector workers. The *Morning Star* reported Serwotka stating that the government's attack on over two million workers had the potential to 'lay ruin to the best laid general election campaign plans' by their attempt to tear up their contracts and by 'refusing to consult or negotiate on the issue'. He added, 'Strike action is a route a number of public sector trade unions, including PCS, have expressed a willingness to pursue if forced and have put in place the mechanisms and are ready to ballot'.[29]

PCS held a membership ballot to provide a mandate for 'discontinuous action', not just on pensions but also over job cuts, the CSCS and other conditions of service.[30] The members returned a clear Yes vote and the union organised for a further national strike on 23 March 2005, along with other unions including UNISON, Amicus, UCATT, FDA and NIPSA.

Shortly before the action was due to take place, Alan Johnson, secretary of state for work and pensions, wrote to the TUC saying he had been 'tasked' by the prime minister to make a 'fresh start'. Now that all the proposals were open to negotiation, he hoped that strike action could be called off. He followed this up in a BBC Radio 4 interview, saying: 'What can I say, *mea culpa*. We got it wrong'. PCS also received a commitment from the Cabinet Office that, along with pensions negotiations, discussions would be opened on the other issues included in the ballot, including the avoidance of compulsory redundancies and relocations 'to maintain momentum'. All of which, if progressed, would be a significant step forward in defending members' jobs and conditions.

Unions representing local authority workers decided to suspend their action on 23 March on the basis that changes to their pension scheme would be 'annulled' till 2006 to allow negotiations to take place. FDA and NIPSA were also due to suspend their actions, as were the education unions. In light of this, PCS's NEC agreed to also suspend. This followed an extensive debate over the advantages and disadvantages of such a move. Fearing that the government might renege if they won the election, the union leadership agreed that while industrial action was suspended on pensions in lieu of a settlement, the ballot mandate for discontinuous action remained.

In the negotiations with Johnson that followed from March onwards, the distance between militant union leaders and those prepared to settle to the government's advantage was stark. UNISON and GMB negotiators, for example, had made threatening noises about the 'dire consequences' of pushing ahead with the pension plans, but the government was aware they had no intention of following through. However, left negotiators, like

Serwotka, Matt Wrack, the newly elected FBU general secretary, and Kevin Courtney of the NUT, held firm on the main points of contention.

The falsehood that militants can only oppose and are incapable of finding solutions to settle disputes was shown as nonsense in negotiations. In fact, it was Serwotka who raised the question of securing the pension rights of existing employees as a basis for an agreement, which Johnson seized upon. This was itself a major achievement, winning a respite for millions of workers who would otherwise have had to entirely re-evaluate their finances and retirement dates.

During the talks, PCS played a further decisive role in encouraging solidarity in the face of the defeatism and cynicism of some union and TUC leaders. Against this background, pressing ahead with strike action on its own account to win further demands would not only have isolated the union from the wider movement, but would also have destroyed the unity it had worked so hard to achieve. Such a move might also have allowed the government to appeal to PCS members over the heads of the union leadership.

Negotiations continued during the spring through the TUC's Public Sector Forum and a proposed agreement went to the executives of the various unions for consultation. The agreement covered workers in the civil service, education, and health; local authority workers' and firefighters' unions were still conducting negotiations. The principal feature of the deal reached with the TUC meant all existing members of the scheme would suffer no detriment in terms of their normal pension age of 60 and retain their existing provision, but there would be a rise in the pension age to 65 for new entrants, while retaining the right to retire at 60. This compared favourably to other public schemes. It did, though, mean higher contributions and a change from career average to a final salary scheme, although union research showed it would be helpful for a significant number of lower-paid members. While squarely facing the reality that it meant the introduction of two-tier pension arrangements, PCS entered into further negotiations on the scheme in order to obtain the best possible deal for new entrants.

One of the main factors that forced the government's retreat on pensions was the upcoming election. New Labour was returned to government in May 2005, but on a considerably reduced majority and with only slightly above 35 per cent of the popular vote. This loss in support was due mainly to opposition to the Iraq invasion and the government's neoliberal policies, but for the right wing, the failure to savage public sector pensions was another mark on the charge sheet. Negotiations with Johnston had been conducted against the background of strident media attacks bemoaning the government's compromise in the face of union opposition. The *Financial Times* raged: 'Abject surrender over public sector pensions', while in a Channel Four television news interview, the then director general of the CBI, Digby Jones, fulminated on a deal 'costing hundreds of billions of pounds'.[31]

An opportunist union leadership might have painted the government's climb-down as an unqualified 'victory'. This was certainly the position of some committed Blairite leaders, like general secretary Dave Prentis, who hailed it as the product of government and union partnership working. However, at the PCS's NEC meeting to consider the proposed deal, Serwotka, Godrich and others stressed that this was a shallow and dangerously complacent analysis. Although the concessions were highly significant, not least following a period of retreat for the unions, the government had not completely abandoned their plans. The recommendation to accept the deal was agreed by the NEC, although it was attacked by the SWP as 'shabby'. Left Unity publicly responded with a leaflet entitled *A Significant Achievement*:

> PCS members would see the union's refusal of an agreement that protected their pensions as an act of madness... and not only would we lose any concessions on pensions, but the job cuts agenda would be pursued with greater vigour with our union divided from top to bottom'.

The SWP's posturing took no account of the balance of forces between PCS and the government and indeed, within the wider trade union movement. The leaflet continued:

> It is worth posing the question sharply – whose interests are served by rejecting this deal? To reject would mean losing the deal itself, the support of members, the left leadership in PCS. Only New Labour, the CBI and the enemies of campaigning, socialist leadership would win in such circumstances.

An unprecedented 98 per cent of the PCS membership voted for the deal. Sharp as the internal debate had been, the SWP did not split from Left Unity.

Along with the union's influential role in the pensions dispute, it had taken a number of steps forward in defending members' interests at a national and group level by the beginning of 2006. Compulsory redundancies had been prevented and the government had conceded to talks on national pay coherence. In the Prison Service, legal action had secured a major equal pay success in which 2,500 claims were won, yielding settlements of between £500 and £5,000, costing the employer £50 million, with the establishment of a new pay structure. In addition, the government had agreed to introduce measures to eradicate the two-tier workforce in Civil Service commercial contracts. Confidence in the union was reflected in a 20 per cent growth in membership.

....

Notes & References

1. *The Socialist*, 12 July 2003.
2. *Financial Times*, 23 October 1998.
3. See, M. Serwotka and G. Gall, *The future of public services under Labour*, Working Paper, University of Hertfordshire, 2007.
4. *Belfast Telegraph*, 14 December 2007.
5. *The Guardian*, 25 May 2022.
6. *Daily Express*, 14 December 2021.
7. *The Guardian*, 18 January 2008.

8.   *The Times*, 21 March 2010.

9.   *Daily Mail*, 15 June 2010.

10. House of Commons Debates, 12 July 2004, vol. 423 cc1129-55.

11. *The Guardian*, 19 January 2005.

12. *Morning Star*, 30 June 2004.

13. *The Socialist*, 14 February 2004.

14. *Morning Star*, 10 June 2004.

15. *Morning Star*, 23 November 2005.

16. *The Scotsman*, 22 October 2004.

17. *Morning Star*, 6 November 2004.

18. *The Guardian*, 6 November 2024.

19. *Belfast Newsletter*, 6 November 2004.

20. *The Socialist*, 27 November 2004.

21. *Morning Star*, 10 June 2004.

22. *Morning Star*, 28 July 2004.

23. *Financial Times*, 10 December 2004.

24. *Civil service pensions – developments to 2010*, SN 3324, House of Commons Library, 2013.

25. *The Guardian*, 10 May 2004.

26. The Parliamentary Pensions (Amendment) Regulations 2002, UK Statutory Instruments 2002, No. 1807.

27. *The Guardian*, 8 December 2004.

28. *Morning Star*, 10 September 2003.

29. *Morning Star*, 19 February 2004.

30. Discontinuous industrial action takes place on only some days where there is an opportunity.

31. *Financial Times*, 19 October 2005.

6. New Labour, new challenges

Performing partnership – the Warwick Agreement

In July 2004, the Labour Party and affiliated unions in the Trade Union and Labour Party Liaison Organisation (TULO) signed the Warwick Agreement covering 'fairness at work', public services, pensions and economic policy.[1] Hailed by some union leaders and even some on the left as a basis for good relations between unions and the government, it was a performative display of 'unity' to create the appearance of peaceful cooperation. There would be no real concessions from a government that intended to press ahead with its cuts and privatisation agenda. Indeed, Tony Blair viewed the agreement as insurance that his planned blitz on the public sector would proceed unhindered. With little on offer for the working class, reformists who supported the agreement revealed a capacity for self-delusion as strong as the right wing.

The Warwick Agreement was still being negotiated when the government launched its assault on pension rights. Given their subsequent retreat, PCS argued that this afforded the movement a real opportunity to extend coordinated campaigning in the fight against low pay, attacks on conditions and privatisation. The run-up to the general election was the most propitious time to press for further concessions. However, the government, TUC and Blairite union leaders were all desperate for a return to the 'normality' of partnership working. The pensions campaign during 2004 had frightened the trade union right wing almost as much as the government. They knew that militancy presented a real challenge to their compromise bargaining strategy and by extension, to their own personal power bases. Their response was an insistence that no more challenges to 'our government' would be tolerated, effectively offering Blair and Gordon Brown a clear field to continue their attacks. Big general unions like the GMB and Unite, for example, had an important public sector presence, but the key union that would determine whether a coordinated fightback would be built was UNISON. This was the largest and potentially the most powerful formation in the public sector, representing a million workers. Unfortunately, general secretary Dave Prentis headed a Blairite leadership and an entrenched full-time bureaucracy whose main function, like their counterparts in the old CPSA, was to ruthlessly stamp out opposition.

Against this background, divide and rule tactics remained paramount. The government was consistent in portraying the civil service as the 'undeserving' public sector, in contrast to the NHS where Labour was just as committed to outsourcing, privatisation and marketisation. Since Gordon Brown's 2004 Comprehensive Spending Review, it was this workforce that had become the main target for New Labour's 'modernisation' agenda of job losses, outsourcing and performance management.

Fighting job cuts is one of the most notoriously difficult tasks that any union can face. Avoidance of compulsory redundancies would now become the PCS's key priority. Typical was their uncompromising response when notices were served to staff in the Department for Food and Rural Affairs (DEFRA) and the Department of Trade and Industry (DTI). A membership ballot for industrial action was launched in November 2004, which resulted in solid support for national strike action, followed by targeted stoppages and overtime bans and a programme of public and parliamentary campaigning.[2] The government initially refused to negotiate, but when a consultative, non-statutory ballot showed strong membership support for the escalation of industrial action, they conceded to direct talks. Although government ministers refused to state publicly that compulsory redundancy notices would not be issued during the negotiations, they knew that if it happened, PCS would call for national strike action. The NEC recommended agreement to a protocol for 'handling surplus staff situations', which included guidance on managing outsourcing and privatisation. Union negotiators had insisted that the agreement should cover all departments.

The protocol's endorsement by the Cabinet Office, permanent secretaries, the head of thecivil service and ministers placed an obligation on them to ensure that it worked, imposing some measure of restraint on those more hawkish elements who were eager for a showdown with the union. The agreement included important concessions, including a binding obligation on departments, agencies and non-departmental public bodies to provide the union with full information on any risk of redundancies, with the requirement to conduct Equality Impact Assessments. Consultation had to be maintained throughout the process and anyone threatened with redundancy who did not wish to leave voluntarily was to be given an alternative job offer and priority in applying for vacancies in other departments. The protocol did not give cast-iron guarantees of job security, but it did offer very strong protection from compulsory redundancy, while the union made clear that if this did occur it would reserve the right to take industrial action, including national action.

Guidance on outsourcing offered a further opportunity for the union to stop the practice of transferring workers and then making them open to compulsory redundancy. Consultation at the earliest stages of outsourcing was agreed, as was the possibility of in-house bids being considered. The agreement also provided a more solid platform on which to build effective opposition to specific privatisation attempts. In the event, campaigning could not stop sell-offs going ahead, but the union was strongly positioned to negotiate deals to protect the terms and conditions of the workers involved – a considerable improvement on the previous free-for-all that had suited the most unscrupulous employers.[3]

The union's campaign strategy on job cuts was justified in its own terms. During New Labour's time in office, no civil service worker who wished to remain in employment was made redundant compulsorily. The union leadership's approach stood in sharp contrast to the remnants of the old CPSA Moderate Group, which continued to stand in national elections in alliance with Membership

First, the small oppositional group that had originated in the pre-merger PTC. In a leaflet distributed to annual conference delegates in June 2004, they stated:

> The hard left NEC will tell you about the great coverage in the media and the parliamentary profile PCS has – But what does this really amount [to]. The fact is that this NEC threatens strikes on all issues without delivering. The government now treats their treats [sic] with disdain and more of PCS crying wolf. We believe that the entire civil service national membership should be balloted on the issue of compulsory transfers and compulsory transfers [sic]. The reason for this is quite simple. If we are being honest, we all know that any offer of early release or severance on a voluntary basis will be welcomed by many of our members who want to take the money on offer and move on. There will be a stampede by our members and our duty is to ensure that the best terms possible are on offer for our colleagues who wish to go. What our members will not accept and, in our view, take action over the treat [sic] of compulsory transfers and compulsory redundancies?

Crudely expressed, the Moderate's strategy was, 'job cuts are inevitable, there is little we can do, let's just plead for the best terms possible'.

Crucially, the union's campaigning strategy saw specific government attacks as part of an overall strategy. This was a productive approach. Without coordinated resistance, individual sections would have been picked off one by one. It also meant that workers considering voluntary redundancy remained motivated to support union campaigns against closures while they were still employed. Their union had delivered for them, and they were prepared to deliver for their union. The cynical right-wing view of individual self-interest would have meant mass compulsory redundancies. The contrast between collaborationist and militant union strategies could not have been clearer.

The New Labour government had seen PCS and its members as a soft touch, believing that there was little public sympathy for the union's attempts to save jobs and services. Blair and Brown also felt secure that the majority of the Parliamentary Labour Party would support the cuts, not to mention the Tories and Liberal Democrats – and of course the media. In the absence of opposition from public sector unions affiliated to the party, they calculated that PCS could be easily isolated. However, the success of the union's campaign to expose the social impact of government cuts meant that even the anti-union national media did take notice. PCS produced detailed speakers' notes for national campaigns, replicated at departmental level, which provided union activists with all the detailed arguments, facts and figures that they needed. Earlier experience had proved the value of contact with the local press, and this brought further opportunities to publicise the union's case.[4] Meanwhile, representatives also developed skills in radio, television, and press interviews, with many becoming very effective communicators.

Chancellor Gordon Brown had hoped to drive his cuts through with minimal scrutiny, but as public awareness grew, Parliamentary Select Committees were forced to look more closely at the chaos in service delivery resulting from 'modernisation'. MPs were lobbied by suffering constituents, while even employers expressed their horror at the dismantling of previously reliable relationships with the public sector. PCS tactics were doing their work.

Organising call centre workers

PCS departmental groups had their own policy-making annual conferences that addressed issues specific to their sectors. Rather than leaving departmental groups to respond piecemeal to government initiatives, the national union assisted with a common approach, developing policy and campaigning guidelines centrally based on national conference decisions. This was particularly valuable in the case of call centre workers.

The introduction of new technology and working practices gave management an opportunity to impose unfavourable conditions in the call centres that were being rolled out across many departments. Call centres aimed to deliver public services on the cheap as office closures and privatisation were pushed through. This worsened service delivery and raised issues of workloads, health and safety and aggressive micro-management. Lack of flexibility was a major grievance. Starting and leaving times and breaks were circumscribed to the very minute.[5] In one particularly ludicrous example, a Jobcentre worker's request to leave five minutes early to pick up her child had to be cleared at national management level. In addition, there were major fears over the government's agenda to reduce pay levels through systematic de-skilling. It was hardly surprising that call centres displayed far higher turnover rates and sickness levels than in the rest of the civil service.

The government had inadvertently created the type of factory-style conditions that gave PCS excellent opportunities to grow membership among a mainly young and female workforce. The national union held its first Call Centre Forum in December 2006 and produced a Charter for workers which set out the issues and raised demands.[6] The charter also provided guidance on campaigning and organising on pay issues; stress and safe working environments; surveillance and privacy; equal opportunities, training and representation. Campaigns, including strike action in defence of call centre workers' rights, although far from resolving every problem, would have been far more difficult to achieve without the union's coordinated approach.

The financial crash – campaigning on pay

The global financial crash of 2008 made nonsense of Gordon Brown's boast that his 'prudence' had put an end to the old pattern of boom and bust. Having replaced Blair as prime minister in June 2007, he and his new chancellor, Alistair Darling, were keen to claim the credit for the subsequent international rescue that led to £1.3 trillion being spent on bailing out the very banking and financial sectors that had caused the crisis in the first place.[7] As with every crisis of capital, however, it was the government's intention to make the working class pay the price with austerity, deeper cuts in living standards and services – and yet more privatisation.

The scrapping of national pay bargaining by the Tories had inevitably led to inequalities and systemic discrimination. There were significant disparities in wage rates which produced pay gaps of between 20 to 30 per cent between different government departments. Already by 2003, over a quarter of civil servants earned less than £13,250, while pay disparities had also opened up between them and other public sector workers. Between 1992 and 2002, the earnings of Administrative Officers and Assistants, and Executive Officers, the majority of PCS members, had risen by only 3.5 and 3.7 per cent respectively, while the pay of local government workers and primary school teachers had risen by 14 per cent and nurses by 21 per cent.[8]

The impact of discriminatory pay and the erosion of previous union-negotiated gains in terms and conditions had a disproportionate impact on women, who formed most of the civil service workforce. Demands for higher output and the de-skilling of work left them badly affected. The advance for equal pay in the Prison Service in July 2004 had exposed the scandalous situation that the pay gap between men and women had actually increased under New Labour.[9] NEC member and Women's Forum activist Emily Kelly set out some of the issues:

> Unrealistic work targets have seriously undermined our ability to fully utilise flexible working hours and leave restrictions, sick-leave monitoring, inefficient and incompetently delivered 'Change' programmes that require constant retraining have left many women workers badly stressed and unable to cope with balancing work and home life (and) the continued push by the government to keep an element of performance-related pay, although there is solid proof that it discriminates against part-time workers, has made many women members feel under-valued and less motivated.

The destruction of national pay bargaining had recreated conditions that would have been familiar to the pioneers of civil service trade unionism when presented with pay offers within fixed Treasury parameters. This made a farce of the idea of any flexibility to resolve union claims, which in turn meant that no real collective bargaining was taking place. The government had no intention of conceding a full return to national pay bargaining, but in the face of union pressure, it suggested talks on pay 'coherence'. Given the shambles that the delegated system had become, some partial return to national bargaining might have benefited the government as well as the union. For its part, PCS aimed at restoring common rates of pay for equivalent jobs in different departments, while establishing national terms and conditions on issues like hours and holidays. The leadership also grasped the need to tackle issues like equal and progression pay if they were to win any real financial gains for members.

Initially, these talks seemed to make progress, but they were overshadowed by the government's 2008 Pay Remit, which set a two per cent pay limit; as inflation was averaging around four per cent, this was effectively a further pay cut. In their defence, Brown and Darling fell back on the old myth that inflation was caused by wage rises. This was succinctly punctured in a PCS members' circular quoting Andrew Oswald, Professor of Economics at Warwick University, who said: 'An undergraduate who wrote in an essay that inflation was caused by public sector pay rises would receive a fail.'

In the 2008 Pay Remit, the government had also provocatively signalled its intention to introduce local and regional pay. Brown had stated as early as his 2001 Autumn Statement that: 'While private sector pay was set in accordance with local labour markets, public sector pay is usually set on a national basis'.[10] This was typical New Labour spin – most large private sector companies with a nationwide profile had national pay structures. Previous experiments at introducing pay levels based on local labour market conditions in the private sector had led personnel managers to conclude that national pay systems were the most efficient, providing simplicity and economy and avoiding the cost of duplication, and reducing the poaching of staff.

Union members were enraged that a Labour government would seek to reduce their already diminished wage levels even further. The government seemed intent on dividing workers depending on whether they worked in areas of high or low unemployment and poverty. PCS tackled this strategy by addressing the assumption that workers in London would benefit compared with those in areas like the north of England, Wales or Scotland. As the capital had some of the most deprived boroughs in the country, they might be severely disadvantaged by local pay.

During early 2008, disputes developed in some departmental groups, such as DEFRA and the Magistrates' Courts, where Treasury pay limits were being strictly enforced.[11] Increasingly complex pay arrangements had been introduced, which meant basic wage increases were conflated within pay progression arrangements, something workers regarded as a form of wage theft. Pressure on the government increased with a coordinated strike in April 2008 involving 400,000 workers, including civil servants from departmental groups that had balloted for action, alongside teachers, local government workers and university lecturers.[12]

Having rescued the banks, the government offered nothing to those struggling with their home loans because of the crash. Support for Labour was rapidly diminishing among civil servants, as it was for workers generally. Tax workers' jobs were cut and HMRC offices closed while tax evasion ran at an estimated £25–£40 billion each year. On the other hand, the highest tax burden, up to 36.4 per cent of income, fell on the poorest 20 per cent of households, while the abolition of the 10 per cent tax rate at the beginning of the 2008 tax year pushed as many as five million low-paid workers deeper into poverty.[13]

A major PCS membership consultation in the autumn of 2008 was followed by a national pay ballot which returned a 54 per cent vote for national industrial action on a 35 per cent turnout.[14] The union demanded that each member should receive a consolidated basic pay increase at least equal to the Retail Price Index. It also sought a minimum rate of £8 an hour; a reduction in the number of pay negotiations with no implementation of regional or local pay; additional funding to remedy equal pay problems; and an end to links between pay and performance appraisal. In response, Sir Gus O'Donnell, cabinet secretary and head of the civil service, himself on £260,000 a year, wrote seemingly without embarrassment to all civil servants to tell them, 'current economic problems mean that higher pay increases could not be made and would not be understood by the public'.[15]

The union campaign was planned to begin with a one-day strike on 10 November, with the aim of coordinating action with the NUT and Unite and any other unions prepared to join in united action. This was to be followed by further national action, including an overtime ban and action short of strike. Before the strike was due, the government agreed to negotiate. This left the unions with the decision of whether to proceed with the strike or suspend it and enter talks. Both National Executives of PCS and the NUT agreed on suspension and taking up the government's offer.

During the intense discussions which followed, Cabinet Office negotiators gave the impression that they were authorised to deliver more than the government was willing to concede. Whatever agreement was reached around the table, it was unlikely that it would be honoured in any substantial sense. The banking and financial crash still dominated the political and economic climate, shifting the balance of power between the unions and the government in the latter's favour. The TUC and Blairite union leaders remained committed to delivering for the Labour government in its time of crisis. They blocked or simply ignored demands from PCS and other left-led unions for a National Day of Action and coordinated campaigning across the public sector. Beyond public posturing over pay limits, their position was to settle without a fight, as strikes would merely hasten the return of the Tories.

For principled socialist union leaders, suspending a strike is always a question of judgment. In this case, PCS had previously secured national agreements on jobs and redundancies, and there was a reasonable hope that a pay agreement would follow. This was a mistake. It had always been in the government's interest to buy time while their trade union allies encouraged their members to accept what little was on offer. This was also part of a divide-and-rule strategy, which also, in some areas, included slightly higher settlements than were offered to other civil and public sector workers. Although there was no guarantee that strike action would have secured further concessions, the loss of momentum operated to the government's advantage. It is equally true that a substantial level of strike action and sacrifice from members would have been required to substantially shift the government's stance, with most other public sector unions on the sidelines.

The decision to suspend the strike may have been a miscalculation, but an honest one that had nothing in common with either the ultra-left approach that, in virtually all cases, would oppose any such suspension whatever the objective circumstances, or the collaborationist method of right-wing bureaucracies, who would grasp at any opportunity to avoid a strike. Clear vision is easy in hindsight, but the purpose for any union activist in addressing such events is not to rerun them, but to learn lessons. Only then can they offer an assessment that considers all relevant objective and subjective factors, and apply this approach to all future struggles. As discussed in detail in Chapter 10, PCS campaigning during 2008 had at least forced the government to abandon its plans for regional and local pay and stopped the imposition of further detrimental change for its members.

Marketisation of welfare

The union's annual conference in May 2009 took place against the backdrop of the worst recession since the 1930s. Delegates called for a comprehensive programme to deal with an unrestrained market economy that had so dramatically failed. They demanded democratic control of the banking and finance sectors, an end to public sector cuts, accompanied by major public investment. But how was this to be accomplished?

The neoliberal political consensus among the major political parties had deprived working people of political representation. If such policies were to be opposed and defeated, then a combined struggle on the industrial and political fronts was imperative. Agreeing to establish a political fund in 2005, PCS had chosen not to affiliate with the Labour Party. This would have provided for delegates to the party's national conference, as well as the election of members to the party's national executive. However, in preference to these close institutional ties, the union had already formed a cross-party lobby group of its own sponsored representatives the previous year, giving it a measure of political autonomy similar to RMT and FBU.[16] Under the chairmanship of John McDonnell MP, the PCS Parliamentary Group quickly became one of the most influential bodies of its type in the trade union movement.

The union leadership had also introduced campaigns such as 'Make Your Vote Count' (MYVC), aiming to hold politicians to account through election hustings and debates. The more radical option of backing independent trade union candidates was discussed. In pressing forward with this, PCS joined the RMT in recognising that a fresh approach was needed to address the shifting balance of political power against the working class. Reflecting on the failed pay bid that the union had made before Christmas 2008, it was also agreed to consult widely on how to strengthen the union's capacity for future struggles.

Particularly troubling was New Labour's determination to dismantle the principle of universality and so impose a stricter benefits regime. In 2006, Tony Blair had commissioned former UBS investment banker David Freud to review the UK's welfare-to-work scheme. His report published the following year came to the extraordinary, if unsurprising, conclusion that although Jobcentre Plus was a 'model of public sector delivery', it should still be privatised because the 'scale of the potential market is huge... an annual multi-billion market'.[17] Despite failing to present any real evidence to support this conclusion, he argued that outsourcing was the best and most efficient way forward.

For the moment, this was too much for even Gordon Brown to stomach, but during the 2008 financial crisis, a 'sea-change' took place in Labour thinking and Freud miraculously resurfaced as welfare advisor to work and pensions secretary, James Purnell.[18] His influence was signalled by the publication of Purnell's Green Paper of that year, *No One Written off: Reforming Welfare to Reward Responsibility*. The author's comment that 'there was more to life than moving from the bedroom to the sofa' left no room for misinterpretation. At the heart of government plans was the increased 'conditionality' of benefits, with punitive sanctions that would end safety-net provision and force lone parents and the disabled to find work. Along with Freud's earlier proposals for private companies to tender for core welfare services, the government also encouraged the third sector – charities, social enterprises and voluntary groups – to bid. Some had been founded on altruistic principles, but many were now openly marketised and eager for commercial contracts in the lucrative benefits field. Indeed, some charities had developed such a close relationship with big business that the CBI described them as the 'weapon of choice' to ensure the further privatisation of public services.[19]

Experts, in particular PCS members who administered the system, knew that the best way to get people back into the job market was through help, patience and tackling the complexities surrounding unemployment, especially affordable childcare and the availability and provision of sustainable, well-paid, flexible jobs. The new proposals piled responsibilities on claimants, but with no corresponding demands on employers. Experience also showed that private sector companies could not be trusted to run welfare services in the interests of those requiring support – their priority was maximising profits. Unscrupulous employers selected the most 'job-ready' claimants, while those who required more intensive assistance were left on benefits. When profits fell or companies failed, low-paid Jobcentre Plus staff were left to clean up the mess.

PCS argued that these proposals were a 'risk too far'. The union nationally and in the DWP group argued that if there was to be a genuine debate about welfare provision, it could not be based on government spin nor on advice from merchant bankers, and certainly against the narrative of 'work-shy scroungers' in the press. Any serious approach had to be based on listening to the real experts – Jobcentre workers themselves, anti-poverty campaigners and unemployed and disabled workers groups. The union's 'Welfare for All' campaign during late 2008 and 2009 argued that the government's welfare reforms were not a 'bold step into a progressive future but a regression to the poverty and degradation of the nineteenth century'.[20] Raising awareness of the deeper human issues at stake acted as a partial brake on Freud and Purnell's plans, although privatisation schemes were attempted, they were to be nowhere near the scale and depth envisaged by their ideologically-driven promoters.

CSCS – national strike action

In the run-up to the 2010 General Election, prime minister Gordon Brown addressed the TUC congress. He proclaimed that every redundancy was a 'personal tragedy', before going on to announce his government's plan to halve the country's deficit in four years consisted of £50 billion worth of cuts and the loss of 300,000 public sector jobs, '...cutting costs where we can, ensuring efficiency where it's needed, agreeing realistic public sector pay settlements throughout, selling off the unproductive assets we don't need, to pay for the services we do need.'[21] Nowhere in his speech did he confront the unregulated market forces that had caused the crash, other than a rhetorical flourish that he would be 'demanding that internationally we look at setting limits on bankers' bonuses'.

Brown appealed to compliant union bosses to focus on winning the election. While many delegates listened with deep concern, some of their leaders welcomed the speech. TUC general secretary,

Brendan Barber, for example, said that Brown had delivered a 'jobs versus cuts' speech and 'he chose jobs', adding: 'The dividing lines for the next election got that bit clearer today'. Dave Prentis of UNISON refuted any fears that the speech signalled 'the death knell for public services', but – with one eye on the reaction of his members – conceded there were, 'certain phrases within the speech, as there often are in a Gordon Brown speech, which do ring alarm bells, such as dealing with inefficiencies and getting rid of waste'. Bob Crow simply said: 'He has the look of a beaten man'.[22]

Brown's speech had focused on his plans for savaging the CSCS, urging other public sector employers to do likewise and slash voluntary and compulsory redundancy payments in preparation for major public sector job losses:

> We will be saving up to £500 million over the next three years by reforming Whitehall early exit scheme pay outs for early retirement. It's a scheme that's often as much as six times annual pay. These high costs prevent us from giving other people jobs and this is not the best way to spend public money. I am calling on all public authorities to make similar reviews of their terms'.

Mark Serwotka attacked Brown's claim that it would be 'mandarins', who would bear the brunt of CSCS cuts rather than the many thousands of low-paid staff delivering vital services. PCS and other left-led unions demanded that the TUC organise against this assault. The union began to develop alternative proposals. These included the collection of the £106 billion lost in commercial tax evasion, a major extension of public ownership, and investment in council housing and in public services.

The union leadership and its activists, except for some isolated Moderate voices, rejected the 'lesser-evil' approach of their Blairite counterparts, on the simple premise that whoever won the election, the attacks would continue. Their task was to build resistance, rather than enabling the politicians to carry out attacks that would place civil service jobs under a heightened threat of redundancy.

CSCS 'reform' would also mean that members with longer service would lose entitlements of up to one third, including their rights to enhanced pensions and voluntary severance packages.

Protection of the CSCS had long been an integral aspect of the ongoing national campaign on jobs, pay and conditions, but was now prioritised due to the immediate threat. The NEC set up a National Campaign Liaison Group to prepare for a national ballot and, if necessary, a Judicial Review. The issue for members was not simply one of self-interest, the argument was also made that closing 200 tax offices and getting rid of 25,000 tax workers, while tax evasion was spiralling, was 'the economics of the madhouse'.

The ballot to reinforce the union's mandate in opposing cuts to the CSCS in early 2010 returned a majority for industrial action with a 64 per cent yes vote, with 81 per cent for an overtime ban.[23] This was on a 33 per cent turnout, lower than previous ballots but still a solid figure. PCS members had taken more industrial action over the past decade than any other union – almost half of all industrial action in the UK in a single year. Ministers detected a sense of weariness among union members, but they had underestimated their anger at claims that the government was powerless to act against the 'contractual rights' of bankers' and MPs' 'golden handshakes', while trashing the contracts of their own staff.

Talks with the Cabinet Office took place before the proposed strike action, but the government was simply going through the motions. Despite PCS negotiators showing that savings could be made while protecting contractual rights, they were informed that it was not just about savings, but the need to show civil servants were actually 'worse off' from cuts to the CSCS. PCS members responded with one of their strongest expressions of support, as the union launched its campaign with a two-day national strike on 8 and 9 March 2010.[24] Industrial action hit operations in many areas affecting courts, Jobcentres, tax offices, passport offices and other government services. The National Assembly for Wales was suspended as Labour and Plaid Cymru assembly members refused to cross picket lines. The strikes drew considerable public support, as the connection between attacks on workers' conditions and the deterioration of public services was now well-established in many people's minds. The union went on to institute legal action for a Judicial Review and demanded that ministers re-enter negotiations. The action presented serious political problems for Brown and Darling. A total of 151 MPs had already signed a parliamentary motion the previous month condemning the 'unfair proposals' for civil service contracts, many of them no doubt questioning the competence of the Blairite clique around Brown in alienating a key group of workers months before a general election.[25]

It was an open secret that Brown had a visceral hatred of the PCS leadership. While this may have encouraged him to recklessly pick a fight, his real motivation was to single out a militant union and crush it, sending the message that any organised resistance to New Labour's embrace of austerity would meet with the same response. A further one-day national strike was arranged to coincide with Alistair Darling's pre-election budget on 24 March as part of a month of action, disruption and lobbying. In extraordinary scenes, the chancellor had to cross picket lines at Downing Street and parliament before he could deliver a speech promising public sector cuts on a scale that even Thatcher would have shrunk from.[26]

The union considered further strike action, but the announcement of a general election in May meant that there was nobody to negotiate with until a new government was in place. PCS did not suspend campaigning but continued its activity in workplaces up and down the country, including a national tour of the Battle Bus. It also pushed forward with its legal action, alarming the government so much that it used every manner of delaying tactic to postpone the result until after the election.

As the votes were counted on the night of 6 May 2010, it became clear that Labour's race to the bottom had sealed Gordon Brown's fate. Bob Crow had been right. While failing to secure an all-out majority, the Tories under David Cameron were able to form a coalition government through a pact with Liberal Democrats. The 'lesser-evil' approach of the Blairite union leaders had brought the exact opposite – a greater intensification of attacks on the working class. Big business, the banks and financial institutions and the privatisation sharks may have publicly welcomed Brown's austerity speeches, but in private they had drawn the conclusion that what they preferred was a remorseless right-wing government. Behind Cameron's carefully manufactured image as a moderniser who had transformed the 'nasty party' to one that was 'compassionate and caring', was an establishment insider and ruthless neoliberal who intended to finish what Brown and Darling had started.

Notes & References

1.   *The Guardian*, 17 July 2004.

2.   *Morning Star*, 13 September 2004.

3.   *Morning Star*, 25 August 2004.

4.   *West Lancashire Evening Gazette*, 4 September 2004; *Northamptonshire Chronicle and Echo*, 28 September 2004; *Chorley Guardian*, 10 November 2004.

5.   *The Socialist*, 28 October 2009.

6.   *Morning Star*, 17 May 2007.

7.   *Financial Times*, 13 October 2009.

8.   *Morning Star*, 4 November 2003.

9.   *Personnel Today*, 26 July 2004.

10.   *Financial Times*, 28 November 2001.

11.   *Morning Star*, 21 January 2008.

12.   *Morning Star*, 25 April 2008.

13.   *The Guardian*, 30 April 2008.

14.   *Morning Star*, 25 August 2008.

15.   *The Socialist*, 4 November, 10 December 2008.

16.   *Morning Star*, 23 November 2005.

17.   D. Freud, *Reducing dependency, increasing opportunity: options for the future of welfare to work. An independent report into the Department of Work and Pensions*, 2007, pp.107-12.

18.   *Daily Telegraph*, 2 February 2008.

19.   *Public Finance*, 4 August 2006.

20.   *Morning Star*, 11 December 2008; 3 March 2009.

21. *The Guardian*, 15 September 2009.

22. *Morning Star*, 16 February 2009.

23. *Morning Star*, 3 February 2010.

24. *The Guardian*, 9 March 2009.

25. *Morning Star*, 9 February 2010.

26. *Financial Times*, 24 March 2010.

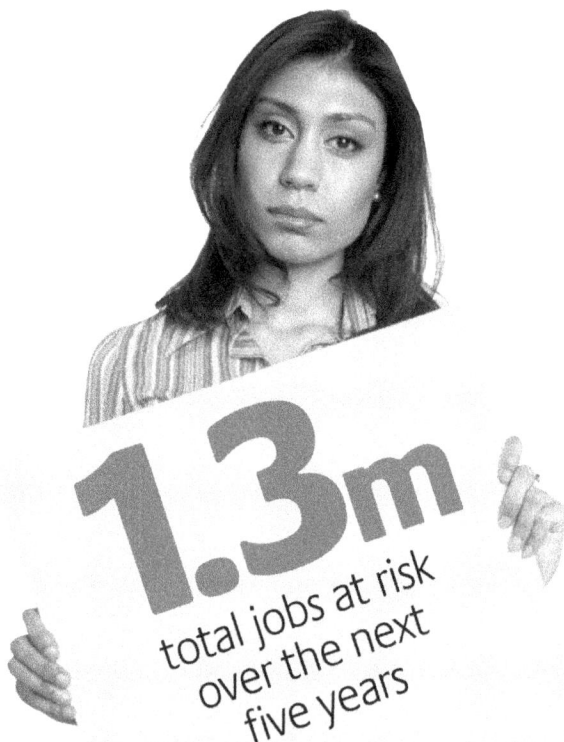

There is an
alternative...

The case against cuts
in public spending

1.3m

total jobs at risk
over the next
five years

pcs **Public and Commercial Services Union** | pcs.org.uk

■ The PCS's influential *Alternative* – challenging austerity.

7. Resistance and betrayal

The coalition government – imposing austerity

From an economic perspective, the crash which culminated in 2008 marked the end of neo-liberal globalisation and brought a sharp end to the massive expansion of free trade on which it was based. While political consequences invariably lag behind economic reality, the impact of the crash and the consequent downturn was apparent in a reversion to protectionism amongst competing countries and economic blocs, the full political ramifications of which would become fully evident only with the election of Donald Trump in 2024.

The crash set the conditions for a qualitative intensification of both economic and political instability. In Britain, existing antagonisms within the Tory party between the globalists and nationalist capitalists developed into a serious split over 'Brexit', resulting in the referendum in 2016 that ended the country's membership of the European Union. In Scotland there was a rise in nationalism and demands for independence. Decades of neo-liberal reaction with its strategy of de-industrialisation and the primacy of finance capital, with the deregulation of banking, saw the City of London operate as an international money laundering enterprise on a colossal scale, leaving the United Kingdom particularly vulnerable in the new conditions of heightened competitiveness.

Three main factors mitigated the impact of the crash. First, to stabilise markets in the short term, Gordon Brown and globalist governments throughout the Western world introduced 'quantitative easing'. This printing of unsecured money was essentially a desperate stopgap measure that could not resolve the structural and systemic contradictions that caused the crisis in the first place. Second, the continued expansion of the Chinese economy was significant in avoiding a complete collapse into unstoppable instability and market chaos. The third main factor that allowed the capitalist class to continue expanding their profits was an intensification of their decades-long plunder of the UK's public services and state assets through marketisation, cuts and privatisation, now re-branded as 'austerity'.

At Westminster, the debate among the mainstream parties was not over whether public sector cuts were required, but how many, how deep, and how quickly. The newly elected coalition government sought to exploit the ongoing economic crisis by promoting a 'we're all in it together' mentality to justify the need for 'austerity'. Cameron and his chancellor George Osborne presented the cuts as an undeniable reality to which no reasonable person could object. The media, with the BBC in its traditional role as a prop of the state in times of trouble, presented neoliberal orthodoxy as the new public consensus; dissenting voices were ignored, sneeringly dismissed, and even openly mocked.

When invited to interviews, Mark Serwotka and other PCS senior officers were informed by television and radio producers of the strict parameters for discussion. Regardless of this, PCS continued to make the case that the trade union movement should oppose all cuts. It was on this basis that the union would consistently campaign, demanding a real alternative to the government's harshness and indifference.

Public sector workers had already faced decades of attacks, including wage depression. There was a growing public awareness of the serious damage being inflicted on services through cuts and privatisation, even among the middle class. As they prepared to press ahead with the biggest austerity programme since the 1920s, the new government was cautious in its approach, even though it faced little opposition in parliament, aside from bodies like the PCS Parliamentary Group. For them, the question was how extra-parliamentary resistance would express itself. Would there be disparate struggles that could be easily contained, or would there be mass protest coordinated with industrial action?

The trade union movement was the only force capable of bringing together the working class and other broad forces, the social movements, anti-cuts organisations, anti-poverty and disability campaigners, all of them opposed to austerity. First and foremost, workers looked to their unions in the face of the potentially catastrophic consequences of cuts; so too did less well-organised groups like the unemployed and the disabled. If the TUC stood firm in the face of the attacks, it might be possible to unite the broad mass of the working class and even significant sections of the middle class against austerity. Any effective opposition to the government would require a firm and unambiguous rejection of its strategy from both the TUC and individual union leaderships. It would also take mass mobilisation to bring together public and private sector workers and to build alliances with the developing anti-cuts movement.

Sensing this, Cameron's tactic was to draw the TUC and trade union leaders into consultation in the hope of sowing division between different interest groups. His 'historic meeting' at Downing Street in December 2010 – the first between the unions and a Tory leader for a quarter of a century – was also intended to split them off from the non-unionised working class.[1] The government's propaganda offensive was essentially an appeal to union leaders to stand behind the government and work in partnership in a time of national crisis. It also contained a subtle warning that if they did not do so, then the cuts would go ahead anyway, leaving them on the sidelines. It was a well-tried approach that had always succeeded in the past with right-wing union bosses. Essentially, the coalition bargained that their opponents would show less aggression in defending workers' interests than they themselves would expend in protecting the profits of the banks and big business. Events would prove them right.

As workers braced themselves for George Osborne's first Budget in June 2010, the unions came under pressure from the New Labour leadership to adopt a 'tread carefully' approach. They argued that only a minority of society opposed the political consensus on austerity and that unions must not do anything to damage the prospect of a Labour return to power. This ignored that the general election was still five years away and that Labour was itself fully committed to the cuts agenda, a position that had just cost them the 2010 election. In response, a sympathetic TUC refused to support calls for orchestrated action around the budget, leaving PCS to organise workplace protests, meetings, and rallies, which drew in members from other unions.[2]

The coalition's budget was ironically entitled *Responsibility, Freedom and Fairness*. In it, Osborne declared that state spending was 'completely unsustainable' and that the national debt must be reduced through cuts in public spending rather than increases in taxation. Labour's proposed increase in National Insurance contributions was scrapped, and VAT rose by 2.5 per cent; this would have little impact on the wealthy but would be a significant burden for low-paid workers.

The chancellor then outlined the horrifying scale of the planned cuts. Government departments were told that they must reduce budgets by 25 per cent to achieve £83 billion in 'savings' over the next five years; this was an increase of £39 billion on the cuts previously agreed by Labour. He also announced attacks on living standards with a two-year public sector pay freeze and an accelerated rise in the state pension age.

But it was for those reliant on benefits that the sheer viciousness of the attacks became evident. It was no coincidence that former Labour adviser, David Freud, had become minister for welfare in the new administration. An £11 billion cut would be made in the welfare budget with a maximum of £400 per week in housing benefit; there would be a three-year freeze in child benefit; and benefits and pensions would be linked to the Consumer Price Index (CPI) rather than the Retail Price Index (RPI). The Treasury calculated that this would reduce expenditure by £6 billion over five years.

Osborne announced that Disability Living Allowance (DLA) claimants must face a new medical assessment from 2013, an initiative that presaged a major attempt to drive down the number of claimants. This was accompanied by an extension of outsourcing and privatisation in the health and welfare sectors, with major corporations lacking any background in delivering social or medical services, but best poised to rake in profits. In a final divisive flourish, he implied that if further cuts could be found in welfare on top of these, then cuts elsewhere might not need to be so deep. This served as a signal to reactionary elements in the media and in wider society to unleash a torrent of abuse against benefit claimants and the disabled.

The early confidence of coalition leaders that trade union leaders would remain bound by the political consensus around pro-market, neoliberal policies was fully justified by the response of TUC general secretary, Brendan Barber. While condemning the savage nature of the cuts, he effectively endorsed their inevitability, albeit suggesting that workers should not have to bear the whole burden.[3] This was precisely what the government wanted to hear. Cameron, Osborne and Nick Clegg, the Liberal Democrat deputy prime minister, were reassured that in the official leadership of the organised working class, they had compliant partners with whom they could do business.

The left-led unions, however, insisted that the renewed cuts and privatisation agenda had to be tackled head-on. This would require united action and building of broad-based alliances to maximise the strength of the trade union movement and the working class as a whole. In particular, PCS suggested that attempts by the government to divide workers through phoney consultations should be rejected, as should Osborne's false claim that public sector workers had been shielded from the worst impacts of the financial crisis. In fact, both private and public sector workers were under attack, with the vast majority of the latter having endured decades of pay freezes, pensions robbery and job cuts.

Osborne's budget brought an angry backlash from unions, anti-poverty groups and women's organisations. The Fawcett Society, for example, unsuccessfully sought a judicial review of the government's cuts, arguing that it had not assessed the disproportionate impact of the cuts on women.[4] The PCS Parliamentary group continued to apply pressure, so that even some Tory MPs, including David Davis and John Redwood, were worried that the cuts would have harmful consequences for minority groups.[5] Only months into their administration, the coalition's claim, supported by the entire Westminster political establishment, that a majority in British society supported austerity was contradicted by a perceptible shift in public opinion.

The government's concern over potential opposition to its programme was evident in September 2010 when Danny Alexander, Liberal Democrat and chief secretary to the Treasury, reacted to campaigns on the tax justice issue by PCS and the newly formed pressure group UK Uncut. He unveiled plans to tackle tax avoidance and evasion, with a target recovery figure of up to £9 billion; the rich too had to 'do their bit', but as the government was planning a 25 per cent cut to HMRC, Alexander was making an empty promise.[6]

The Alternative

PCS sought to build a campaign in which public awareness and involvement, political lobbying and pressure and industrial strategies were interconnected. Under Gordon Brown's Labour government, the union had already begun to develop the idea of a democratic alternative to austerity. In strategy meetings to discuss how resistance might be built against the coalition, the union's leadership agreed that this work should now be given an even higher priority. The result was *There is an alternative: The case against cuts in public spending*, a short, powerful document published in September 2010, which set out the case for new thinking on public sector cuts, government spending and tax justice.[7] 'The Alternative', as it became known, was the product of existing union policy, discussions with various activists and senior officers and drew on the extensive research of policy officer, Andrew Fisher, who, when Jeremy Corbyn was elected Labour leader, became his policy advisor.

Right-wing and centrist union leaders become quite aggrieved when they are accused of compliance in government attacks, but it is the only logical outcome of their narrow, self-regulated view of their responsibilities and of the parameters within which they seek to contain working-class resistance. Unable to envisage any alternative, not just to capitalism itself, but in the form of austerity, the question of a real alternative, raised by PCS and supported by other left-led unions and social movements, posed as much a threat to them as the government. As did the simple question, if an alternative is possible, then why are we not fighting for it?

The concept of the Alternative became a core element of the union's campaigning work, not just a response to austerity itself, which had assumed an even greater significance and focus after the election of the Coalition in 2010. The attempt by the political establishment to silence any opposition to austerity backfired as the destructive impact of government policies grew in public consciousness, greatly increasing the effectiveness of the Alternative argument.

In their introduction, Mark Serwotka and Janice Godrich dissected the plans of the coalition. They challenged the propaganda that the deficit crisis meant the country was spending beyond its means and that the only solution was to cut public spending. Instead, as PCS had long argued, public spending was an investment, not a financial liability. The real reason for the vilification of the public sector was a drive for privatisation, which Cameron disguised as a bid to 'tear down... big government bureaucracy'.

There was no need to take a penny from public services nor to lose a single job. Ministers boasted they would cut services by up to 40 per cent. Yet, the Treasury's own analysis, exposed in leaked documents, showed their policies meant that within six years 600,000 jobs would be lost in the public sector and 700,000 in the private sector. Given increasing unemployment, there would be a decrease in tax receipts and a rise in benefits. At the same time, cuts in HMRC staff numbers resulted in uncollected taxes, with tax avoidance and evasion reaching record levels. In contrast,

Richard Murphy of Tax Research had demonstrated that the state recouped 90 per cent of the cost of creating new public sector jobs.

The Alternative also focused on the disastrous record of privatisation, citing its threat to public services and its many failures. All evidence showed that privatisation meant cuts for workers and profits for bosses. One notorious instance was QinetiQ – a company set up from the privatisation of the Defence Evaluation and Research Agency. Here, the ten most senior managers made £107.5 million on a joint investment of £540,000, while simultaneously attempting to impose a pay freeze on staff. The pamphlet also exposed how the government funnelled public funds through the Treasury's Infrastructure Finance Unit to state-owned banks, who loaned finance to PFI consortia, who then claimed inflated returns over the next thirty years that 'greatly exceeded' the money given to them.

While the government, opposition and media castigated unemployed and disabled workers over the issue of benefit fraud, the government's own figures showed it was actually running at less than one per cent of the money lost through tax avoidance and evasion. HMRC compliance officers could each bring in over £658,000, but instead their jobs were being cut. A tax on global financial transactions would raise up to £30 billion a year from the UK financial sector. This alone could reduce the annual deficit by between 12.5 per cent and 20 per cent. But perhaps the most shocking revelation was that the poorest fifth of the population paid 39.9 per cent of their income in tax, while the wealthiest fifth paid only 35.1 per cent.

Welfare costs were contrasted with the 'real waste' of government spending: £1.8billion spent on private sector consultants, some little more than money-spinning scams; the government's 230 plus civil service bargaining units instead of one central outfit; the annual £1.5 billion cost of the Trident nuclear submarine programme, with its estimated renewal costs between £94 and £104 billion over thirty years; and the £2.6 billion cost of the Afghan War.

In short, the Alternative's key points and demands were:

- There is no need for cuts to public services or further privatisation.
- Creating jobs will boost the economy. Cutting jobs will damage the economy and increase the deficit.
- Invest in areas such as housing, renewable energy, and public transport.
- The UK debt is lower than in other major economies.
- There is a £120 billion tax cap of evaded, avoided, and uncollected taxes.
- The UK holds £850 billion in banking assets from the bailout – more than the national debt.
- Free up these billions by not renewing Trident.
- End the use of consultants.

For a short pamphlet of only ten pages, the Alternative made a big impact. Some 250,000 copies were distributed to members, activists, MPs, campaign groups, other unions and trades councils; many tens of thousands of people also read it online. Achieving an unusually high readership within PCS, it gave members an even stronger sense of confidence that their own union was fighting and campaigning on the issues that affected them directly. It also became a tremendous resource that could be used by even less experienced reps, providing them with arguments and statistics which were invaluable for local campaigns and workplace negotiations. A series of highly successful Privatisation Forums were held in the UK, including London, Glasgow, Bristol, and Belfast, and the pamphlet played a prominent role at fringe meetings at the TUC congress and various party conferences.

Even more importantly, the Alternative model spawned a series of similar PCS initiatives, with more specific 'alternatives' produced for departmental groups, using the same evidence-based methods to expose government plans. For example, the highly influential *Welfare: An Alternative Vision* (2011), discussed in Chapter 9, robustly addressed the issue of welfare cuts, challenging media myths and arguing for sustained public investment. Another vital campaigning tool was *Alternative Vision for HM Land Registry* (2014), based on the work of academics Roger Seifert and Mike Ironside, which was credited with helping to defeat plans for privatisation in the department.

Although almost universally welcomed on the left, the Alternative did not escape some criticism, inevitably from a small number of those who see themselves as Marxist 'theoreticians'. They argued that the document was 'reformist' and also that the argument that austerity was a 'political choice' was essentially misleading, as the capitalists were only responding to the internal contradictions of their system which compelled them to extract more value from the labour of the working class for themselves.

While no worker raised this objection to the Alternative, it is not entirely an abstract argument but one that touches profoundly on how to produce programmes that gain support from the working class, while also raising their consciousness about the nature of class society. In fact, this issue was discussed amongst socialists and Marxists in the union's leadership.

The British capitalist class did have a political choice on whether to attack the working class with cuts, privatisation and austerity, but a severely limited one. The profit system is international, particularly in terms of finance capital, and no national capitalist class has complete freedom of action. Neoliberalism is an internationally coordinated assault on the working class, its intensity in any one country determined by the balance of class forces between the ruling elite and the working class. The labour and trade union movement in the UK in 2010 had been greatly weakened, and the ruling class had for some time been deprived of the massive profits extracted from the super-exploitation of its former colonies – it was still a wealthy country, but a rapidly declining, second-rate post-imperial economic power.

Had any government from Thatcher onwards attempted to do anything other than launch a full neoliberal programme, it would have resulted in a ferocious coordinated attack by the big banks and monopolies. Labour's formulation under Miliband that cuts were 'too quick and too deep' perfectly reflects the severe, almost strangulated nature of the 'choice'. Had PCS's Alternative been framed based on a full Marxist analysis of the death agony of capitalism and the need for a complete overthrow of the profit system, there may have been a few recruits to revolutionary groups, but most workers would not have read past the first paragraph.

Cuts as class war

Mark Serwotka memorably described austerity as 'political shock and awe'.[8] Now armed with an alternative vision, a show of opposition and resistance from the trade union movement during the autumn of 2010 could have brought millions onto the streets. At the TUC General Council, PCS president Janice Godrich called for a national demonstration in October to coincide with the coalition's Comprehensive Spending Review, which would provide greater detail on where the cuts would fall.[9] Although she was initially unsuccessful, pressure from PCS, RMT, FBU and the POA and other left-leaning unions resulted in an event being planned for March 2011. The damage was done; the delay sent a strong signal to the coalition that the TUC was hesitant and in no mood for a real fight.

With the TUC leadership dithering, unions at a local level organised demonstrations in conjunction with long-established campaign groups, such as the Bristol and Avon District Anti-cuts Alliance, as well as new groups that had been formed in response to Osborne's budget. There were sizable turnouts in various towns and cities, including Bristol, London, Cardiff, Wrexham, Sheffield and Leeds. Significantly, the Scottish Trades Union Congress (STUC) responded to the growing mood of discontent by holding a 20,000-strong demonstration in Edinburgh, which also drew in trade unionists from the North of England.[10]

The budget had to some extent prepared workers for what was to come, but any hope the government might draw back was dashed by the 2010 Spending Review.[11] This laid out how they intended to implement a further £7 billion in cuts. No area of the public sector would be untouched, nor would any part of the country. Regions and areas disproportionately dependent on public sector employment, like Northern Ireland, faced massive job losses if the cuts were fully implemented. Estimates ran at around 700,000 overall job losses in the public sector. With the Home Office targeted for 25 per cent cuts and other departments badly hit too, it was estimated that 100,000 civil service jobs alone would go. In the private sector, cuts of 60 per cent in capital spending and a general fall in economic demand meant that 900,000 job losses were estimated.

The extent of the cuts would mean some services would simply disappear from many communities. They would also mean poverty for many on a scale not seen since before the welfare state, including a further rise in child poverty, which had already doubled between 1979 to 2008. Housing budget cuts meant council house tenants could face substantial rent increases, with the prospect of massive increases in homelessness. Cuts in media, culture, arts and sports ran to £1 billion. Court closures, including the loss of 14,000 jobs, would deny many access to justice. A 6.8 per cent real-terms cut to the Scottish government's overall budget would turbocharge the nationalist cause, while a 7.5 per cent cut for Wales risked a similar reaction there.[12]

As boardroom pay increased by 55 per cent and bank bonuses topped £7 billion, tax relief for the super-rich was now running at £10 billion. There was no doubt that this was a class war. When Mark Serwotka was described as a 'fundamentalist' and 'deficit denier' at the TUC General Council, he responded that if the leadership of the movement accepted that there should be cuts, then the question must be posed: 'Who deserves to lose their jobs, conditions and services?' He went on to argue:

> It is essential that we all expose the fraudulent argument that the economy will collapse unless the

public services suffer hundreds of thousands of job cuts... Ask the people if they want their local library, tax office, swimming pool or job centre to close and the answer is No. Ask people if they want their pension, job or pay slashed and again the answer is No... The first lesson that we should take from this situation is that support for cuts is shallow, but people need to be given confidence that there is an alternative.[13]

PCS wrote to the TUC Public Sector Liaison Committee to say that with growing working-class anger a national demonstration must be called before Christmas. This was again refused. Meanwhile, massive student and school pupil protests were held in response to education cuts and an increase in the cap on tuition fees. Over 50,000 students marched in central London in November, while mass action in Bristol saw students leave schools and campuses in such numbers that the police lost control of the city centre for several hours, with their vans being overturned.[14] Further protests were violently suppressed, notably by the employment of militarised methods by the Metropolitan Police, such as the notorious 'kettling'. The coalition government was able to ride out these disturbances, secure in the knowledge that a combination of repression and patience would prevail, not least because trade union leaders had failed to swing the enormous strength and status of their movement behind the protestors.

Yet, conflict was building on other fronts for the government, most notably around further detrimental changes planned to CSCS. As discussed in the previous chapter, the scheme had been the subject of a fierce PCS campaign and legal action in the run-up to the 2010 general election. The coalition now intended to unilaterally impose cuts, despite a High Court ruling in May that the government must reach a settlement with the union.[15] Five unions, including Prospect (successor to IPMS) and FDA, representing the higher-paid grades, had already reached a deal, but PCS continued to hold firm. They conducted a consultative policy ballot in January 2011 with two questions. Members were asked if they agreed that the proposed changes to the CSCS should be rejected; and whether they supported the union's continued opposition to cuts in jobs, conditions and services. Linking both questions emphasised how the specific attack on the CSCS should be inextricably linked to the wider cuts programme. Members voted Yes with 90 per cent on the first question and 96 per cent on the second, a solid platform from which to build for industrial action, while also continuing the fight of PCS in the courts.[16]

The great pensions robbery

The first major battle took place over pensions. In October 2010, the former Labour minister, John Hutton, now ennobled as Baron Hutton of Furness, had been appointed to chair the Independent Public Service Pensions Commission.[17] In his final report in March the following year, Hutton concluded that while public sector pensions were not 'gold-plated', workers must nevertheless pay more, receive less and work longer. Although he claimed that workers should be entitled to 'adequate levels of income', pensions for the mainly low-paid public-sector workforce were already wholly inadequate and among the lowest in Europe.

Seeking to short-circuit resistance to this pensions robbery, the government pursued a press campaign aimed at forestalling any serious debate over the report. The TUC had calculated that the change to pensions indexation from RPI to CPI alone would devalue pensions by around fifteen per cent, but the media constantly repeated the lie that the public sector pensions were unaffordable and unsustainable. So satisfied was the government with Hutton's report that it warned against 'cherry-picking' its conclusions and implied that it would adopt a firm approach in negotiations with the unions. Affecting a commitment to 'inclusivity and equality', Cameron claimed that pensions reform was part of his aspiration to build a 'Big Society'; a vacuous slogan barely disguising his real aim – using the crash to impose yet another major transfer of wealth and power to the ruling class.[18]

In a *Guardian* article in March 2011, John Cridland, the new director general of the CBI, suggested that Hutton had sounded the last rites for final salary schemes. The issue was simply one of 'fairness'; while greater life expectancy was something to celebrate, he explained, 'somebody has to pay the bill'. Crucially, he failed to mention that 'the bill' meant workers doubling or even trebling their contributions and working until 68, with cuts of between 20 to 50 per cent in the value of their pensions. Nor did he mention that public sector pensions in 2009 cost a relatively modest £4 billion, while providing tax relief for the 1 per cent earning over £150,000 cost £10 billion. And he certainly did not mention that big business was sitting on over £850 billion of the super-profits extracted from the working class in recent years that could have been used to invest in jobs, services, and communities. Instead, the real purpose of pension reform was revealed in his statement that:

> Public sector pensions remain the biggest barrier to the private sector and third sector providing public services. Pension costs and liabilities are far higher for providers outside the public sector. When third sector and private sector organisations currently bid for work, they have to be able to cover the full cost of public sector pensions liabilities, and many simply do not have the money to do so... This puts a brake on competition and makes it harder for those in the private sector to bid for public service contracts.[19]

Cridand's message was clear – in order to plunder the public sector for profit, low-paid workers must endure an old age of poverty. PCS's view was equally clear – pension reform was simply another aspect of the wider cuts and privatisation programme. It had to be resisted by using unified industrial action and by alliance-based public and political campaigning. Only through coordinated national strikes and a programme of targeted action could sufficient pressure be applied to defeat the government, or at best win concessions.

Nevertheless, the government's confidence was such that Cabinet Office minister Francis Maude disdainfully let it be known he believed that the unions, 'had no stomach for a fight'.[20] On the surface this was hardly surprising. Even now, some union leaders were intent on offering the government concessions up front, without even testing the mood of members. Similarly, Labour's new leader, Ed Miliband, was described as walking a 'tricky tightrope', criticising the coalition for cutting too deep and too recklessly, while still trapped in a defensive posture that offered no alternative to the spending squeeze.[21]

But Maude was underestimating the strength of feeling among rank-and-file trade unionists. Memories of Gordon Brown's attack on pensions rights were fresh in many workers' minds; they knew that an 'affordable' deal had been reached on that occasion and saw the coalition's return to the issue as highly provocative and confrontational. They also remembered that a united response in 2005 had forced the government to retreat, protecting the pension rights of millions. Debate was not restricted to the committee rooms of the TUC nor to the various union headquarters, but took place in workplaces, union branches and trades councils. Here, PCS members, along with other trade unionists and community activists, worked to create a mood of confidence and resistance. Nor was anger restricted to public sector workers; many of them had extended families, neighbours and friends who worked in the private sector and who had seen their pensions cut or snatched outright over the preceding decades.

The UK was far from alone. Although no one had voted for it, austerity was being imposed on unwilling populations across Europe. The implementation of policies designed to benefit only the very richest in society lacked real popular support. The ruling class's contempt for the democratic values upon which they based their authority rested was most noticeably exposed in Greece, where the European Union insisted on devastating cuts and privatisation. When the Greek government dared to suggest that the people should be consulted, they were told that this was not acceptable and that austerity must be implemented regardless of the popular will, leading to the impoverishment of millions, albeit in the face of fierce working-class resistance.

TUC-led pensions negotiations with government ministers began during the summer of 2011. They were described by Mark Serwotka as a 'farce', as Treasury minister Danny Alexander had insisted that the unions concede on 'core' points before the talks went ahead.[22] These points included increased contributions, cuts in the value of pensions and increases in working age – in other words, the very areas under dispute. Alexander hoped that the discussion would focus on how cuts were to be distributed rather than on whether the proposals had any justification. PCS argued for complete rejection of these conditions, reiterating that the only serious response was for the unions to launch a coordinated campaign, including industrial action.

The TUC eventually organised their 'March for the Alternative' on 26 March 2011, but even now their underestimation of likely attendance was used by the media to imply that they represented only a minority in society. In fact, the opposite was true. Over 750,000 attended the march, with tens of thousands converging on London from all parts of the country in up to 1,000 coaches and specially chartered trains. This demonstration of class anger, solidarity and resistance was the biggest in postwar British history, surpassed only by the two million who had marched in 2003 against the impending war against Iraq. PCS pushed for the maximum attendance – HMRC group member Richard Evans gained valuable publicity for the union by walking the approximately 160 miles between Cardiff to London.[23]

The demonstration threw into sharp relief the problems faced in the labour and trade union movement over how to fight austerity. Its scale showed the tremendous potential of the organised working class to build a united opposition, but the failure of so many leaders to unequivocally oppose the government programme and set out clear campaign objectives in simple language left many demonstrators unclear as to whether there was any real strategy of resistance. Typical was the platitudinous speech of Ed Miliband, who had reluctantly agreed to attend the rally, but not the march. In contrast, Mark Serwotka made PCS's position unmistakably clear: 'Look around this park – imagine what it would be like if we all went on strike together?'.[24]

While this message of defiance was what demonstrators wanted to hear, the TUC union negotiators preferred to deal with the pension issue in isolation from the rest of the austerity agenda and settle it as quickly as possible, even if this meant divisive sectoral bargaining. PCS and other left-led unions rejected this approach, pointing out the catastrophic consequences for jobs and conditions, and public services. The attacks on pensions emanated from the same source – the government. As they affected all workers, they must be opposed by all and in the common interest of all.

Having successfully balloted for sustained action on pensions and the wider austerity agenda at the beginning of the year, PCS and three education unions, UCU, NUT and ATL, called a one-day strike on 30 June 2011. A publicity campaign heightened awareness over the scale of the pension grab, including the production of a PCS Pensions Calculator. This allowed members to check for themselves the financial implications of the government's proposals; in the four weeks after going online and the strike itself, it had over 20,000 visits.

Three-quarters of a million workers took strike action on 'J30', as it was termed. This was a show of solidarity that drew support from other trade unionists, who joined rallies and marches in significant numbers. On the morning of the strike, Mark Serwotka clinically exposed the government's pension policy in a debate on BBC Radio 4's Today programme with Cabinet Office secretary, Francis Maude, who then refused interviews for the rest of the day.

At certain critical junctures, one event can exert an influence far beyond its formal significance. J30 was just such an event. The strike received considerable media coverage, which promoted public awareness of why workers were opposed to the pension changes.[25] But it did more than that – strong support for the strike demonstrated that workers were prepared to resist and take strike action to do so. Those workers from other unions who demonstrated such active solidarity on the day showed the enormous potential to build the type of united, coordinated approach advocated by PCS, the education unions, and others with left leaderships. Most importantly, J30 led many activists and members to question their own union leaders in the most direct manner and ask: what is my union doing to stop this attack? If other unions are fighting to defend our pension rights, why can't we? In this way, J30 qualitatively shifted the debate on the pensions campaign. Every worker now knew that large-scale joint action was the only effective way to challenge the government. No union leader, even the most conservative, could deny this reality.

Ed Balls, Labour's shadow chancellor, had to date shown little concern for the consequences of the pensions robbery for millions of low-paid workers. He now expressed disappointment at the talk of further action, which he claimed would be a 'Tory trap' to divert attention away from the economy, damaging his party's future electoral prospects.[26] For its part, the government continued in its attempt to separate 'reasonable' union leaders from those whom Danny Alexander described as 'hell bent on premature action'.[27] PCS was singled out for attack in parliament and the media, but pressure had already built to a point where avoiding industrial action was no longer a credible option, even for those 'reasonable' leaders on whom the coalition rested their hopes.

Although the J30 strike was not the only factor in galvanising a reluctant TUC and union leadership, it was the main one. Following a number of union ballots, a further one-day public sector strike was called for 30 November 2011 ('N30'). Activity among members grew as the strike date approached. Rallies were arranged throughout the country, mobilising activists from unions who normally had little contact with each other. PCS had already come together with Unite, NUT, UCU and the National Pensioners Convention to launch a booklet entitled, *Fair Pensions for All*, explaining their demands.[28]

N30 saw between two and three million workers take strike action in opposition to the coalition's pensions policy, the biggest industrial action in modern British history. Picket lines were the strongest and best supported in many years. Confidence was high as workers from different areas of the public sector compared their experiences of how wages, terms, and conditions were being eroded and how employers were using similar methods to demoralise and control staff. The resulting marches and rallies drew huge support. An estimated 30,000 marched in Manchester and 20,000 in Bristol, but it was the turnout in the smaller cities and towns that demonstrated the breadth of support for the strike and opposition to the coalition government; in Taunton, for example, over 4,000 joined a march and rally.[29]

The government's composure was rattled by the scale of what was effectively a public sector general strike; they knew it was not only about pensions. The picket lines, marches and rallies punctured the Westminster 'bubble'. In the run-up to the day, Labour leader Ed Miliband had characteristically attempted to dampen the resolve of those who had planned to strike whilst avoiding explicitly condemning it; while David Cameron's initial portrayal of the strike as a 'damp squib' failed to survive the early reports of huge attendances at over 1,000 protests across the country.[30]

PCS speakers at rallies did not restrict themselves to condemnations of the coalition but advanced their union's strategy on how it could be challenged and defeated. At the Bristol rally, John McInally, PCS national vice-president, said:

> My union, PCS, believes the TUC must announce at its upcoming meeting – as an absolute minimum – another National Day of Action, involving all the unions on strike today. We must escalate by getting even more unions on board, including private sector workers fighting for their pension rights too. Targeted, selective or rolling action must be coordinated by the TUC for maximum impact. The way to win is to demonstrate our power

as we have done today, striking together. National coordinated industrial action is the key to defeating the attack on pensions and the cuts themselves.[31]

Delivering the deal

The government attempted to destroy the unity achieved by N30 by reiterating its demand that the unions should enter separate sectoral negotiations for education, health, and local and central government, a strategy designed to divide union from union in a scramble for the best deals. While trade unionists waited expectantly for the next stage in the anti-cuts campaign, rumours began to circulate that senior trade union figures were brokering a deal with the government around a so-called 'Heads of Agreement'. Concerningly, this sounded like a capitulation to the government's terms, with no concessions on any of the three main areas of contention upon which the campaign, including the huge N30 strike, was built – paying more, receiving less, and working longer.

As the government grew more confident that their union 'partners' would deliver on sectoral arrangements, concern turned to anger among many workers. The TUC General Council held in December 2011 was lobbied by activists, while in the meeting itself Mark Serwotka condemned the negotiations and argued that the campaign should continue, a view supported by other left leaders of unions such as NUT and POA.[32] However, TUC general secretary, Brendan Barber and UNISON leader, Dave Prentis, the main advocates of the deal, were already quietly working to secure majority support. Their surrender to sectoral bargaining meant the end of a genuinely coordinated campaign, with each union now trying separately to reach the best negotiated settlement for its members.

The Heads of Agreement had serious implications for all public sector workers and deserved to be subjected to the widest possible scrutiny, but those who had agreed to it behind closed doors now wished to close down debate by drawing a line under negotiations. This process of betrayal played out over the Christmas period as leaders of key unions, most significantly UNISON, prepared to push through the deal.

The PCS leadership refused to accept the agreement, a decision endorsed by members in a consultative ballot in March in which 90 per cent rejected the deal and 72 per cent supported further action.[33] The union continued to oppose the deal while working to build a new coalition of 'rejectionist' unions who were prepared to use further industrial action. It was clear from the outset, however, that any such alliance must have a realistic chance of success. This would be dependent, for example, on members' capacity for financial sacrifice in any extended strike action.

In circumstances in which the 'official' leadership of the movement capitulates in the way it did over pensions, a vacuum is created, and one that can only be partially filled by militant unions like PCS. In the hiatus between New Year and the series of meetings in early January in which various unions would decide on their response to the deal, Janice Godrich raised the need for an initiative to bring together activists from across the movement on an 'unofficial' basis as quickly as possible in order to build awareness, assess the strength of opposition, test levels of combativity and to coordinate resistance.

Given the scale of betrayal over pensions, any initiative would have to be called by an organisation with real authority and a record of struggle, with a non-sectarian status and credibility. Godrich, in her capacity as chair of Left Unity, the union's rank and file socialist organisation, the biggest of its type in the British trade union movement, suggested that it was best placed to call an activists' conference for 7 January 2012.

There was an element of uncertainty as to whether such a hastily convened event would attract any significant level of support, but on the day the 450 activists who had officially registered were joined by many more, with over 700 delegates filling the Friends Meeting House in London. Activists from every major union attended, with many from a number of others ensuring a more than credible representation of the activist layer across the movement. Chaired by Godrich, the conference heard from speakers that included: John McDonnell MP; Kevin Courtney, NUT general secretary; Patrick Mulholland, NIPSA vice-president; Roger Bannister from UNISON left; and Zita Holbourne, representing Black Activists against Cuts.[34] The conference unanimously agreed to reject the betrayal on pensions and to carry on the fight.

However, the scale of the challenge in successfully opposing the betrayal was enormous. The abandonment of a united strategy was understood by many as the first step on the road to acceptance of the government's terms, despite promises of further strike action by right-wing leaders if sectoral negotiations did not produce a good outcome. With major unions pulling out of the alliance that had built J30 and N30, the prevailing mood was one of exasperation and disillusionment. Despite the initial impact of the January conference, the limitations of building widespread resistance became clear over the coming weeks as key public sector unions pushed through the TUC deal. The challenge to the great pensions robbery had become blunted by a fundamental shift in the balance of power towards the coalition government and its ruling-class backers.

PCS members had earlier voted for further action on the basis that NIPSA, Unite, UCU, NUT and the Scottish teaching unions, EIS and SSTA, would be part of the alliance. Building on the highly successful mass industrial action of the previous year, a one-day strike was announced for 28 March 2012. Unfortunately, NUT decided to withdraw from the strike, as its upcoming conference was due to decide whether to continue with nationally coordinated action. Meanwhile, EIS decided to enter into separate negotiations with the Scottish government, while Unite had yet to ballot its small but important group of civil service members. Given these developments, the PCS leadership decided to call off the strike on 12 March. There was a sense of disappointment among activists as much preparatory work had been done, but most valued the 'contract of trust' between leadership and membership, which stated that they would not be asked to take strike action on their own, or in the absence of a reasonable chance of success. The union agreed to continue building an effective inter-union alliance, while organising mass constituency lobbying of MPs. Inevitably, criticism for the decision came from the same ultra-left sources who regarded strikes as an end in themselves.[35]

Work to restore a measure of unity resulted in a one-day strike on 10 May 2012, with PCS, UCU, Unite, and ISU (the Immigration Service Union) all taking action.[36] RMT under its militant leadership also brought out its members in the Royal Fleet Auxiliary and the POA defied the no-strike ban that had been imposed by a previous New Labour government. Although it was well supported, it was obvious that the unions taking industrial action on the day did not constitute a force capable of wresting further concessions from the government. While PCS would continue to campaign for pension justice through political and legal campaigns, including joining TUC initiatives, it needed to reorient its priorities and conserve its energies for the battles that were to come, not least over the government's imposition of a two-year one per cent pay limit.

Like the 1984–5 Miners' Strike, the pensions dispute was betrayed in the most cynical manner by the TUC and Blairite union leaders. This took place despite large-scale industrial action that gave workers a glimpse of their collective power. Many workers who took strike action in June and November 2011 were very much aware that these powerful displays of class solidarity and strength could defeat the government's pensions grab and stop austerity in its tracks. While the surrender of their leaders did not represent a defeat on the scale of the Miners' Strike, their cravenness and self-interest encouraged the coalition to deepen its attacks on the working class, particularly the most vulnerable and marginalised.

Reversal on the industrial front was accompanied by political setbacks, as workers became even more estranged from the Labour Party. Preferring 'austerity lite' to a genuine rejection of neoliberalism, Miliband and his shadow cabinet helped create the conditions for further reaction under subsequent right-wing governments.

The pensions betrayal achieved the main objective of the ruling class – there would be no coordinated action to oppose the austerity onslaught. Instead, the coalition planned how to further restrict trade unions and workers' rights. An emboldened David Cameron appointed Lord Beecroft, a Tory donor and venture capitalist, to investigate how this could be accomplished through changes in employment law. Among his recommendations published in May 2012 were attacks on industrial relations, facility agreements, further restrictions on the right to strike, and a reduction in free access to employment tribunals.[37]

Meanwhile, Brendan Barber retired as TUC general secretary in 2012. Appointed chair of the Advisory, Conciliation and Arbitration Service, he was knighted in the 2013 Honours List in recognition of his 'services to employment relations'. In 2012, Dave Prentis became a non-executive director of the Bank of England and in 2022 was created Baron Prentis of Leeds.

When the government reflected on its troubles with the trade union movement over the previous year, the PCS remained at the top of its target list. This was one problem that they were determined to solve once and for all by launching an attack aimed at financially breaking the union.

....

Notes & References

1. *The Guardian*, 20 December 2010.
2. *Morning Star*, 23 June 2010.
3. *The Guardian*, 22 June 2010.
4. *The Guardian*, 6 June 2010.
5. *The Guardian*, 21 June 2010.
6. *The Guardian*, 19 September 2010.
7. *There is an alternative: The case against cuts in public spending*, PCS, London, 2010.
8. *The Guardian*, 18 October 2010.
9. *Morning Star*, 18 June 2010.

10. *Morning Star*, 25 October 2010.

11. *Financial Times*, 20 October 2010.

12. *The Guardian*, 20 October 2010.

13. *Morning Star*, 13 September 2010.

14. *Daily Telegraph*, 24 November 2010.

15. *Morning Star*, 11 May 2010.

16. *Morning Star*, 19 January 2011.

17. *Financial Times*, 7 October 2010.

18. *The Independent*, 20 July 2010.

19. *The Guardian*, 9 March 2011.

20. *The Independent*, 4 November 2011.

21. *Guardian*, 27 March 2011.

22. *Morning Star*, 16 June 2011.

23. *Morning Star*, 21 March 2011.

24. *Morning Star*, 28 March 2011.

25. *Daily Mirror*, 1 July 2011.

26. *Daily Record*, 1 July 2012.

27. *The Guardian*, 6 November 2011.

28. *Morning Star*, 27 October 2011.

29. *The Socialist*, 30 November 2011.

30. *Daily Express*, 30 November 2011.

31. *The Socialist*, 30 November 2011.

32. *Morning Star*, 31 December 2011.

33. *The Guardian*, 19 March 2012.

34. *Morning Star*, 11 January 2012.

35. See, for example, Workers' Liberty 28 March 2012: https://www.workersliberty.org/story/2012/03/28/pcs-verbiage

36. *Morning Star*, 11 May 2012.

37. UK Parliament, Employment Law (Beecroft Report), vol. 545, 12 May 2012.

8. The beacon of resistance

Maude's assault on PCS

PCS had become a beacon of resistance in the fight against austerity. It was not just its strength in the workplace and its mass industrial protests that had established its reputation as a fighting union. Nor was it the influential briefings of its parliamentary group, which prompted even Tory MPs to ask awkward questions about the impact of government policies. Even more important was its willingness to challenge the race to the bottom by posing real alternatives in the shape of universal benefits, public investment, tax justice and the public ownership of banks and utilities.

In the aftermath of the pensions betrayal, PCS came under sustained attack, first from the coalition government and second from the Tory administration which followed it. Behind Cabinet Office minister Francis Maude's 2011 description of the union's leadership as 'very, very hard left' was the fear that it posed a serious challenge to partnership working and business unionism.[1] If PCS, representing most of the government's own employees, could not be kept in line, then how could other workers? And if the workers could not be kept in line, how could the government carry forward its austerity agenda? For PCS, these attacks merely demonstrated the convergence of interest between the government and the right-wing union leaders who had rejected any idea of a fight back.

There was also a more immediate reason to bring PCS to heel. In June 2012, Maude launched *The Civil Service Reform Plan*. In it he envisaged a relentless drive for efficiency and productivity, creating an organisation that was 'smaller, pacier, flatter'. Taking advantage of the lack of coordinated action by other key public sector unions, he personally orchestrated the assault on one of the most critical barriers to this agenda. It was a mark of how seriously he regarded the PCS threat that no quarter was to be given. The key aim was not simply to silence the union, but to destroy it. He hoped to achieve this by undermining PCS's financial capacity to function as an effective union, thus directing its energies away from fighting the cuts and forcing it to defend its membership base. As in the case of Gordon Brown, there may also have been personal antipathy at play; Maude had been repeatedly trounced by Mark Serwotka in media interviews, leaving him visibly shaken by accusations that he was lying about pension reforms. Nothing enrages a Tory grandee as much as a capable working-class representative exposing him as a privileged mediocrity.[2]

Maude's intention was to bankrupt the union through the removal of the 'check-off' system of union dues collection, payments made automatically from a member's salary. Whilst convenient financially, the system held dangers in that it could be withdrawn at any time – which had already happened to the RMT in 1993. Check-off had been agreed during the period of the Moderate leadership, prior to the dismantling of the Whitley system in the mid-1990s. Any attack on the system had the potential to do catastrophic damage to PCS's finances, given the inevitable delay and difficulty of signing up members to direct debit payments. Former president of the NUM, Ian Lavery MP, said this attempt to break PCS was the most serious attack on a union since Thatcher tried to smash the miners.[3] But even if the union avoided total financial meltdown, it would take years to rebuild PCS's dues-paying membership. The government might even exploit lower membership levels to deny union recognition altogether – rumours of this were already leaking from various departments.

An unspoken element of the civil service reform plan was that the government would hit PCS hard on multiple other fronts. This included a refusal to negotiate at a national level, while continuing to push through cuts in departmental groups on a piecemeal basis. The intention was to drive down wages and conditions across the entire civil service, with the added bonus that this would undermine the national union leadership by creating the impression among members that it had been left with little bargaining power or influence.

Another of Maude's critical targets was 'facilities time' or 'facilities'. This was the arrangement which allowed lay officers time off to perform union duties, such as workplace negotiations and representing members in disciplinary cases. Preparing the ground for Cabinet Office plans to cut this by up to 60 per cent, the arrangement was portrayed by pressure groups such as the TaxPayers' Alliance as a 'scandalous subsidy' to the unions.[4]

In pursuing his vendetta, Maude ignored government research that showed that union reps were an 'important workplace resource' for employers in both the public and private sectors. Productivity and safety tended to be better in unionised workplaces, recruitment costs lower, and the acquisition and updating of skills more efficient. Research by the Department of Business, Enterprise and Regulatory Reform (BERR) under the previous Labour government had shown that the work done by union reps brought savings to employers and the exchequer of between £22 million and £43 million as a result of reducing the numbers of Employment Tribunal cases; and at least £136 million as a result of reducing working days lost because of workplace injury, alongside wider societal benefits from reduced work-related stress.[5]

It seemed that partnership with unions worked very well for the government – so long as unions were not led by militants who opposed government policy. Besides, the benefits of partnership working meant little against the political imperative to wreck the PCS's capacity to organise. It was hoped that cuts to facilities would drive a wedge between activists and members, limiting protection for those subject to disciplinary or grievance issues and impeding workplace union activity more generally. The union's national elected lay leaders were among the first to be specifically selected for attention. In an increasingly hostile anti-union environment, individual local reps were also targeted, even resulting in some dismissals. In the past, the union's right-wing leaders had frequently colluded in such victimisation, but now PCS would defend its activists. Sacked reps were given full backing, including the payment of wages up until an Employment Tribunal judgement. This supportive stance became a factor in staying the hand of some senior managers from carrying out future attacks.

In preparation for the planned roll-out of check-off's removal during 2014, PCS built a nationally coordinated campaign that involved organising the signup of members to direct debit. A clear explanation was given to the membership that the attacks on their union were intended to crush its resistance to cuts in jobs and conditions. It was emphasised that the direct debit campaign was not just some routine, bureaucratic exercise but critical for survival. Fortunately, PCS had become a well-run union under left leadership, although Maude's attack was intended to ruthlessly expose any weaknesses. In contrast to when the same employer tactic was directed at the RMT, virtually every member now had a bank account; the social and professional composition of the civil service workforce also encouraged receptiveness to the direct debit campaign.

Writing in the union's *PCS People*, RMT president, Alex Gordon, explained how their union had faced and dealt with a similar attack when the 1993 Railway Act broke British Rail up into hundreds of separate operating units. The union had taken industrial action against privatisation, and when it refused to settle on the government's terms, check-off was withdrawn, leading to the loss of 50 per cent of members in a few months:

> We had to encourage workplace reps to see recruitment as their core responsibility. It was a culture change. We had to become an organising union. And we developed a more militant industrial strategy, fighting for bread-and-butter improvements for members and advertising our successes to non-members. We didn't entirely recover our membership levels, but we recruited thousands and were able to secure recognition in new places as a result. My message to PCS members is that

we have been through this and have come out of it a different but stronger union.

This was an important message of solidarity from a union that had direct experience of facing such an attack.

Civil service chief executives and their management boards in scores of different departments and agencies enjoyed a certain autonomy. This was reflected in the priority they gave to implementing Maude's plans. Hardliners could barely wait to attack the union, while others showed more caution, fearing further tensions would lead to instability and low morale. The direct debit push was often at its most sluggish in areas of low membership where the Whitley culture had endured and where relationships between executive teams and the trade union had become rather too close for comfort. Most PCS members though readily signed up, confirming something obvious about union recruitment – the main reason that workers do not join a union is usually because they have not been asked. Alongside the hard slog of signing up members, the union began to challenge the government over its check-off removal in a series of successful court cases. The first left the Department for Communities and Local Government in September 2013 with a legal bill of nearly £100,000. Further victories were won with the DWP and other departments ordered to pay millions in compensation, but at appeal the judges denied the union compensation, cynically claiming that while these departments breached staff contracts, they were not intended to be enforceable by PCS. The union's appeal to the Supreme Court was upheld in November 2024 which meant, after a ten-year campaign, that PCS can now sue the departments who refused to accept responsibility for their attempt to bankrupt a free and independent trade union, which is likely to win the union a considerable sum, running potentially to several millions of pounds.[6]

The diversion of resources and the energies of activists and full-time officers to the direct debit campaign limited the time for other campaigning, but the government failed in its intention of stopping the union coordinating industrial resistance and its promotion of a socialist alternative to austerity. Instead, the campaign fostered a tremendous sense of solidarity among members, deepening their contempt for the government. Fault lines were exposed too; full-time officers who adopted a 'business as usual' approach could be instructed to rearrange their priorities to concentrate on the campaign, but it was no easy task to convince a small number lay activists to do likewise, either because they did not fully appreciate the scale of the attack, or they were simply too immersed in their own routines.

The NEC cancelled annual national and group elections in 2015 for that year only. This was at the height of the check-off attack. As the NEC explained, the union faced an existential crisis and diverting the energies of activists from signing up members to engage in electoral activity could simply not be justified.[7] This position had widespread support, even among opponents of the national leadership, but disappointingly a small group expressed disagreement, using arguments that demonstrated breathtaking levels of ultra-left sanctimony. Their appeal to activists stated: 'The decision to cancel the NEC elections this year is a mistake and will make it much harder to sign up PCS members to direct debit because it will undermine their belief in the democratic and accountable nature of their union.' It went on: 'This is a serious situation but not an emergency' and bizarrely demanded the union divert resources and finances from the check-off campaign to, 'launch an immediate national consultation on the financial crisis the union faces and all the options PCS members face'. Such self-indulgent posturing was overwhelmingly rejected by delegates when the union next met in conference.

Membership levels did drop due to the government attacks on check-off, but some of the union's departmental groups recovered very quickly. In the Home Office, over 80 per cent of the previous membership level was restored by autumn 2015. Recovery rates were not only affected by the efforts of activists but also reflected the character of the workplaces themselves. Large but compact offices made the task of communicating much easier, while scattered multiple workplaces with fewer staff proved more of a challenge. This was compounded by the harsher treatment of reps in the more militant areas. In 2010 the union had just under 300,000 members, but cuts and job losses had already reduced this number before the check-off assault reduced it still further. By the end of 2019, membership was just under 200,000, but it started to rise thereafter.[8] Financially, this meant that more had to be done with less, a reality that would become weaponised in later internal conflicts.

Surviving such a direct government attack was a real achievement, confirming that a leadership willing to fight for its members was the firmest foundation upon which a union could be built. Although it would take four to five years to fully recover in terms of financial stability, Maude's plan to bankrupt PCS had failed. His dream of breaking the union had exactly the opposite effect.

The witch-hunts are back!

PCS would have struggled to fight the check-off attack without the solidarity of other unions, especially those with left leaderships. Unite provided premises and other practical aid, while the RMT, POA, FBU and others also gave invaluable support. Despite tensions between PCS and TUC leaderships, the latter too offered important backing. Some suspected though that elsewhere in the movement, warm words on the platform concealed a more equivocal attitude in private towards the plight of PCS.

The coordinated nature of the continuing attack on the union was revealed in late 2014 with the leak of a document for HMRC's Executive Committee (ExCom) entitled *Update for ExCom on Employee and Industrial Relations*. Despite the unconvincing claim that it was 'only one' of various policy considerations, it detailed the strategy for an anti-union witch-hunt, some of which was already being implemented. The document advocated 'a further reduction of facility time for key PCS office holders' and the 'isolation' of PCS's leadership from all but statutorily required discussion with

HMRC. This was to, 'target those responsible for leading union members into a series of disputes... and permanently reducing the influence of union leaders'.[9]

HMRC members had taken industrial action in summer 2014 over jobs and staffing levels, permanent contracts for casual fixed-term staff and office closures. Following a well-supported series of rolling strikes, negotiations began that led to the PCS HMRC departmental group suspending action. Management, however, withdrew from the talks after four weeks, using the excuse that the union's magazine for HMRC members, *Oracle*, had reported that the union had secured jobs for fixed-term staff as a result of industrial action at the Dundee office. Management's manufactured outrage over the article gave the excuse to remove facilities arrangements for HMRC PCS Group officers.[10] At the same time, the Cabinet Office also removed facilities from elected national union leaders, including the president Janice Godrich, deputy president Kevin McHugh, along with the vice-presidents. This was an action calculated to hamstring both the union's operations and its democratic foundation as a lay-led organisation.

The author of the ExCom document was Jonathan Donovan, HMRC deputy director for employee relations. He justified its anti-union content by making the case against PCS. First, he claimed that while relations with the Association of Revenue and Customs (ARC), FDA's HMRC section representing senior and professional staff, were near 'normalised', PCS presented with a 'much more intractable problem', as it was, 'campaigning on a Civil Service-wide agenda, while also conducting a HMRC-specific dispute, notionally around the issue of jobs and staffing'. Not only did the HMRC dispute lack 'logic and cohesion', but it also signalled the union's intention to mount an orchestrated resistance against the department's Change Plan. In response, what was needed was a formula that, 'involves...strengthening the direct employer/employee relationship, based on a conclusion that business interests are best served by direct dialogue with our people which, over time, reduces the influence of the unions'. He added ominously that if PCS were, 'unable to persuade the new GEC [Group Executive Committee] and full-time officials to change their stance this suggests that the usual rules for engagement with a trade union will not work'.

The reference to PCS 'full-time officials' is noteworthy as it shows that the solid united front that they and elected lay reps presented resulted in a high level of frustration for senior managers and negotiators. This was a reversal of the collaborationist role played by full-timers in some other unions, whose role was to act 'responsibly' and rein in the activists, while lowering members' expectations.

PCS published the ExCom document in November 2014, followed by protest meetings throughout the civil service.[11] The document confirmed that Maude's civil service reform plan – deep cuts in jobs and conditions, services, and union rights – was intended to undermine coordinated workplace struggle, weakening the ability to negotiate collective agreements that maintained national standards. Above all, ministers wanted to avoid nationally agreed protocols on jobs and redundancies. This push for fragmentation explained Donovan's accusation that the union's HMRC activity 'lacks logic' and his stigmatising of PCS as a maverick outfit which believed, 'that outright opposition to everything serves members' interest more strongly than achievement of change in a way which, as far as is possible, protects the legitimate interests of people impacted by change'.

During the previous year, PCS had refused to accept demands from the National Crime Agency (NCA), a key structure in the state security apparatus, to sign a no-strike agreement. The NCA's senior management had anticipated PCS's refusal by promoting the formation of a state-sponsored staff association. Its advocates resorted to familiar anti-left rhetoric, describing the PCS leaders as 'militants', 'communists', and 'Trotskyists'. This witch-hunting drive, along with a carrot and stick approach towards terms and conditions, drew most members into the new formation, leaving a small but highly dedicated PCS grouping.

HMRC senior managers attempted to replicate this manoeuvre by encouraging and colluding with a former PCS rep and a few others to form a similar rival 'alternative' to PCS, effectively a scab union, under the title the Revenue and Customs Trade Union (RCTU). It was a move personally applauded by Francis Maude, who commented: 'There's a market operating. If people feel their concerns aren't being represented effectively by the union they were a member of, then they're going to look elsewhere.'[12] However, the HMRC workforce was of a very different social composition to that in the NCA, and the initiative failed in the face of members' distaste for such divisive tactics. This action demonstrated how far senior civil servants had become enmeshed in the neoliberal project. HMRC chief executive, Lyn Homer, under whose leadership the witch-hunt began, had previously been chief executive of Birmingham City Council, where she had been upbraided by the Electoral Commission over a vote-rigging scandal that would 'disgrace a banana republic'; in her next job as head of the UK Border Agency, she was accused by a Home Affairs House of Commons Select Committee of a 'catastrophic failure of leadership'.[13]

Maude subsequently picked Jonathan Donovan to oversee a Cabinet Office project entitled 'Responsible Trade Unionism', suggesting that while PCS was the government's main target, it intended to eliminate all vestiges of campaigning trade unionism from the civil and public services. Nevertheless, PCS's firm response to the attempt to break union influence in HMRC led to a retreat by management, as they correctly assessed their strategy would only provoke the most intense opposition from the workforce. In early 2015, Mark Serwotka met senior HMRC managers and sufficient progress was made to resume dispute resolution talks. Management repeated their claim that the ExCom document had only been a draft and stated they would not be proceeding with its recommendations. The scale of membership support for the union beyond the activist layer set an example for other departments, proving that PCS was no pushover.

Defeating this assault on the union did not mean an end to attacks. In late 2015, HMRC announced its 'Building Our Future' plans, which involved the closure of most of the 170 local offices and their replacement with fewer than 20 regional centres.[14] PCS opposed the closures, but although they eventually went ahead, it was with an improved redundancy agreement.

Anti-union witch-hunts are only effective when unions assist employers by placing good relationships above defending members. PCS may have lost its negotiating rights with the NCA, but it did not accept the no-strike agreement, a surrender which would have encouraged the government to press for similar arrangements elsewhere.

'My door is always open...'

In December 2014, an article by Matt Ross appeared in *Civil Service World* entitled, 'Disunion in the unions'.[15] Despite the magazine's reputation for balanced journalism, this was a carefully calibrated and personalised attack on the PCS leadership. Yet, behind its combination of self-serving and misrepresentation, it provided a revealing insight into the ideological differences that separated compliant and militant trade unionism.

The article accused Mark Serwotka of adopting a 'hardline stance' that 'has itself attracted the ire of other civil service unions and, indeed, many of his own members'. This was part of a wider picture of conflicting union reactions to austerity, ranging from direct confrontation to pure pragmatism, that had both 'weakened collective action, and created resentments that could prompt substantial change across the civil service union landscape'. Although the article contained rebuttals from the PCS head of bargaining, Paul O'Connor, it left the reader in no doubt where the blame lay for these developments. FDA general secretary, Dave Penman, a veteran of civil service trade unionism and one of the most articulate 'pragmatist' voices stated plainly: 'Whichever party was in power in this parliament we'd have faced an approximation of what we have got just now... You have to find a way of influencing the employer, trying to shape what's happening to your members – and that means you have to engage with them. Our experience is that continual confrontation does not influence'. This was echoed by Prospect deputy general secretary Leslie Manasseh who stated: 'We think our members best interests are best served by compromising, which is what negotiations are about'. In other words, Maude's 'entirely predictable' attack on check-off was a reaction to PCS's own aggression.

The most provocative comments, however, came from Francis Maude himself. PCS had achieved a legal victory at judicial review in challenging proposed detrimental changes to the CSCS, which then prompted Maude, in what O'Connor described as an 'act of larceny', to simply use legislative change to remove the inconvenient obstacle of the government's illegality. In the article, Maude cynically and almost comically claimed that if the union's challenge had not been made, he would have stuck to the original agreement reached under the Labour government. He also assured readers that he had, 'a completely open door to all union leaders... I'm always happy to meet, but Mark Serwotka doesn't want to show up'. His implication that PCS operated in self-imposed isolation from the mainstream had already been obligingly trailed by Penman and Manasseh. In a final unguarded revelation, he boasted that he had been invited to make speeches 'at the retirement parties of three union leaders'. The rewards of 'strong relationships' and partnership working were great indeed.

Besides its reputational smears, the article contained more specific allegations, which further highlighted inter-union flashpoints. Penman, for example, blamed PCS for the 2011 break-up of the Council of Civil Service Unions (CCSU), claiming that, 'the lack of a credible single voice for civil service unions has damaged the influence of union members'. In fact, most unions had already accepted that since the demise of the Whitley structure, the council was no longer effective. Although PCS represented the broad mass of civil service workers, the CCSU had become little more than a 'talking shop' in which smaller unions like FDA and Prospect would block or delay initiatives.

The tensions across the civil unions highlighted in *Civil Service World* were also evident in an acerbic exchange between Mark Serwotka and Mike Clancy, general secretary of Prospect. Responding to Serwotka, who had written seeking support for PCS in its struggles with the government, Clancy's letter set out the Prospect's leadership view in 'candid' terms. He acknowledged that, '...relations with PCS have been strained, largely in our view because you have chosen a singular response of meeting every challenge with prolonged bouts of industrial action... We have come to the conclusion that PCS regards any form of compromise through negotiation as capitulation. We reject that notion entirely'.[16]

He then proceeded to lecture Serwotka on the 'proper role of a trade union', which is 'to negotiate the best outcome for members in the circumstances that present themselves':

> ...in our view refusing to reach agreement if any detriment is contemplated is an abrogation of leadership responsibility. All too regularly, this then embarks hard pressed members on industrial action campaigns that have rarely met their objectives. In fact, this has diminished the overall capacity of civil service members to resist adverse changes as lengthy campaigns have brought little tangible benefits.

> ...to date we have refrained from commenting on the choices of PCS as they are your business (though it directly affects our members) but of late, the rhetoric emerging from PCS that some Unions are in contrast to yourselves 'compliant' has made keeping our counsel increasingly difficult.

Far from offering solidarity, he presented the attack on check-off as the fault of PCS, as, '...it is impossible to divorce this present circumstance from past choices that have caused these conditions and government actions.'

Following discussion among the union's senior officers and the NEC, Serwotka responded to Clancy:

Your response is the only one received from across the trade union movement which has not supported PCS.

It is not entirely clear from your letter why you have rejected my request. It contains a number of fallacies and confusions. I will say to you that we are proud of the role PCS has played in reaching settlements at national and departmental level over the years, often amounting to significant achievements made through negotiations. These settlements sometimes followed industrial action by PCS members where it has been the case that such action was necessary to create the conditions within which successful negotiations can take place. The alternative is to accept that nothing can be done to oppose the Tories cuts agenda and to fail in our duty to do everything we can to defend our members...It appears to me that the fallacies and confused arguments in your letter echo the political line promulgated by the Cabinet Office to justify its imposition of cuts and its refusal to negotiate properly with PCS at national level. Your letter seems to be more revealing about your relationship with Francis Maude than ours.

If Maude's direct attempts to undermine union solidarity were not enough, the corrosive effects of falling membership affecting all public sector unions meant an open season for opportunism. In particular, the breaching of previously accepted boundaries in terms of recruitment and representation led to acrimony and time-consuming attempts to resolve disputes. PCS and UNISON, for example, had signed a Memorandum of Understanding in September 2009 in the hope of joint working, but this had not been developed as intended, mainly because of their different positions over pensions.[17] Disputes arose over spheres of membership and representation, the product of changes in the structure of the wider public sector. In line with the memorandum, PCS advised its members to transfer to UNISON, where the latter had bargaining rights with a new employer, but this was a cooperative approach that PCS felt was not always reciprocated.

The ground shifted in 2014, when Francis Maude awarded UNISON bargaining rights within the civil service without consulting other unions with existing recognition agreements. It was naturally assumed that he was acting on his own behalf to sow inter-union rivalry, but when UNISON itself demanded bargaining and negotiating rights within the civil service's biggest department, DWP, it was obvious that this was not the case. PCS represented most workers in DWP, but its concerns went far beyond questions of representation. The UNISON leadership's actions were unapologetically hostile and had the potential to undermine effective representation in the wider public sector.[18] When common ground cannot be found in these cases, unions can refer the matter to the TUC for adjudication; in this case the matter was eventually resolved with PCS retaining its longstanding recognition rights in DWP.

The timing of UNISON's attempt to acquire bargaining rights in DWP coincided with a similar attempt by FDA, which represented the most senior civil servants. This involved recruiting among grades represented by PCS for its new 'Keystone' section for Higher and Senior Executive Officers.[19] Again, this issue was resolved with each union sticking to its 'sphere of influence', but reflecting on recent events, some in PCS drew the conclusion that if Maude's plan to bankrupt the union had been successful, there would have been no shortage of fellow trade unionists waiting to 'divide the spoils'.

Notes & References

1. *The Independent*, 4 October 2011.

2. *Nursing Times*, 1 December 2011.

3. Lynn Henderson, 'Defeat Government Union-Busting', *Scottish Left Review*, 86, April-May 2015.

4. TaxPayers' Alliance, *Taxpayer Funding of Trade Unions*, Research Note 97, 25 November 2011.

5. *Reps in Action: how workplaces can gain from modern representation*, BERR, London, 2009.

6. *Morning Star*, 20 November 2024.

7. *The Socialist*, 10 February 2015.

8. PCS Annual Returns to the Certification Officer, 2013–7.

9. *Scottish Socialist Voice*, 11 December 2014.

10. *The Courier*, 1 August 2014.

11. *Morning Star*, 2 December 2014.

12. *Civil Service World*, 18 December 2014.

13. *Daily Mail*, 25 March 2013.

14. *Building our Future: Transforming the way HMRC serves the UK*, HMRC, London, 2015.

15. *Civil Service World*, 18 December 2014.

16. The episode is covered in PCS NEC Papers: NEC 36/41/14; NEC 36/54/15; NEC 37/4/15; NEC 37/8/15; NEC 37/4/15; NEC 39/5/15; NEC 39/47/15; NEC 56/14/18.

17. *Personnel Today*, September 2009.

18. *The Socialist*, 10 February 2015.

19. *Civil Service World*, 24 July 2015.

9. Finding a public voice

Political representation and influence

The idea of a politicised civil service workforce was a recurring nightmare for the British establishment. For decades, the civil service unions were banned from having political funds and from affiliation to bodies such as the TUC and the Labour Party. Although restrictions were lifted by the Atlee government, hesitancy over openly political activity remained among many trade unionists. For PCS, however, the search for an authentic public voice became a necessity, forced by attacks on public services, public sector workers and not least the union itself.

The election of Mark Serwotka and a left national leadership of PCS had been due in part to growing disenchantment with New Labour's performance in government. Civil servants were at the sharp end of their policies, so the mood for an alternative was strong among activists and members. Inevitably, the question of political representation became more important, and while there was little appetite for affiliation to Labour, it was generally agreed that the union had to campaign politically, as well as on the industrial front.

The debate on working-class representation gathered pace with the impact of Labour's neoliberal policies and the widespread disgust at the decision to attack Iraq. The establishment of a political fund in 2005, following a membership ballot, had been a longstanding objective for Left Unity and the wider Democracy Alliance. It greatly expanded the union's capacity for independent public campaigning. Parliamentary Groups were set up at Westminster, the Scottish Parliament and the National Assembly of Wales. These allowed the union to brief and lobby politicians, putting the union's case directly and hopefully influencing decision-making. This approach quickly paid dividends with jobs saved, closures avoided, and privatisations blocked or at least delayed. When the government attacked the Civil Service Compensation Scheme, Gordon Brown's tabloid-style disinformation campaign on civil service 'privileges' was challenged by PCS activists who contacted every single MP at Westminster to explain how these plans would deprive workers of their statutory rights and have a disproportionate impact on low-paid workers.

The Make Your Vote Count (MYVC) initiative, launched in 2007, had provided a further mechanism to win support for the union's policies during elections.[1] Candidates were exposed to the reality of working lives in the civil service and why workers felt so devalued. Surveys and discussions in members' meetings confirmed that members' principal concern was the systematic degradation and destruction of the services that they delivered. For most members, the traditional public service ethos remained central, contradicting the 'user interest' smear of Brown and market ideologues. Building on this, interventions in by-elections allowed PCS to raise its opposition to cuts and defend public services. In the 2008 Glenrothes by-election, for example, activists linked the national issue of public sector cuts to the deteriorating conditions in local communities, exposing politicians to sharp questioning and scrutiny.[2] In no case did the union recommend candidates – neither the national leadership nor local branches had any mandate to do so – but it did publish the replies that politicians gave to PCS questions.

The political fund also allowed the union to extend its anti-racist campaigning work, with interventions in elections to highlight the growth of the far right. The union did not seek the views of openly racist politicians like those of the British National Party, but instead actively funded anti-fascist demonstrations and events like the *Love Music Not Racism* carnivals in the run-up to the London Assembly and local government elections in 2008 and the European Parliament election the following year.[3] Drawing on this work, the union published its *Anti-racist and anti-fascist strategy* in 2014, regularly updated to take into account the nature of the threat and to consolidate the union's challenge against racism.

While anti-racist campaigning was successful in mobilising PCS members, other initiatives brought their own issues. In the case of MYVC, some politicians felt that the views of civil service workers could be safely ignored; some mouthed platitudes in meetings and in written replies; some made clear they felt no obligation to consider 'unrealistic demands' to stop the cuts and reverse privatisation. Others simply refused to engage. This was particularly the case with most Labour politicians, who, apart from the socialist grouping in the party, were simply not prepared to entertain any criticism of the government. The MYVC campaign continued as an important part of the union's wider political campaigning, albeit with a healthy cynicism towards the grip of party politics at Westminster.

PCS activists largely grouped around Left Unity had been involved in discussions in the wider movement on the issue of political representation for many years. From around 2000 onwards, there had been attempts at building socialist electoral alternatives, such as Socialist Alliance, Respect and the Left List. In 2010, the Socialist Party formed the Trade Unionist and Socialist Coalition (TUSC), but none of these initiatives secured any sustained level of support among workers and, although George Galloway won the Bethnal Green and Bow parliamentary seat for Respect in 2005, electoral successes were few.

Debate in the trade union movement intensified following the Iraq War. In 2004, RMT was expelled from the Labour Party after it allowed its branches in Scotland to affiliate to the Scottish Socialist Party (SSP).[4] Pressure built from below for disaffiliation and this was keenly debated in some unions. FBU, which had been through a very bitter dispute with the New Labour government, agreed to disaffiliate in 2004, reaffiliating in 2015 in order to give support to the new party leader, Jeremy Corbyn. For most left-leaning unions, however, in the absence of a plausible alternative and with the continuing commitment displayed by the socialist minority in the PLP, the link survived.

For all its weaknesses, the Labour Party was still viewed by many workers and certainly most trade unions as capable of achieving reforms and providing more stable living conditions for the working class. Allied to this was the confidence of many on the left that the party could survive Blairite reaction and emerge transformed. These views were shared by some PCS activists, but the majority, including most of the leadership, considered Labour irredeemably lost as an effective vehicle for working-class representation. Many other members had little time for an abstract debate over affiliation that bore no relationship to their day-to-day struggles in the workplace. There was therefore remarkable unanimity about building the union's public campaign work, now widely regarded as an essential component in the defence of jobs, conditions and services.

This consensus created space for further debate on why and how PCS should undertake independent political activity. The union's leadership was determined on the most inclusive discussion so that it would not be seen merely as an 'issue for activists', but something that was directly related to members. While many described themselves as 'not very political', the union's campaigns had raised awareness about political representation and its importance to their lives – after all, their problems stemmed directly from specific government decisions and the general neoliberal political consensus. This was the type of daily experience that produced a deepening class consciousness. The positions developed by the union leadership and activists organised around Left Unity convinced many members of the need to resist and challenge the government's policies.

The union's campaigning methods had already made a very positive impact on how members viewed their union. They supported the linking of industrial action and engagement with the public and politicians to build a political alternative. It was a short step from endorsing these methods to debating whether the union should directly intervene in the electoral process. The annual delegate conference in 2009 called for consultation with branches on standing or supporting independent union candidates in national elections. This saw strong engagement from members. Toward the end of the consultation period, PCS intervened in the 2010 general election, again under the MYVC banner, writing to 1,800 candidates and with 47 hustings organised by activists where members questioned candidates, raising union demands for an end to cuts and privatisation, and for investment in public services.[5]

The results of the consultation were discussed at the 2010 Brighton conference, in the wake of the coalition's victory. It was reported that 64 per cent of branches had backed the proposals to stand or support independent candidates.[6] The conference called for further consultation to consider how backing candidates might work in practice. They invited ideas on how selection processes would be arranged; on the criteria for choosing candidates, on what policies they would campaign on; and what kind of campaigning methods could be employed against the far right, in particular. The outcome represented a fundamental challenge to the traditional idea that civil service workers should be 'politically neutral'. The debate also raised the undemocratic nature of restrictions on civil servants' political activity. This prevented even administrative workers, most of the workforce, from standing in elections. It was not only the consultation and debate around standing and supporting candidates that had convinced members of the need for effective political representation, but also the union's public campaigning through MYVC and its parliamentary groups.

The issue of political neutrality continued to be raised in consultation debates in branches and at annual conferences. While this had a remarkably tenacious hold on the more conservatively minded, it proved no obstacle to the support of activists, and more critically, members for standing independent candidates. Few saw any contradiction between performing their daily work as civil servants without fear or favour, and campaigning for their rights as workers in defence of their jobs and the services they delivered. Communications for the consultative ballot outlined the need to build an alternative to austerity and a political consensus against the coalition government's cuts agenda. It envisaged either standing candidates in 'exceptional circumstances' when it would directly assist PCS campaigns, or working with others to stand them.

The ongoing debate eventually led to a national membership ballot in 2012 in which the two questions were put to members: first, on supporting the union's existing political campaign strategy, such as lobbying through parliamentary groups and the MYVC campaign; and second, whether members supported standing or supporting candidates in national elections in support of union campaigning. The strong message that PCS was 'political, not party political' undermined the accusation that the leadership had a hidden agenda to affiliate to Labour. In any case, this was highly unlikely given that the new opposition leader Ed Miliband had begun to present himself as a critical friend to the coalition's austerity agenda.

Members voted by an overwhelming 78 per cent to stand or support candidates and by 81 per cent to endorse the union's political strategy. This was with a 20 per cent turnout, a reasonably strong mandate that showed engagement in the debate went far beyond the activist layer.[7] Three principal factors help explain how PCS members were the first of any union not affiliated to the Labour Party to vote for supporting and standing candidates in general elections: the politicisation of a now largely proletarian workforce; the neoliberal assault on the public services and especially the civil service itself; and critically the union's socialist leadership rooted in a militant activist base.

Promoting the Welfare Alternative

The public activity of PCS was by no means confined to electoral politics but also involved intensive grassroots campaigning. The union knew that to build an effective case for public services meant challenging the myths promoted by successive neoliberal administrations. For this, evidence-based ammunition was needed. The publication of *There is an alternative*, shortly after the election of the coalition government, had been an important first step, ensuring that the union became an influential participant in The People's Assembly against Austerity from its foundation in 2013.[8]

Building on this success was *Welfare: An alternative vision*, launched in Glasgow in September 2011.[9] The Welfare Alternative pamphlet would become another vital campaigning tool, providing facts, figures and arguments to rebut the government and media propaganda, raising awareness, and in the process establishing a focal point around which alliances might be built and campaigns could be coordinated to challenge the attacks on welfare.

It was the product of many years of work by activists in the employment and social security fields, who had shown outstanding solidarity with the communities they served. Indeed, most PCS members working in DWP were opposed to the stricter benefits regimes imposed on them and benefit claimants by the coalition. Many of these low-paid workers had first-hand experience of being on benefits themselves, as did their friends and families. They also had a very detailed professional knowledge of the system they administered on a daily basis and were well aware that the application of harsh, punitive measures to 'incentivise' people into finding jobs was entirely counterproductive.

Drawing on their experiences, the Welfare Alternative also reflected the background of systematic attacks being made on the working class through austerity measures. From the 1970s onwards, successive governments had ended the commitment to 'full employment' and developed a strategy of demonising the poor, unemployed and disabled; they were blamed for their own condition, a process ramped up under the coalition administration to justify its proposed cuts in welfare spending. According to chancellor Osborne, those on benefits had made a 'lifestyle choice'. While benefits were never 'generous', further cuts meant people were genuinely struggling to make ends meet as poverty levels rose inexorably.

Despite its favoured language of 'inclusivity', the coalition had targeted disabled people for special attention, seeking to identify them as the very embodiment of 'dependency culture'.[10] The *Financial Times* responded to the government's plans to cut £1.4 billion from Disability Living Allowance by subjecting disabled people to 'reassessments' with this cold-blooded analysis: 'Although this will generate political heat amongst those affected, it is the easiest bit of welfare reform to sell, Britain's out of work disability benefits have been abused.'[11] It was hardly surprising that Ellen Clifford revealed in her book *The War on Disabled People* that disability hate crime and harassment had become widespread in Cameron's Britain. She noted that the Equality and Human Rights Commission report *Hidden in Plain Sight* had detailed ten murders of disabled people, including the case of Brent Martin, a man with learning difficulties, attacked for a bet by three people he considered his friends. Similarly, Kathryn Stone, CEO of Voice UK, warned of real increases in the most horrendous murders and very serious sexual assaults.[12]

In response to this onslaught, the PCS Welfare Alternative reiterated the principle of 'social insurance' that underpinned the creation of the welfare state - that meant when people became unemployed, ill, disabled or in retirement, they should not be driven into poverty, and that people caring for children disabled or elderly relatives should have a 'dignified income'. It also explained how struggles of the working class through their unions, and particularly the struggles of the women's movement, had demanded the right to welfare as a fundamental human right. This had been a struggle strongly linked to that for independent working-class political representation, on the assumption that a presence in parliament was the only guarantor of such legislation being passed. The stress on the role of the women's movement was a particularly important feature of the pamphlet, as in the past some union leaders had opposed certain benefits, arguing that wages should be sufficient to cover the cost of raising children and other caring responsibilities; it was in these areas that the insistence of women campaigners and women within the labour movement prevailed.

In their introduction to the Welfare Alternative, Godrich and Serwotka stated:

> Now the government's £18 billion welfare cuts will damage the welfare state as a safety net that ensures a decent standard of living for those unable to work. We have no wish to return to the welfare state of the late 1940s: it reflected the social attitudes of its time (especially towards women and disabled people). However, the welfare state did establish the principle of 'social insurance' giving people the security of knowing that if they become unemployed, ill or disabled, and when they retire they will not be in poverty. If people need to care for children, disabled or elderly relatives then they too should be guaranteed a dignified income. These principles are the hallmarks of civilised society – we need to make the case for welfare for the 21st century. This pamphlet looks at the past, present and future of welfare and we hope it starts a new debate about the sort of welfare and society that we want.

Godrich related the union's campaign to her own experience of work and her community, writing:

> Anyone, whatever their background, can find themselves in difficult circumstances during their lifetime. It is at these times that you realise just how important the welfare state is. I have seen this first hand having worked for the DWP and its predecessors since leaving school. I am proud to be part of the campaign to defend it and proud that my union treats this campaign with the importance it deserves.

The pamphlet went on to set out a series of general demands and statements:

- Job creation based on public investment in new energy, transport and housing infrastructure, and public services.

- A dignified standard of living for those out of work, with much increased benefit levels.
- More free training and educational opportunities for the unemployed.
- Campaign for a substantially increased national minimum wage
- Provide greater advice and assistance to ensure people receive the benefits they are entitled to.
- Build strong trade unions in each workplace with stronger trade union rights, as a balance against low pay.
- Tackle employer discrimination with tougher enforcement and penalties for non-compliance and greater awareness raising.
- Abandon flawed privatised assessment programmes and return to a system of assessment by NHS staff and GPs.
- Improve, not attack, DLA to support more disabled people to lead independent lives, including working lives.
- Tackle child poverty by removing the causes of adult poverty: end low pay and low benefit levels.
- Provide universal publicly funded childcare to allow parents to work and study, and to support and encourage children's development.
- Provide housing for those in housing need.
- Stop housing benefits from being used to subsidise the lifestyles of wealthy landlords.
- Provide thousands of jobs, reduce unemployment and help boost the economy.
- Abolish means testing and raise the state pension to £170pw.

- End the tax relief on private pensions for higher-rate taxpayers.

- Renationalise the energy companies to prevent profiteering that causes fuel poverty.

The pamphlet also contained a 'What you can do' section, which suggested PCS members and other workers should:

- Challenge the myths when you read them in the press, hear them in the media or if they are repeated by people you know.

- Discuss the issues raised in this pamphlet in your trade union, community organisation or political party.

- Lobby your MP against welfare cuts and privatisation, and for full employment.

- Support PCS campaigns and those of others like Gingerbread, the National Pensioners' Convention and Defend Council Housing.

As with the 2010 Alternative, the pamphlet was not meant for use in isolation but as part of the wider campaigning work of the union, and along with PCS's other policies and strategies, it was intended to form a wide and comprehensive basis for resistance to austerity and the government's entire austerity agenda. It was promoted in both the national union and in the PCS DWP group, and was instrumental in significantly boosting and extending the joint campaigning work with claimants and anti-poverty groups already underway. PCS activists embraced the campaign with enthusiasm, building links and launching local initiatives, and also raising the arguments in the media, with other unions, and campaign groups and with management too.

The government had intended to sow division between employed, unemployed and disabled workers. Hence, the importance of such coordinated work between the union mainly responsible for delivering benefits and welfare, the wider trade union movement, and socialist Labour MPs, as well as those from other parties like the Greens, SNP and Plaid Cymru cannot be overstated. Raising awareness was critically important, but so too was building solidarity and showing a common front that emphasised what united rather than what divided workers.

Testimonials at the launch of the Welfare Alternative revealed the range of support for its arguments. Colin Hampton, of the Derbyshire Unemployed Centres, said: 'PCS have started the development of a campaign that must bring together the unions and communities to demand a welfare system that allows people to live in dignity in and out of work'. Linda Burnip of Disabled People Against Cuts (DPAC) added: 'DPAC believes that everyone is entitled to rights not charity, and that public services should be run by public sector employees and not to make massive profits for private firms'. Similarly, Fiona Weir, Gingerbread's chief executive, commented: 'Single parents frequently tell Gingerbread that childcare is the make-or-break issue when looking for work. It is vital that the government puts sufficient effort into high quality, affordable childcare to ensure work pays for all parents'.

Reflecting the link between PCS's public and parliamentary campaigning, John McDonnell, chair of the PCS Parliamentary Group at Westminster, also gave his endorsement:

> This small booklet challenges the big lies that form the basis of this government's welfare reform policies. Every time a politician or political commentator tries to spew out the same tired old myths about scroungers and benefit fraud or the abuse of the system, just swat them intellectually with the facts and arguments set out in this excellent booklet.

The Welfare Alternative was a major weapon in exposing the government's attack on those on benefits and low incomes, and the wider working-class too: the coalition thought the unemployed, disabled and low-income workers and women were the easiest target to hit, and the most unlikely to organise against them; they were mistaken. In a conscious departure from the identity politics already becoming increasingly prevalent in disability campaigning, new groups such as DPAC and Scottish-based Black Triangle were being set up with the explicit aim of building alliances and joining the wider anti-capitalist movement. They were led by socialists and trade union activists who, along with their awareness-raising and advocacy campaign work, were prepared to protest and even take direct action, exposing both the brutality of welfare 'reform' and the state's response to a fight back.

DPAC activist Paula Peters, for example, described her experience at demonstrations against the government's welfare policies in which disabled people were tipped out of wheelchairs outside DWP headquarters in London in 2012, with a baton being used against a protester whose shoulder was broken. In later demonstrations, disabled protesters were 'kettled', held for hours without food, water and medication; in 2014 Territorial Support Group officers even pointed guns outside parliament, after work and pensions secretary, Iain Duncan Smith, had claimed protesters would be violent.[13]

PCS actively supported these groups and many others, providing them with financial and other forms of practical assistance.[14]

The Welfare Alternative provided a firm foundation upon which resistance to the coalition's welfare reforms could be built, linking the struggles of organised workers in their trade unions and campaign groups like DPAC. A range of initiatives sprang from this joint work, including the Welfare Charter (2014), supported by PCS, Trade Union Councils, London Unemployed Strategies, Unemployed Centres Combine, Unite Community and other organisations, which demanded:

- A political commitment to full employment.
- A livable wage.
- A social security system that works to end poverty.
- No work conscription, keep volunteering voluntary.
- Representation for unemployed workers.

- The appointment of an ombudsman for claimants.
- Equality in the labour market and workplace.
- Equality in access to benefits.
- An end to the sanctions regime and the current Work Capability Assessment.
- Full maintenance for the unemployed and underemployed.
- State provision of high-quality information advice on employment, training, and careers.

PCS and its predecessor unions had a long tradition of working with unemployed, disabled and other claimant groups and the ongoing assault on the welfare state allowed it to raise these issues in the wider movement at all levels, from the TUC itself to local trades councils and social and community movements.

It was following the pensions betrayal that the coalition had felt able to intensify its attacks on the welfare state. The failure, or more accurately refusal, of some union leaders to support calls from PCS and other left unions to build a coordinated, unified struggle against the austerity agenda left union and campaign groups to fight isolated struggles; this remains the most important and clearly identifiable factor in enabling its dreadful impact on the working-class.

At the core of the government's welfare policy was the introduction of Universal Credit. Spearheaded by the right-wing ideologue Iain Duncan Smith, this was intended to amalgamate five means-tested benefits and tax credits into one monthly payment. The vast majority of claims were to be initiated and managed online, even though benefit claimants were the people most likely not to have computers or be trained to use them. While the new benefit would be implemented by DWP, it was clear that the intention was to privatise these services, with the resulting impact on DWP, HMRC and local authority jobs.

Although PCS did not oppose all changes to the welfare system, it did reject those that were detrimental to claimants and benefit workers. The union warned, for example, that introducing an 'untried and tested' scheme like Universal Credit at breakneck speed would reproduce the chaos that engulfed New Labour reforms, when IT systems turned out to be 'completely unreliable'. Inevitably, Duncan Smith's refusal to listen resulted in multi-million pound IT write-offs and delays, leaving 700,000 facing a long wait for the new benefit.[15] Claimants in work were also subjected to a new sanctions and conditionality regime, which meant that they would be expected to increase their hours or their income until they were no longer eligible for the benefit. In a shameful exposure of low pay in the civil service, PCS revealed 40 per cent of DWP staff administering the benefit were themselves recipients.

The cooperation between PCS and unemployed and disabled workers campaign groups in creating the Welfare Alternative had helped establish the defence of the welfare state as a class issue, affecting the whole class; not a sectional one, dividing workers into those in work and those not, the unionised and the un-unionised. As a result, a united front was built that mitigated the potential for division in which claimants and benefit workers were presented as enemies. Such cooperation also led to a greater appreciation and understanding of the situation between both groups, the only basis upon which common strategies and tactics could be formed. The role of leading PCS speakers, such as Godrich and Serwotka, was invaluable in building both awareness and class solidarity, as they constantly stressed the impact of welfare reform on both PCS and benefit claimants and publicly expressed their complete support of DPAC and similar campaigns.

Claimants' groups raised with PCS the legitimate issue of how claimants were sometimes treated by some benefit workers. PCS and its reps in DWP sought to raise awareness amongst members about the conditions being imposed on claimants. For the vast majority of workers, this was hardly necessary as they were perfectly aware from a class and professional viewpoint that claimants should always be treated respectfully. Some in the workforce, however, were influenced by the sheer intensity of government and media propaganda, although such attitudes were far less prevalent in workplaces where the union was most highly organised.

The union also provided support for claimants and campaign groups in their opposition to the government's various 'Workfare' initiatives. These revived the 1930s-style demand that the unemployed should do unpaid work for their benefits. Resistance, including legal challenges and direct action, led to several employers withdrawing from the scheme and its eventual shelving by DWP.

Despite close working links with welfare campaign groups such as DPAC, there were some voices that hid their anti-union ideology behind a sectarian 'radicalism', demanding that benefit workers should refuse to implement government policy. It was reminiscent of the demand during the battle against Thatcher's Poll Tax that council workers should simply not administer it. This effectively placed the burden of a major class battle on the shoulders of a relatively small group of workers who were expected to defeat not just the government but the state itself. In the event, the Poll Tax was not defeated by non-implementation nor, for that matter, riots, as has been disingenuously claimed, but by a programme of mass non-payment, a strategy that united millions in unbeatable opposition that resulted in the demise of Thatcher herself.

What such a demand would have meant in this case was that PCS members should take indefinite strike action on the basis that the government should withdraw its entire welfare reform programme. Even if the majority agreed to do so – which they would not – the government would have mobilised the might of the establishment to crush such a challenge, no doubt with the assistance of the Labour party and even elements in the trade union movement itself. The result would have been mass sackings, with the unionised DWP workforce replaced by a scab workforce, far more likely to implement the government's programme in the most ruthless manner.

The idea that a small section of the working class could assume the entire responsibility of overturning government welfare reform was divisive and fanciful. It stigmatised workers as antagonists - in this case, a group of workers whose union was supporting claimants and building resistance to the government's policies and who, in the majority, were doing what they could to mitigate and ameliorate government policies. PCS explained these issues to campaigners, and apart from a tiny number who were clearly determined to treat PCS and the unions as the enemy, this analysis was accepted.

The 2014 Scottish independence referendum

PCS was committed to a principled stand on issues that affected the civil service workforce and the wider working class, but it also remained conscious of the need to avoid unnecessary divisions among its membership. This delicate balancing act was put to the test when Alex Salmond called a referendum in Scotland for 18 September 2014, with the consent of David Cameron's UK government. It was to be based on the straightforward question: 'Should Scotland be an independent country?'

The phenomenon of nationalism and demands for self-determination are neither inherently progressive or reactionary in themselves but dependent on specific economic, political, social and historical circumstances it can play either role – the determining factor is whether such demands advance or reverse the interests of the working class – not only in Scotland itself but in the other nations of the British Isles.

The Labour Party and some union leaders were quick to throw their weight behind a No vote, especially as opinion polls in the early days of the referendum campaign suggested this was the most likely outcome.[16] However, PCS's leadership were aware of the difficulties that might result if the union mishandled its approach to the independence question. Widespread discussion now began across PCS, and not just in Scotland. For the union, the starting point was to develop an independent class position, based firmly on consultation and democratic decision-making. It was accepted that there could be no veto on the right of the Scottish people to self-determination from any other part of the UK, but at the same time there must be a continuing dialogue between workers throughout Britain. It was also imperative that constitutional issues should not sideline the union's campaigning priority of opposing austerity and pressing for concessions in its members' interests.

PCS organised in all areas of the UK government located in Scotland and among civil servants working for the Scottish government and the Welsh government. The union already had a long tradition of working in a devolved environment, representing UK civil servants in Northern Ireland alongside its sister union NIPSA, which covered the devolved public sector areas. Activists of both unions were some of the bravest and most dedicated in the movement, operating to build working-class unity during the worst of the Troubles.[17] They also ensured that the voices of Northern Irish workers were heard throughout the UK, as well as on an all-Ireland basis through the Irish Congress of Trade Unions.

Against this background, it was agreed that the union could not be a 'mere observer' or remain on the fringes of the independence debate, a position which many in the trade union thought was the safest option. This was based on the assessment that neither the Yes nor the No camp offered any alternative to free market orthodoxy. What would independence or maintaining the status quo really mean for Scottish workers? The union leadership and many Scottish activists were also anxious to challenge chauvinism wherever it emerged in the campaign. The smug boast of some left-wing supporters of Scottish independence that the Scots were somehow more egalitarian and socialistic than the 'Tory English' was matched by the lamentations of some English left-wingers that the departure of Scotland from the Union would leave them permanently with Tory governments. This was a depressing and demoralising position that demonstrated a spectacular lack of confidence in the huge English working class. It also ignored the fact that there was no natural Tory majority in England and that opposition to austerity was every bit as strong as in Scotland, arguably more so in some areas.

The strongest support for national self-determination came from the Scottish working class and sprang from class-based opposition to austerity.[18] Backing for independence was also a direct consequence of the crisis in working-class political representation. In particular, it reflected a failure of leadership in the British labour and trade union movement during the previous decade. The SNP-led campaign offered an attractive vision of the fair and just society that would follow with independence. Devolution had allowed Scotland's devolved administrations just enough space to take a step to the left – committing to the concept of the social wage through free prescriptions, personal care and tuition fees. These relatively modest concessions were enough to create the impression that more was possible if the link with Westminster was broken.

In reality, the SNP's independence prospectus was underpinned by their adherence to neoliberalism and the establishment consensus. Currency and fiscal policy would be tied to the Bank of England, guaranteeing austerity policies; defence would be shared with the rest of Britain, with NATO membership continuing; the Queen would remain head of state in what would effectively be a federal arrangement. One worrying portent for an independent Scotland was the commitment of the Yes campaign to a low tax economy, with corporation tax reduced to that of the Republic of Ireland.[19] Similarly, when PCS Scottish Officer Lynn Henderson asked SNP leader Alex Salmond, following his 2013 Jimmy Reid Lecture, whether the UK-wide anti-union laws would be repealed in an independent Scotland, he evaded the question, merely stating that there was no appetite for further legislation. This was a very concerning response as no 'social-democratic egalitarian nation' could ever tolerate such repressive laws.[20]

PCS placed the same demands on both campaigns for an end to austerity, tax justice, workers' rights and increased investment in the public services. If scrutiny of the Yes campaign revealed many contradictions on these issues, there was no ambiguity from the No camp. Under the *Better Together* banner and the uninspiring leadership of Alistair Darling, was gathered an unprincipled alliance of Tories, Liberal Democrats and Labour grandees, with additional support from the media, British state institutions, big business, the EU and even Barack Obama.[21] Sensibly, the STUC refused to back it.

Without adopting a position on whether or not members in Scotland should vote either way in the referendum, PCS advocated an independent class position based on principled support for the democratic right of workers to pursue national self-determination while campaigning to protect and advance the interests of workers throughout the islands and uncompromisingly advocating a socialist alternative to the chaos and instability of capitalism. Developing such an analysis was critical to PCS navigating the referendum debate and avoiding disunity. The union, for example, rejected the scaremongering that an independent Scotland would mean a split in the union and the wider trade union movement. There was little support for such a self-defeating demand from among Scottish trade unionists who could see little contradiction between workers seeking political autonomy while maintaining a unified trade union movement, as had been the case historically between Great Britain and Ireland.[22]

Many PCS activists also grasped that it was not narrow nationalism that drove strong support for independence in working-class heartlands like Glasgow, the West of Scotland and Dundee; a fact confirmed by analysis of voting patterns after the referendum.[23] It was instead the hope that independence could offer a credible route to a more fair and equal society. Support also reflected widespread contempt for the elite Westminster consensus, exemplified by the *Better Together* campaign.

Against this background, PCS agreed not to make a voting recommendation to members in the absence of a full consultation. This contrasted with some unions who simply imposed a No recommendation, or others who passed No recommendations at UK-wide union conferences. In UNISON, the UK's largest public-sector union, the leadership attempted to impose a No recommendation but were faced down by Scottish activists who warned against such a divisive move. Two unions, RMT and POA, held special Scottish conferences that resulted in Yes to independence votes.[24] More by luck than good judgment, open splits were avoided in the No supporting unions. Over 12,000 joined an SNP trade union group, but this subsequently failed to develop an active role among Scottish workers.[25]

PCS consultation with Scottish members and activists included the circulation of information from both camps, policy forums, branch debates and a Scottish conference. PCS material was based on the principle, 'PCS Informs: You Decide'. Surveys of the union's 30,000 Scottish members showed that their main concerns were job security and pensions, with their main priority being the provision of good public services.[26] Delegates attending the Scottish conference in February 2014 were presented with three options. One: the union would provide information on both campaigns so members could decide which to support, and PCS would continue to campaign on industrial issues with both the Scottish and Westminster governments, and would press its demands on PCS's alternative to austerity with both the Yes and No campaigns. Two: support 'Yes'. Three: support 'No'.[27] Through their branches, members favoured the first option with 18,025 votes against 5,775 for Yes and none for No.

The Scottish conference had overwhelmingly endorsed the leadership's approach that PCS should not be a mere observer in the campaign but an active participant with an independent class position, promoting and defending the interests of its members and the working class, campaigning for an end to austerity, cuts and privatisation, and for tax justice, the repeal of the anti-trade union laws, equality and civil liberties, and the return of the utilities to public ownership. These were issues that concerned Scottish workers as much as those in England, Wales and Northern Ireland.

This snapshot of a mixed consciousness within a key sector

of Scottish workers also showed a wariness over both Yes and No campaigns, although the total lack of support for the No option strongly echoed members' revulsion towards *Better Together*. Meanwhile, it reflected the pro-independence views of the overwhelming majority of activists, especially but not exclusively in Left Unity. In the national leadership, there were also many who strongly supported independence, whilst others were very sympathetic. There were, however, those in PCS who argued against the principle of Scottish self-determination and demanded that the union should make decisions only at a UK-wide level, but this was a very isolated view at the union's annual national delegate conference.

On the eve of the referendum, Gordon Brown suddenly redis-covered post-war consensus and working-class solidarity. He proclaimed: 'And we not only won these wars together, we built the peace together, we built the health service together, we built the welfare state together, we will build the future together'.[28] He also opined that 'a Scottish worker has more in common with a worker in Birmingham than a Scottish millionaire'. This observation was certainly true, but cynically substituting a slogan for an analysis and a sermon for a strategy failed to dampen the class anger that underpinned support for independence among Scottish workers. However, the job was already done. The methods used by Brown and his colleagues in the British political and business establishment would succeed in defeating the Yes campaign by 55.3 per cent to 44.7 per cent.

The Scottish independence referendum had been one of the most highly charged battles for hearts and minds in recent memory. However, the focus of PCS on presenting an independent class analysis and empowering members to make their own decisions had provided the surest guarantee of continued unity and political influence. For example, concessions were won from the Scottish government on redundancy and other issues which strengthened existing UK-wide campaigns. But the issue of Scottish independence is one that will inevitably resurrect itself as British capitalism staggers from crisis to crisis. The approach PCS adopted, based on a socialist analysis, is the surest guarantee of maintaining unity, not just amongst Scottish workers, but across the islands, whether or not any future demand for self-determination leads to independence.

In for the long haul...

The general election of May 2015 was the first major opportunity for the union's political representation policy to be tested. However, other than endorsements for left-Labour MPs, John McDonnell and Jeremy Corbyn, both of whom had steadfastly worked to advance the anti-austerity cause, PCS's intervention was limited. As suggested in the previous chapter, the ongoing government union-busting assault had absorbed efforts of activists and full-time workers, severely curtailing PCS campaigning. In a parting shot before he retired at the general election, Francis Maude had even attempted to gag civil servants from speaking to the press.[29] Despite these challenges, constituency coordinators were appointed, lobby packs for branches were produced, and commentaries on party manifestos and MPs' voting records were published. Activist exhaustion aside, local branches did what they could. PCS members in Liverpool, for example, played an important role in the successful campaign to unseat Tory Esther McVey. Her record as parliamentary under-secretary for state for disabled people and subsequently minister of state for employment, and her attacks on the Hillsborough campaigners had alienated voters in her Wirral West constituency.[30]

Just as the union had previously tried to deflect the coalition government from its deep cuts drive, it now aimed to influence the various party manifestos on pay, public services, welfare, tax justice and anti-union legislation. The NEC were prepared to consider requests from branches to stand or support specific independent candidates, but no such requests were made. It may have been that, while few PCS members had any illusions about the Miliband-led Labour Party, there was resignation to the idea that Labour could not be any worse than the Tories. The desire to defeat the coalition at all costs also reflected a certain weariness, stemming from the pensions betrayal and the lack of a cohesive response to austerity from the wider trade union movement.

With a growing voter share in preceding elections, the United Kingdom Independence Party (UKIP) had become a gathering point for various right-wing and racist elements by 2015. The PCS leadership regarded opposition to UKIP as a political imperative and a key element of the union's anti-racist and anti-fascist work during the election. It issued a comprehensive statement for activists and members that stated the new party offered nothing for working people, beyond playing on fears regarding immigration. It was, 'opening the ground for the politics of fear and division', while the real underlying cause of low wages and insecure jobs was predatory employers, deregulated labour markets and the decrease in trade union rights and freedoms. It also warned that UKIP's policies included limiting unfair dismissal claims, scrapping most equality and anti-discrimination legislation, and jettisoning a whole series of workers' rights. Throughout the campaign, PCS members joined with anti-racist organisations and campaigns, with union speakers on platforms and organising events.

The Tories were elected with a majority of twelve seats. Between 1997 and 2015, Labour had lost around 4.5 million votes. It was clear that workers needed more than fear to motivate them to vote for the party. This was demonstrated most dramatically by the near wipeout of Scottish Labour, where forty of their forty-one seats were lost. Traditional Labour voters not only rejected austerity, but also Labour's ill-judged alignment with the Tories and Liberal Democrats in the *Better Together* campaign. The Tories had won the election with support from only 24 per cent of the total electorate but were now able to govern without their previous Liberal Democrat partners, whose collaboration in austerity saw them reduced to eight seats from their previous fifty-seven. Cameron and Osborne quickly pressed ahead with further attacks on public services; but the political landscape had changed, presenting them with big challenges.

One of these came from the victory of the SNP. Despite the immediate effect of the failure of the independence referendum, the party had bounced back to win overwhelming representation at Westminster, as well as holding power in the Scottish Parliament. Paradoxically, the party had become the beneficiary of anti-austerity, without really challenging austerity. Nevertheless, it continued to foster a threat of constitutional instability that had begun to alarm big capital.

An even more pressing and unsettling issue was the future of Britain's membership of the EU. Even as it savoured its election victory, the same rows over Europe that had haunted John Major were again tearing the Conservative Party apart. With UKIP waiting in the wings, one former minister commented: 'Europe is the one issue upon which the Tories can... go walkabout and be unable to function properly'.[31]

Cameron's immediate priority, however, was the promotion of further anti-trade union legislation. Opposition to austerity was growing and there was an urgent need to block renewed resistance on the industrial front. Announced in the Queen's Speech of May 2015, the intention of the Trade Union Bill was to make legal strike action practically impossible, while avoiding the impression of banning it outright. Under the bill, 50 per cent of members would have to vote in any strike ballot, with higher thresholds in 'essential' services. Among its other proposals were a two-week notice period before strike action; the potential criminalisation of union reps when acting as picket organisers; opt-in, not out for political funds; and formalising the end of check-off for all public sector unions.

The bill caused immediate protest from trade unionists who recognised the biggest crackdown on union rights for 30 years. The bill completed its readings in the House of Commons in November and went to the House of Lords for consideration during the spring of 2016. This was a unique moment to defeat it by mobilising collective trade union strength. Not least as David Cameron's decision in February 2016 to hold a referendum on

EU membership had left the Tories squabbling more than usual. Unfortunately, the opportunity was squandered when a coalition of public sector unions reached an understanding with the government; as Dave Prentis of UNISON explained, it was, 'thanks to a good deal of union campaigning behind the scenes'.[32] In his blog to members of 19 April 2016, he crowed: 'For months now, I've been meeting with MPs, peers, ministers and even Bishops (they said they'd pray for us) trying to win the argument over check-off. Today's decision is a vindication of that work and a vindication of our union's campaign'. The *Financial Times* reported that a deal had been struck to drop the check-off clauses after union leaders claimed that they could not be expected to campaign vigorously for a Yes vote in the EU referendum if they were busy fighting the anti-union legislation.[33] Some of these same leaders had already signalled their desperate need for an accommodation with the government in public statements.

The TUC's campaign against the bill was based on the 'human rights' aspects of the legislation, an important point but secondary to its real purpose – to stop unions taking strike action against austerity.[34] Union leaders praised now 'principled peers', such as former head of the civil service, Lord Kerslake, who had raised concerns over the legislation.[35] Such figures astutely recognised that the public-sector union leaders who had delivered on pensions and were holding back the struggle against austerity should not be destabilised by the removal of check-off. This would have had a considerable impact on membership levels, with the real danger that they would not only lose their authority, but their positions to the left wings in their own organisations. Whether or not these 'tensions' were orchestrated as part of a cynical crisis resolution framed for public consumption is of no consequence, the end result was never in question. Indeed, the only genuine opposition was organised by the Trade Union Coordinating Group of left-led unions, including PCS, and the People's Assembly Against Austerity.[36]

There was little doubt over the final outcome. The Trade Union Act received Royal Assent on 4 May 2016 and was implemented the following March. The deal made between the union leaders and Cameron had been one of mutual self-interest. From the Tories' point of view, why not offer a relatively minor concession when PCS, one of its chief opponents, had already been damaged by Maude's check-off campaign? For the union leaders, the agreement protected their financial base, while allowing them to pursue their favoured partnership approach to bargaining.

Always something of a gambler, David Cameron had already found himself a new battle to fight. Buoyed perhaps by seeing off Scottish independence, he was confident of victory in the EU referendum due to be held on 23 June 2016, calling on the British electorate not to commit 'economic self-harm' by leaving Europe. The surprise result of his 'roll of the dice', a majority against continuing EU membership based on a huge voter turnout, was a personal and political disaster.[37] After his crushing miscalculation, Cameron was replaced by Theresa May, but she proved incapable of resolving the conflicts among her own party and its big business backers over how to negotiate an exit from the EU.

Brexit also sharpened the threat to the neoliberal consensus that had emerged with the 'political earthquake' of Jeremy Corbyn's election as Labour Party leader in a landslide victory on 12 September 2015, with 59.5 per cent of first-preference votes in the first round of voting.[38] In a sense, Corbyn's election had been an accident of history. It was enabled by a rule change designed by the right wing to weaken trade union influence and introduce a US-style primary process. The intention was to widen the range of individual supporters able to vote, who would be unsympathetic to radical ideas. As it turned out, the opposite was true.

Like all such political 'accidents', Corbyn's victory had also occurred for more concrete reasons. There was still a significant proportion of left-leaning supporters in Labour's activist base. With the general election defeat in 2015, many saw an opportunity to register a protest against the road the party had taken. Alongside them, activists and some leaderships in the affiliated unions also saw an opportunity to hit back at the right wing, using support for

Corbyn as leverage to force the party to adopt more radical policies. Most importantly, Corbyn's bold outward-looking campaign aroused a mood of resistance to austerity on the basis that there now was an alternative.[39] Mass meetings throughout the country and activist-led use of social media mobilised many thousands of new members and supporters, enfranchised by the new voting arrangements. This was the real secret of his stunning victory.

Clearly, the political landscape had shifted dramatically even during the few short years since the PCS decision on standing independent candidates. The advent of Corbyn as Labour leader now gave hope that the party would adopt policies that would benefit PCS members and all workers. Alongside left-led unions in the Trade Union Coordinating Group, PCS worked closely with Corbyn and his shadow chancellor, John McDonnell, to develop a new economic and political strategy. Indeed, the perspectives developed in the union's *Alternative* publications helped shape what would become Labour's 2017 manifesto. Unite's left leadership under Len McCluskey were also firm Corbyn supporters, but while right-wing union leaders gave public pledges of support, they would be the first to undermine him – behind the scenes and then openly. Like PCS's own position, Corbyn's policies were basically a demand that the concessions taken from the working-class since Thatcher be restored. This was hardly a revolutionary programme, but it would take intense class struggle to reverse decades of defeat.

There was tremendous support for Corbyn among PCS activists, and this extended to the wider membership. At the union's 2016 conference, he promised that any government he led would reintroduce national pay bargaining. This was alongside commitments to end the one per cent pay cap; scrap the Trade Union Act; improve protections for workers and pensioners in company takeovers; and enact a whole series of employment rights and protections.[40] The union's 2016 consultation on political representation revealed members' distrust of the PLP, as they witnessed almost daily attacks on Labour's new leadership. Even with Corbyn now at the helm, a founder member of the PCS

Parliamentary Group, there was still little support for affiliation to the party. Members were determined not to be beholden to any political party, and certainly not a party that had treated them so badly when last in power. The union therefore reaffirmed its 'political, not party political' stance, so it might continue to exert influence on all parties without having formal loyalty to one. It was telling that when John McDonnell stood down as PCS's Parliamentary Group chair to take up post as shadow chancellor, he was replaced by former UNISON activist Chris Stephens from the SNP, while Green Party MP, Caroline Lucas, became vice-chair.

Theresa May called a surprise general election for 8 June 2017 in the hope of securing her personal position in the Tory party and exploiting what she saw as Labour's weakness under Corbyn. Reflecting conference decisions, a statement by Janice Godrich and Mark Serwotka to members set out the union's position on the government's record, '...the worst possible outcome of this election for us would be another Tory government with its vicious spending cuts'. It went on to explain: 'We are not affiliated to any political party, but the NEC has previously agreed to support Jeremy Corbyn's continued leadership of the Labour Party as best serving our members' interests'. The conference also decided that branch requests to support Labour candidates would be considered.[41]

The most distinctive feature of the election campaign was the surge in support for Labour, driven by Corbyn's leadership, including a very big increase in Labour Party membership and activity. Also significant was the great popularity of Labour's manifesto, which contained measures which signified a genuine departure from the neoliberal consensus, with calls for a rebuilding of the welfare state and an end to anti-union laws.

PCS's election campaign focused on the government's record of cuts, privatisation, job losses, destruction of services, office closures and pay caps. It also raised the fear that Brexit negotiations would establish conditions for even more extreme measures, including the undermining of civil rights, equality and human rights legislation, and health and safety standards. Meanwhile, the union continued its campaigns against the far right, and while UKIP suffered electorally, the English Defence League and other organisations remained a threat; this prompted the issue prior to the election of a pamphlet, *Brexit: why we must unite against racism and fight for an alternative to cuts.*

Corbyn's startling success in the 2017 election provoked real fear among the entire political establishment, not least their surrogates in the Labour Party's bureaucracy and PLP. These elements in the party openly operated as a fifth column against Corbyn and his thousands of supporters. They launched a campaign to destroy both Corbyn as an individual and the left of the party as a whole, with alleged antisemitism deployed in the most cynical and shameful fashion. The series of attacks and attempted coups in the PLP culminated in the defeat of Labour in the 2019 general election, with the populist Boris Johnson returned as prime minister with an eighty-seat Commons majority.

Although it would be naïve to underplay the impact of the ferocious campaign waged by the ruling elite, it was by no means predestined that the Corbyn movement would be defeated. Seeking an accommodation within the Labour Party bureaucracy, composed as it was of diehard right-wing careerists determined to undermine him, was an error; as was failing to push through five-yearly mandatory reselection for MPs, a basic democratic demand that ensured some degree of accountability for Labour MPs. Political power and authority cannot be maintained unless secured organisationally. He was widely regarded as a principled conviction politician, but when he equivocated on the issue of Brexit, which Tory leader Boris Johnson made the main focus of the election, his position was irrevocably compromised.

The election of Keir Starmer as leader of the Labour Party in April 2020 on a cynical programme of 'continuity' with Corbyn's policies was the beginning of a counter-revolution that marginalised the left and fully re-established the Westminster consensus on capitalist orthodoxy. For the British ruling class, the Corbyn movement meant a hegemonic shift in favour of the working class.

In the interests of profitability, it had to be destroyed.

At the September 2023 Trades Union Congress, Mark Serwotka was interviewed by *Morning Star*'s editor Ben Chacko. He reflected on recent experiences:

> Britain is broken, it needs radical surgery, and we've got a Labour opposition that is fiscally conservative, wants to keep the two-child benefits cap, talks about tough decisions to hold down spending but won't make the tough decision to tax the rich.

> Keir Starmer's keynote speech this week was given to a private dinner [of the TUC general council], he didn't address the conference, he sent Angela Rayner. He doesn't want to be associated with the labour movement.[42]

This was a prescient comment. Starmer would 'triumph' in the 2024 election with 600,000 less votes than Corbyn got in 2019 and almost three million less than in 2017. Speaking to another news outlet, Serwotka described the Labour leader as: 'A car salesman who just sells soap'.[43]

The outcome of the 2019 general election may have been a disappointment to most of PCS's members, but at least the union had been able to make a political impact, not least on the direction of Labour's policy development under Corbyn. Independently of formal party politics, it had built and sustained an articulate alternative in its anti-austerity and anti-racism campaigns.

Unless unions fight on the political front as well as the industrial, they are fighting with one hand tied behind their back. Like the struggle in the workplace, political engagement by a union is a constant, it is for the long haul.

Notes & References

1. Mark Serwotka interview, *Socialist Worker*, 1 May 2007.

2. *The Guardian*, 7 November 2008.

3. *Morning Star*, 28 April 2008.

4. Rob Griffiths, *Morning Star*, 23 February 2004.

5. *Morning Star*, 27 April 2010.

6. *Morning Star*, 21 May 2010.

7. 'Historic vote for union to support election candidates', *PCS media release*, 2 July 2012.

8. *There is an alternative: The case against cuts in public spending*, PCS, London, 2010.

9. *Welfare: An alternative vision*, PCS, London, 2011.

10. *Morning Star*, 7 May 2023.

11. *Financial Times*, 16 September 2010. It was completely untrue there was widespread abuse of the system, DWP's own figures showed fraud rates for DLA were only 0.5 per cent, approximately 14,500 fraudulent claims from between 2.9 million, an infinitesimal amount: *Fraud and Error in the Benefits System: 2010/11 Estimates*, DWP, Leeds, 2012.

12. E. Clifford, *The War on Disabled People: Capitalism, Welfare and the Making of a Human Catastrophe*, Zed Books, London, 2020.

13. *Morning Star*, 30 June 2014.

14. Lynn Henderson, *Morning Star*, 14 November 2016.

15. *Morning Star*, 10 December 2013.

16. *The Herald*, 10 November 2013.

17. Over the years, PCS and NIPSA would produce some outstanding class fighters. These included from PCS, Barney Lawn, Brian Magee, Billy O'Gorman, Alistair Donaghy, Paul Wolfe, John McCloskey and full-timer, Gayle Matthews, and from NIPSA, Brian Campfield, Carmel Gates, Maria Morgan, Gerry Malone, Billy Lynn, Lucia Collins, Tony McMullan, Patrick Mulholland and Tina Creaney.

18. *The Socialist*, 10, November 2014.

19. Vince Mills, *Morning Star*, 13 March 2014

20. Robin McAlpine, *Some thoughts on the first minister's lecture*, The Jimmy Reid Foundation, 30 January 2013.

21. *Morning Star*, 18 February 2013.

22. *The Herald*, 4 September 2014.

23. S. Ayres, *Demographic and voting patterns in Scotland's independence referendum*, House of Commons Library, London, 2014.

24. *The Scotsman*, 9 September 2014.

25. Bill Ramsay, *Bella Caledonia*, 19 November 2014.

26. *The Herald*, 13 October 2013.

27. 'Unions have their say on Scotland's future', *Labour Research*, August 2014.

28. *Daily Mirror*, 17 September 2014.

29. Lynn Henderson, *Morning Star*, 21 April 2015.

30. *Liverpool Echo*, 8 May 2015.

31. *The Guardian*, 11 June 2015.

32. *The Guardian*, 19 April 2015.

33. *Financial Times*, 16 April 2016.

34. *Trade Union Bill is a "major attack on civil liberties", human rights groups warn*, TUC press release, London, 7 September 2015.

35. *Civil Service World*, 26 February 2016.

36. Mark Serwotka, *Morning Star*, 13 September 2016.

37. *The Guardian*, 3 June 2016.

38. *The Socialist*, 18 September 2015.

39. A. Nunns, *The Candidate: Jeremy Corbyn's Improbable Path to Power*, OR Books, New York and London, 2016, pp.163-189.

40. Mark Serwotka, *Morning Star*, 23 May 2017.

41. *Morning Star*, 23 May 2017.

42. *Morning Star*, 13 September 2023.

43. *The Independent*, 12 September 2023.

PCS – FIGHTING BAC

END AUSTERITY NOW

■ Andy Aitchison, *Mark Serwotak with Janice Godrich opposing Tory austerity*, 2017 © Andy Aitchison

10. Building strength – learning lessons

Campaign strategy

Except for the Corbyn interregnum, the battleground on which PCS developed its militant strategy, tactics, and methods was conditioned by the shared neoliberal position of the major political parties. This made a focus on alliance-building imperative to strengthen and widen resistance to austerity. Effective campaigning involved continuous reflection and debate at all levels of the union. Ineffective approaches had to be identified and corrected, not abstractly, but in real living conditions of struggle. This was especially so in relation to industrial action where maximum impact was required in the struggle against employers and the government.

Building an interconnected campaign strategy for PCS meant that the national leadership had to respond appropriately to demands for industrial action from departmental groups. The National Disputes Committee (NDC), consisting of the general secretary, the assistant general secretary, the president and vice-presidents, never once rejected a submission for strike action. It also involved itself in the planning and execution of these campaigns, ensuring a direct line of responsibility from the union's policy-making annual conference through to departmental and branch levels. In a union comprising members in hundreds of departments and agencies, and with a substantial outsourced sector, it was crucial to coordinate differing interests to develop a consistent approach to collective bargaining. Settlements were agreed or rejected by the NDC in line with the union's overall national strategy as set by the national conference. The approach enjoyed widespread support. Despite the potential for tensions over proposed settlement terms, differences with the NDC were generally resolved amicably. Where any issues persisted, they were tempered by an understanding among reps and the general membership that they were a consequence of the forcible breakup of the civil service into hundreds of discrete bargaining areas.

The government's hope was to single out weak spots and destroy each in turn, particularly targeting militant areas such as DWP. It had taken industrial action in 2004 to get Tony Blair's government to the negotiating table to agree to a protocol for 'handling surplus staff situations', which would protect the interests of hundreds of thousands of members facing redundancy. But no matter how good national agreements may have appeared on paper, they had to be rigorously policed at the workplace and departmental levels, as management would invariably test how well the union could defend them.

The resolve of PCS's members was repeatedly tested as successive administrations encouraged individual executive teams to dilute or even disregard these agreements. One and two-day national strikes in response did have a limited impact, but they were not always enough to secure negotiations or concessions. Nevertheless, they did raise awareness among members and strengthened solidarity, while the union's outward-looking communications educated the public on the danger to public services. Although national strikes did not themselves cause severe levels of disruption to management operations, they had a very strong political impact, and when allied to departmental strikes and action short of strike campaigns, they could force negotiations and concessions.

Fighting closures

Questions of how to apply national campaigning tactics and how to respond to different levels of combativeness within the union's departmental groups were sharply tested by the advance of austerity and a labour movement in retreat. Announced in 2017, the Tory government's massive office closure programmes were a case in point. These were aimed at several of the largest departments, including the DWP and HMRC. In the latter, a national scheme was put in place to shut 170 offices and open 13 regional centres, with up to 5,000 staff expected to leave as a result of the proposed moves.[1] The local impact would also be considerable; in Wales alone, it was proposed to close DWP offices in Caerphilly, Cwmbran, Merthyr, Newport and Cardiff, transferring 1,700 jobs to a new site in Treforrest.[2]

The union had secured redundancy rights with the 2004 jobs protocol and had been successful in defending the CSCS. Members who had backed their union and taken industrial action on these issues had done so from differing outlooks. For example, some of the union's most supportive and loyal members also wanted to leave the civil service and therefore were mainly concerned with the protection of redundancy rights. Many also saw the closure of the offices where they worked as inevitable. This led to the apparent contradiction that while it was the union's job to defend redundancy rights, it also opposed closures, except when there was a genuine case that had been agreed with the union. PCS argued against the closure programme on the basis that services should be delivered by well-trained staff, capable of efficiently understanding and then dealing with the complex needs of real people; this meant offices being accessible. PCS did not oppose the introduction of new technology – unions rarely do – but it did reject its reckless implementation where it diminished rather than improved services. The union also argued that closures damaged local economies with the loss of jobs and other services, as well as discouraging inward investment.

Tactical flexibility is extremely important in union campaign work, as each dispute has its own specific conditions and characteristics. There is no set list of rules or measures; the success of any dispute depends on reading all the contributory factors accurately. Yet, it is also true that there are certain principles that apply in almost all situations. The basis of any campaign lies first in organising the workplaces targeted for closure and then winning over members, while considering the concerns of those who wish to leave. Campaigning to keep an office open, even when many there wish to take redundancy, is difficult but not as illogical as it may first appear. Also, winning over the local community is not a supplementary consideration, it is critical. Establishing a solid level of support locally is often the first step before extending the campaign more widely to include workplaces potentially threatened with closure.

The proposed closure of the Passport Office in Newport, South Wales in 2010 had already shown how difficult it could be to get the tactics right in practice. With national support, the Home Office departmental PCS group organised meetings in Newport attended by almost all the staff. Meetings involving local Labour MPs, the trades council and the local community were sympathetically covered in the local and national media. After a well-attended march and rally, members were prepared to move to industrial action.[3] Meetings were held in passport offices across the country and, following feedback from reps, it was decided that a group-wide ballot for strike action would be held. The ballot, however, was unsuccessful. Events in Newport suggested that even where there had been a strong local campaign. It did not necessarily imply though that other workplaces had reached the stage of considering industrial action, even where they too were potentially at risk. Calling industrial action at Newport in the first instance would have allowed strikers to visit other workplaces and present the issues from a more powerful perspective, including explaining why they needed solidarity action to oppose the closure and to protect other offices. These messages would be taken to heart for the future.

On a much larger scale, the closure programmes of 2017 also revealed a hesitation among some reps in areas like HMRC, who were daunted by the task of organising local campaigns from the ground up. This was an understandable reaction in places where quite significant numbers of members wanted redundancy. In some cases, this was because workplace organisational strength was not as solid as it might have been. Here only patient work in building and extending local campaigns could provide a way forward. A belief developed among some reps, however, that the only way to stop the closures was to organise national industrial action across the union. This demand was premised on occasional management threats of compulsory redundancies, something the union had described as a 'red line' when securing the job protocol agreement.[4] However, the Newport experience suggested that demanding national action in such circumstances was unlikely to deliver victory. A ballot would have to be won among hundreds of thousands of members, the majority of whom were not directly affected by the closures. Calling a national ballot, even over a very limited number of compulsory redundancies which could be resolved within the protocol framework, would have been a gift to the government. This type of 'performative militancy' may even have emboldened management hawks to move to threaten compulsory redundancies.

While these examples show that not every campaign achieved its potential, PCS's general approach, holding the government to the job protocol framework, made a real difference to members' lives. Those facing local office closures in 2017 were able to find other work in the civil service, something that would have been impossible without the agreement secured by the union. In the absence of these campaigns and much grassroots work by reps and members, there is little doubt the government's closure programmes would have been carried out in a far more brutal fashion and with crippling cost to the civil service workforce.

Defending the CSCS

The rejection of concession bargaining by PCS created tensions with some union leaderships as well as with the government. When David Cameron launched a new attack on the CSCS in 2016, the union was still rebuilding its membership following the withdrawal of automatic payroll deductions. Broadly, the proposed CSCS cuts would have amounted to members receiving a third less in redundancy payments. It initially sought to draw out the consultation process, in the hope of building an alliance with the other unions covered by the scheme. The government's insistence that the unions should sign up to proposals that would severely cut redundancy terms had already caused widespread anxiety among members. While PCS was prepared to enter negotiations, these could not be based on the government's preconditions, as this would mean accepting cuts as a starting point. However, every union on the National Trade Union Committee accepted the government's preconditions except PCS and POA. This resulted in both of them being barred from the talks.[5] PCS launched a judicial review on the basis that the legislation governing the scheme stated that the government must consult 'with a view to reaching agreement', hence barring the union from negotiations breached the government's statutory obligation.

The High Court ruled in PCS's favour. PCS and POA then entered negotiations in a bloc separate from those unions that had accepted changes in advance. They were later joined by Unite and GMB, who had now decided to oppose the detrimental measures. The union's case was as close to cast iron as it could be, but the decision also reflected a concern among certain sections of the establishment over the potential of austerity to alienate large sections of the working and middle classes.

Following the High Court decision, the government launched a new consultation on the CSCS again with a view to imposing changes, but this time doing it lawfully. Protracted negotiations resulted in the Tories deferring a decision on cuts to the CSCS, but they included a commitment to do so in their 2019 election manifesto. Subsequent campaigning resulted in the government conceding in 2023 that they would not seek to make any changes in the lifetime of the new parliament. After the election of a Labour government in 2024, PCS continued to campaign hard on job security and redundancy arrangements. In April 2025, the Cabinet Office confirmed that it was ending consultation on changes to the CSCS, effectively abandoning the latest attack on the scheme. This was a significant victory for PCS and its allies. By refusing to engage in concession bargaining, the rights of workers in their own unions and beyond had been protected; the financial benefits to members and the cost to the government have been calculated at £1 billion.[6]

Campaigning on pay

The priorities of union members inevitably shift over time. From the time of Gordon Brown's cuts, redundancy arrangements and the CSCS dominated, but issues of pay and living standards were a further persistent concern. Cutting wage levels has been a continuous feature of all the developed capitalist countries from the 1960s, and in Britain a principal aim of every government from Margaret Thatcher onwards. Such measures transfer wealth from working-class pockets to ensure that profit levels are maintained. In the public sector, the reduction of living standards also had a deliberate political purpose – to demoralise workers and encourage them to leave their jobs. The drive for government savings through trimming its workforce had some initial success, but it also created a reservoir of anger among PCS members, reflected in growing militancy and opposition to government policy.

Campaigning on pay presented some intractable problems for PCS. Only coordinated action could defeat the imposed pay caps, but the lack of a united front among the public sector unions made this almost impossible, leaving unions to fight isolated battles. This passivity was a gift to successive governments. Each of them in their own fashion sought to foster division and confusion by claiming that there were 'deserving' and 'undeserving' public service workers. Civil servants were left in no doubt as to which category they belonged.

The key question for PCS and other left-led unions was whether they could organise the type of national action capable of exerting sufficient leverage on pay. The union's central demand for a return to national pay bargaining was widely supported, but it could not be achieved without intensive industrial action. This would be a gargantuan task, not least because of the atomising effect of hundreds of separate bargaining units. It had been a bitter learning experience in 2008 when the union had called off its strike action in return for talks which promised to review this dysfunctional system, only to discover that the government had decided to hold the line on pay in advance of any general election. In these circumstances, it was agreed that while nationally agreed pay rates would remain a key objective, concessions on pay were more likely to be achieved at departmental level in the short-term.

The austerity imposed by New Labour after the financial crash intensified the war on the public sector. Neither the subsequent coalition nor later Tory governments had the least intention of returning to the national pay bargaining that had originally been abandoned with the connivance of the union's Moderate regime. Despite David Cameron's refusal to enter negotiations, the union, through the annual delegate conference, was anxious to retain an overarching national approach. Without diluting its demands, PCS leaders nationally fully supported departmental group struggles to secure pay deals, but they oversaw these deals before they went to ballot to ensure they were in line with nationally agreed criteria. No offer was ever put to the ballot without national authority, or without making it clear to the employer that departmental agreements did not imply compromise on the central demand for a return to unified bargaining.

The government concentrated its most sustained attacks on pay levels in the bigger departments, as they had the larger staff levels and pay bills. These were also the areas with the most militant memberships, all led by Left Unity activists. Although every government was determined to take its own tough approach on pay, they were also aware of PCS's ability to sustain strikes at departmental group level. Momentum might well develop if the larger groups were to act at the same time, combining targeted one and two-day strikes with other disruptive measures.

During 2015 and 2016, a series of strikes were held in the face of the Tories' push for a national one per cent pay cap.[7] These departmental disputes presented the union with opportunities to improve members' deteriorating living standards, particularly those on the lowest pay. They also raised serious strategic and tactical considerations – the employers wanted concessions on conditions in return for offering the union increases above the 'going rate', money desperately needed by low-paid members. The balance of power suggested that compromises might be required, but there could be no capitulation to concession bargaining.

In five large departments, the employers indicated that more money might be available, but they had specific demands. Home Office management, for instance, indicated that they wanted to end 'time-served progression' on wages, which in some areas was contractual, proposing the creation of effectively a two-tier workforce in which new entrants would not have this right. Union negotiating teams, composed of both lay and full-time negotiators, warned the employer that members were prepared to take strike action. This was a significant factor in securing a deal that delivered substantial increases, with the biggest for the lowest paid. Other gains included 'continuous journey and reduced journey' times through pay ranges; greater coherence of pay and grading arrangements; and a single rate for the job at the lowest-paid administrative assistant grade. An agreement was also reached on increased pay coherence. This entailed the eradication of the worst elements of discrimination within the existing pay structures and those resulting from the assimilation of other agencies into the department. A similar deal was achieved in the Department for Transport.

In the union's biggest group at DWP, the campaign was centred on another explicit threat of strike action if no deal was reached. Although DWP management was among the most hardline in the civil service, they were facing the union's most militant membership; this became a key factor in reaching a settlement. The 'Employee Deal' which was negotiated secured a four-year agreement that delivered substantial pay rises to 60 per cent of members, in return for more flexible working to support extended opening hours at Jobcentres. A downside was the exclusion of those at the relatively well-paid Senior Executive Officer grade and above, who received only one per cent, with the largest increases going to the lowest paid. The effects of changes to working arrangements were also greatly mitigated by a series of agreed safeguards, including a commitment to negotiate with PCS on their potential implementation. Specific safeguards were also secured for carers, on mobility and access, and in protecting staff who had problems with extended hours. The option remained, for those who wished to take it, to opt out of any new arrangements. Union negotiators had correctly calculated that with no clear data on the effectiveness of extending opening hours, cost and viability would be prohibitive. They were proved correct, and while some changes did take place, the negative impact was less than feared. Deals on similar lines were reached in HMRC and the Ministry of Justice.

All these deals were approved by the national union, endorsed at group conferences and passed by substantial majorities in membership ballots. Those who opposed them fell into two broad camps. There were those militant reps, including some in Left Unity, who believed that the union should never agree to any detrimental change in principle, although they did recognise the achievement of smashing the one per cent pay cap and the benefits won for low-paid members. The second group consisted of ultra-lefts whose slogan 'Together we can beat the employee deal' was based on the facile premise the union should be 'imaginative' about strike action. This was rather cynical, given they could not deliver strike action in their own areas.

In 2016, Fran Heathcote, DWP group president, addressed this tendency:

> We must maintain a united membership for the many struggles ahead, so our position is a clear one – we need to get money in our struggling members' pockets, enforce the negotiated safeguards, including the ability to opt out. We need to build union organisation and density following the attack on check-off and work for coordinated union-wide responses to government attacks and build such a coordinated response across the public sector unions to demand fair pay for public sector workers.

DWP group officer Martin Cavanagh added in the same vein:

We broke the Treasury pay cap and secured a deal which, with all its limitations, has not only put substantial amounts of money in members pockets but kept the membership united where the employer sought to divide us. We don't try to sell it as a victory – it was a compromise, but one that on balance was almost entirely in our favour. But more, in the finest democratic traditions of PCS, we consulted at every stage; we held meetings in over 400 workplaces in three weeks, and where members heard the details of the deal, they supported it in large numbers, so too did conference and members in a ballot.

There is a chasm between concession bargaining and compromises which reflect the reality of a union's bargaining position. This is a concrete issue, not an abstract one. The former sells rights and conditions very cheaply, the latter seeks to extract maximum concessions, so that the membership gains more than they lose. For right-wing leaders there is no dilemma, they tend to settle on the employer's terms. Meanwhile, for ultra-lefts all compromises should be rejected, even if the result is a substantial weakening of union power and no relief for hard-pressed members. Consideration of the deal on offer always requires balanced judgment. In the examples outlined above, real material gains were secured for many low-paid workers; not what they deserved, but considerably more than would have been delivered through concession bargaining.

By 2018, the political situation was now more favourable for the union to launch a major national pay campaign. Corbyn was leading Labour and the Tory government faced mounting opposition over its austerity policies. The July 2018 membership ballot for national strike action achieved an 85 per cent vote in favour – the largest in PCS history. However, the strike was thwarted because some major departmental groups did not reach the arbitrary 50 per cent participation threshold for legal industrial action imposed by the draconian 2016 Trade Union Act. Nevertheless, valuable organisational lessons were learned. Nor was the union deterred from calling for a joint union campaign for pay increases above the rate of inflation – as Mark Serwotka promised, 'we are dusting off and regrouping for future battles...'[8] Unfortunately, as discussed in the next chapter, internal struggles within the union would significantly blunt this fightback.

When the Covid pandemic ended in 2022, the biggest strike wave since the 1980s erupted. This signified a new period of intensified class struggle in which workers turned to their unions in the fight for improved living standards. Successive groups of workers followed the example of the rail workers in punching through the legal threshold for strike action. This confounded the pessimists in the trade union movement who had predicted that legal strike action had become impossible under the terms of the 2016 Act.

In PCS, the 50 per cent barrier was surpassed in 130 bargaining areas, including most of the larger departmental groups. The union's pay campaign from November 2022 was based on targeted action designed to hit the employer hard, causing serious disruption in specific areas.[9] The first phase saw 118 days of action, followed by 186 in the second, supplemented by action at a national level. For the first time since the introduction of delegated pay bargaining, the government was forced to negotiate at national level and shift its initial hard line on pay. Their initial offer of two per cent was increased to four and a half per cent, while in some departments, lower-paid staff received more. A non-consolidated lump sum award of £1,500 was agreed for members in the UK and Welsh departments, with a separate deal reached with the Scottish government. The NEC calculated that, having moved the government twice from their original starting point, this deal was the best on the table, but they began immediate preparations to continue the fight for further concessions from a strengthened bargaining position.[10] The deal was overwhelmingly accepted by members.

The 2022–3 strike-wave was not a one-off event but the first major expression of collective anger by organised workers since the pensions betrayal. Greater coordination across the trade union movement might have inflicted an even more serious defeat on the Tory government, but it marked the beginning of an extended and deepening surge of opposition to neoliberalism. The success of this will be determined by whether unions abandon isolated struggle and concession bargaining and embrace a militant, coordinated response to multiple attacks on the working class in both the workplace and the community.

Achievements and limitations

Any assessment of PCS's role, particularly during the period of the coalition and Tory governments, must take account of the highly unfavourable industrial and political context of austerity and anti-union laws. Compounding a general decline of class consciousness was the lack of independent working-class political representation and the failure to build a unified front against the cuts. Yet, this did not mean that the working class had moved permanently to the right – opinion polls consistently showed solid public opposition to privatisation and public provision of key services.[11]

Virtually every industrial struggle since the mid-seventies has been of a defensive nature; workers have supported industrial action against attempts to diminish working conditions and living standards. They know that the stakes in striking are high, but when there is no alternative, they tend to do so with added determination. But it is also true that in periods of sustained assault from employers, pressures to 'accept reality' can develop even among a fighting union like PCS, resulting in a retreat into administrative 'routinism'.

It was the membership's combative mood that had won the national agreements on redundancies and jobs and had frustrated the worst aspects of New Labour's pensions plans. The union's subsequent record in mobilising against the coalition government established PCS as a serious opponent of austerity and privatisation. Its campaigns also made it powerful enemies in the political establishment, but even in the face of union-busting tactics that threatened its viability, the capacity of activists and members to continue the struggle was remarkable. There were 24 branch and departmental disputes during 2012, with the same number recorded in 2013; this fell by one in 2014. The impact of the government attack can be traced in subsequent years; a total of eight disputes in 2016 was followed by fifteen in 2017, falling to five in 2018; and recovering to seventeen in 2019, the year before Covid-19.[12] Some of these involved tens of thousands of members, and while they met with varying degrees of success, all were important markers of resistance in the most intense years of austerity.

Confidence in the union remained high among the membership, although they faced a hostile balance of power. During 2016, the year of Cameron's Trade Union Act, privatisations were prevented in the Forestry Commission, the Ministry of Justice and the Land Registry, among others. Where it could not be stopped, terms and conditions were protected by safeguards, as in the case of DWP contact centre workers. Job cuts were reversed among police community supporter officers; weekend allowances were secured for museums and galleries staff; and weekend payments were protected at the Driver and Vehicle Licensing Agency (DVLA).[13] In negotiations with the Scottish government in 2018, a 'no redundancy agreement' was secured, and agreement was reached on the Scottish Living Wage, which also covered contract workers and temporary agency staff.[14] These were just snapshots of the concrete gains won by PCS. In addition, successful campaigns were mounted around parental leave, flexible working hours, and workplace nurseries, while equal pay was secured in the Prison Service. For individual members, millions of pounds were won in compensation with victories at Employment Tribunals, while discriminatory practices were tackled in departmental performance management systems.

The Covid-19 pandemic and subsequent lockdowns challenged PCS, like all unions, particularly on health and safety issues. During 2021, for example, staff at DVLA's Swansea HQ accused a panicked management of bringing them back to work too quickly to deal with a massive backlog of licence applications; the result was over 1,700 cases of Covid and one death.[15] Members took strike action on the obvious workplace risks, despite a media onslaught that accused them of 'holding millions of drivers to ransom'.[16] The government's promise of 'local recognition awards' was not enough to deflect a prolonged dispute, which resulted in several vital concessions on working practices that made members safer.[17]

PCS also built strong campaigns around the Green Agenda and Tax Justice, complementing its longstanding anti-racist and anti-fascist work. Internationally, the union continued to support Palestinian liberation, while it became one of the first major unions to express its solidarity with the Black Lives Matter movement. When in 2022 home secretary Priti Patel proposed that PCS members carry out 'pushback' manoeuvres on small boats in the English Channel which would likely result in loss of life, the union launched a judicial review challenge in the High Court.[18] This successfully stopped the plan in its tracks, with the government conceding days before the hearing. The following year when the Tories pushed their Rwanda deportation scheme, PCS and others launched another Judicial Review challenge. This resulted in the Supreme Court ruling the scheme unlawful.[19]

The union also supported many arts and cultural events, as well as national labour festivals like the Durham Miners' Gala. Forced effectively to re-recruit its own members after the removal of check-off, the maintenance of a strong public profile of this type was essential if PCS was to recover its membership base, as it offered a powerful reminder of why being in the union was in everyone's best interests.

Following the conclusion of a three-year Strategic Review of the union's organisational priorities in 2018, various objectives and targets were identified.[20] The most important were rebuilding membership density levels in the workplaces and expanding into the growing commercial sector of services that had been outsourced. The review also aimed to make the best use of full-time staff; develop closer links between the full-timers and activists; and enhance the membership database. Most activists adapted well to the need to work with diminishing resources, although a few complained that some areas were being treated less favourably. The introduction of the 'Union Advocates' initiative was intended in part to address issues of 'burn-out' within the activist base. It encouraged members, who did not hold official branch positions, to help with campaigns and other aspects of work in their own time. Over the coming years, these advocates would play an invaluable role in rebuilding organisational strength at a local level.

Speaking in 2017, PCS president Janice Godrich had reflected on the achievements and limitations of PCS:

> From the 1980s to 2002 the government ripped up national pay bargaining and other national agreements. Members and activists fought back without the support of their national union; they were in effect fighting with one hand tied behind their back. We changed all that too. As we emerge strengthened from the Tories attempt to smash PCS let us recall why they are so scared of this union.

> When Gordon Brown boasted he would cut 100,000 jobs and rip up our redundancy rights we campaigned and won the Protocols Agreement, we stopped their plans to steal our sick leave and much else. We did not just sit back as others did and accept the inevitability of cuts – we fought back... And when Cameron and Osborne told us there was no alternative to Austerity, we did not accept that either. It was we, the PCS leadership, working with members and activists, who set out the Economic Alternative, and the Welfare Alternative. It was this union that demanded coordinated action when both New Labour and the Tories attempted to cut our pensions. The biggest ever general strike of public sector workers on 30 November 2011, would not have happened but for this union. And when the TUC sold out that dispute you backed Mark's refusal at the

General Council to accept that sell-out, and together we fought on.

Of course we have not fully stemmed the attacks from successive governments, fighting almost entirely in isolation. How could any union do that? But without our campaigning, without our democratic decision-making, reached through consultation and all based on conference decision, and by building a solid activist base, we could never have defended what we have – and what we did defend has made a real difference to our members, in their workplaces.

We believe in the idea that a trade union's role should not be limited only to defending terms and conditions but be a democratic force capable of fighting not just for our members but our class – the working-class. And that is why we also have been unstinting in our support for anti-war and anti-racism and fascism campaigns and in defence of disabled and unemployed workers. The war against our class does not end when we leave our workplaces each evening. We believe in the idea that our union, and all unions, can and must be a force in building a better society based not on profit but on the needs of people.

In any period of reaction, advocating militant opposition and resistance is of profound importance. It challenges the slide towards class collaboration and compliance by the labour movement's leaders. It can also demonstrate to workers their collective potential to influence events. In promoting an alternative vision through political engagement, building alliances and extending the parameters of organised struggle, PCS has continued to play a significant role in advancing the interests of the working class. There are those who see the past forty years of reaction as one of endless defeat and retreat, but this is only one side of the story. The capacity of workers, their unions and other working-class organisations to resist builds on a long history of struggle. As capitalism's crisis deepens further, this will be the foundation upon which the fight for a socialist society rests.

....

Notes & References

1. *The Guardian*, 10 January 2017; *Civil Service World*, 2 August 2017.
2. Shavanah Taj, *Morning Star*, 22 May 2018.
3. *The Socialist*, 20 October 2010.
4. *Civil Service World*, 1 February 2016.
5. *Civil Service World*, 26 September 2016.
6. 'Victory for PCS as Labour government agrees to end attacks on CSCS', PCS press release, London, 7 April 2025.
7. *Morning Star*, 3 February 2015.
8. *The Guardian*, 10 September 2018.
9. *Morning Star*, 2 November 2022.
10. *Personnel Today*, 23 January 2024.
11. J. Curtice and R. Ormston (eds), *British Social Attitudes 32: The verdict on five years of coalition government*, National Centre for Social Research, London, 2015.
12. PCS internal memorandum, 2020.
13. L. Henderson, *Morning Star*, 24 May 2018.
14. L. Henderson, 'Public and Civil Service: Transformed by Trade Unionists', in P. Bryan (ed.), *Keep Left: Red Paper on Scotland 2025*, Luath Press, Edinburgh, 2025, p.102.
15. *The Guardian*, 14 October 2021.
16. *Morning Star*, 26 April 2022.
17. *Morning Star*, 18 June 2022.
18. *Morning Star*, 26 April 2022.
19. *Morning Star*, 16 November 2023.
20. M. Serwotka, *Morning Star*, 24 May 2018.

11. Sectarianism – the infantile disorder

Dynamics of sectarianism

After the defeat of the Moderate machine in the merged PCS, it was uncertain whether the new socialist leadership could maintain itself in office and stand firm in the face of relentless attacks on conditions and services. By 2018, the union had established itself in the fighting vanguard against cuts, privatisation and austerity. The Tory government's union-busting attempt to bankrupt it had been defeated. Membership and workplace density levels had recovered, and finances had stabilised. Its anti-austerity alternative, once dismissed as being 'out of touch with reality', now enjoyed support across the movement and in wider society. The external political climate had also changed. Jeremy Corbyn's manifesto saw Labour support rise by twenty per cent in the 2017 general election, denying the Tories a majority. The campaign to destroy his leadership was already underway, but the outcome was far from a settled question.

It was precisely at this time, when industrial and political conditions had begun to improve and with the PCS ready to launch a national pay campaign, that a bitter internal dispute broke out. This conflict arose from within the left itself and was based on sectarian divisions that had developed from both objective and subjective factors connected to the impact of the extended period of reaction on activists and members. It was also the product of how the various political forces on the left had responded themselves to these conditions, with the role of individuals an active factor.

Although this was a conflict peculiar to PCS, it is of wider interest as a concrete case study from which lessons can be learned about how left sectarianism can damage a mass working-class organisation.

The term 'sectarianism' is bandied about so promiscuously that it is often reduced to a general term of abuse devoid of any real substance. But this 'destructive error', analysed by leading Marxist thinkers, including Lenin, is a phenomenon that every socialist union activist will experience.[1] In relation to events in PCS, the term describes the tendency for political groupings to place their own factional interests above those of the wider union organisation and by extension the working class itself.

If the main obstacle to defending attacks on workers' rights is right-wing class collaboration, then 'left' sectarianism is its distorted mirror image. When labour leaders find an accommodation with employers, the government and the state, they place this above the interests of their class in return for personal power and prestige. In some unions with well-established right-wing bureaucracies, political factions are banned on the pretext that they are divisive, disruptive and motivated by their own political agendas. The intended effect is to limit open, democratic discussion and to constrain the left. To maintain their partnership with employers, union bureaucrats need to limit the growth of socialist ideas, typically by a 'carrot and stick' approach – compliance and loyalty attract reward while militants are identified as troublemakers and managed, if necessary, by witch-hunts or other repressive measures.

Against this background, the left must find organisational solutions to undertake its work. For example, there is a long tradition of unity initiatives stretching back to the Minority Movement in the 1920s, these took the form of alliances of left-wing rank-and-file groups, shop stewards, combined committees and national trade union leaders. In many unions, left unity took the form of broad lefts on the united front principle, based on a democratically agreed socialist programme, with prominence given to the pressing material concerns of workers in that particular union or sector. They aimed to build alliances across the union movement, combining campaigning on pay, terms, conditions and rights with the wider issues affecting the working class; war, international solidarity, social and economic policy, equality, the fight against racism and fascism, and in doing so advocate for socialist ideas and the socialist transformation of society.

Socialists and communists are typically among the most dedicated and committed activists in carrying out basic union work, but this is not an end in itself. The workplace is where conflicts with employers arise and workers experience class struggle itself, including in its sharpest form – strike action. Some trade unionists join left organisations. Many more, through their experience in a dispute or campaign, will be drawn to socialism through the personal examples of principled leading activists. Every union representative, whether at the workplace or at national level, is a workers' leader and their fellow workers judge them on that basis, not just in relation to the strategy, tactics and ideas they advocate but also their actions, methods and conduct. There is no greater duty or responsibility a socialist or communist can take upon themselves than leading workers, whether in the workplace, in their union work or other arenas of class struggle.

Real ideological, strategic and tactical differences exist in all working-class mass organisations. Such differences cannot be dealt with by appeals to an abstract unity. Most people on the left understand the importance of the united front principles of solidarity and struggle. Of course, unity can only be built through overarching agreement. When differences of principle exist or mutual trust has broken down, then division is inevitable and perhaps even necessary. There are, however, clear instances where such acts of disunity are wholly unjustified, especially if based on factional and sectarian self-interest. Class-conscious workers easily see through the opportunism of right-wing leaders, but left sectarianism can produce a deep cynicism towards the left. It can also have profound effects on the union itself. Sectarian division affects every aspect of activity in a union and in its most extreme form may even derail campaigns, leading to lost ballots for industrial action. This is a positive asset for the employer.

There are many features of left sectarianism that undermine unity. One is the dogmatic insistence that one particular socialist or communist organisation can alone truly represent the interests of the working class. Sectarianism is also evident when tactical differences, even of a relatively minor character, are elevated to matters of principle. Another feature is when decision-making on policy issues or around strategy and tactics is made with a view to outmanoeuvring other left 'rivals'. When allies are regarded as the main obstacle, rather than the employer, the conscious manufacturing of differences starts to dominate debate.

Sectarianism in its most pathological form inevitably results in the abandonment of principled methods of work and in the placing of naked 'rule or ruin' factionalism above any consideration of solidarity. In a reverse image of right-wing opportunism, which sells any principle to seek a compromise, left sectarianism sanctifies factionalism in the distorted language of 'socialist principle'.

Accusations of sectarianism often arise from factional self-interest itself, but it is the most serious error to suggest sectarianism is simply 'in the eye of the beholder' – when the real article appears, it is recognisable, and in the worst cases, self-evidently so.

Early impact on PCS

As discussed in Chapter 4, Left Unity in PCS was possibly the largest socialist rank-and-file broad left in the trade union movement, with around 1,300 members at its peak. Bringing together Labour left-wingers with activists from the Socialist Party, the Communist Party, the SWP and other smaller groups, it helped the union to become an effective industrial and political force. It also played a decisive role in developing the even more broadly-based Democracy Alliance, the coalition from which the leadership of the union was drawn during some of the most difficult struggles with successive governments. The main factor holding together this broadly representative leadership was the understanding that their role was to implement the union's policies and programme, as democratically decided at the annual delegate conference. Given its strong activist base, Left Unity's commitment to a socialist alternative to austerity also gave PCS a deep and cohesive sense of purpose.

No matter how effective a leadership is, it is inevitable that criticism and disagreements will occur. Democratic scrutiny is imperative to ensure that any leadership, particularly one that claims socialist credentials, is held to account. The PCS tradition of open, and even passionate, debate ensured that this oversight was maintained to an uncommon degree. Settlements with employers were subject to the widest consultation amongst members, with the right to decide outcomes by membership ballot. This gave the national leadership a convincing mandate which enabled them to resist accusations of 'sell-out' from those for whom no compromise in any settlement was acceptable.

The average worker understands that compromise is not 'selling out' but securing what is possible while consolidating the unity that achieved concessions in the first place. What is more difficult to grasp is why workers who have never read Lenin understand these basics of class struggle, in fact of any struggle, but some revolutionaries who claim to be his political heirs seem incapable of doing so.

For example, when union members in the SWP refused to support the pensions deal in 2005, it was widely regarded as opportunism designed to 'out-left' the leadership for factional advantage. Their actions had the unintended consequence of strengthening the union's authority in the eyes of most members who were genuinely anxious about the pensions threat. More serious and damaging was the split engineered by the Independent Left grouping (formerly Socialist Caucus) in 2007.[2] By this point, the left alliance had been in power for only four years, and the union was campaigning on pay, jobs and privatisation. Memories of Moderate rule and their attempted coup were still fresh in people's minds. Although the right wing remained an organised electoral force with a base amongst the union's membership, Independent Left decided to stand candidates against the left in the national leadership and DWP group elections.

The group's history of divisive action had already alienated many members, which may explain why they had recently rebranded themselves as 'PCS Independent Left'. Ironically, it had begun life in the 1970s as a 'soft left' alternative opposed to 'extremism' at a time the state was increasingly concerned about trade union strength. Among the proliferation of tiny sectarian groups was also the pseudo-Trotskyist Alliance for Workers' Liberty – already deeply embedded in the Labour Party, with methods characterised by opportunist industrial strategies. As apologists for Western imperialism, they had developed a reputation for attacking the left, including the SWP, and the Communist Party in particular.

Socialist Caucus/Independent Left justified its divisive electoral move on the false premise that the union's leadership had 'sold out members', accusing Mark Serwotka of 'organising defeat', while insisting that only their strategy could stop government cuts. In fact, the only substantive point of difference was their advocacy of a form of 'paid selective action' in which the union leadership would pick 'key groups of workers' to take strike action on 85 per cent strike pay on behalf of the entire membership. This was precisely the same discredited policy pursued with little success under the right-wing rule of Barry Reamsbottom. The claim that their 'voices were not heard' by the rest of the left was also inaccurate – their strategy had been debated and rejected in every democratic forum in PCS, unofficial and official, and at every level. Their split from Left Unity was formalised by a 15–13 vote at their caucus. They were accused of 'consciously risking a revival of the union's right wing' with 'the only beneficiaries from this reckless and unprincipled behaviour [being] management, the Government and the union right wing'.[3]

Such divisiveness as the union mobilised against attacks on pay and conditions was the most indefensible act of sectarianism in the merged union's short history. That was until a public dispute began in 2018, in which the Socialist Party, formerly a stalwart of the united front within PCS, plunged the left into a most destructive but avoidable conflict that would have serious consequences for the ability of the union to fight for its members' interests.

Roots of the conflict

The ostensible cause of the conflict was a disagreement over whether Chris Baugh, PCS assistant general secretary since 2004 and a Socialist Party member, would have the support of the union left when the post came up for re-election in 2019. Socialist Party members in PCS, mainly low-paid activists, refused to support Baugh as Left Unity candidate and decided to back union president Janice Godrich, also a long-standing Socialist Party member; this was also the position of general secretary, Mark Serwotka. The Socialist Party's national leadership, however, refused to accept this. There followed a bitter battle within Left Unity that ultimately led to the Socialist Party splitting off under the banner of 'Broad Left Network'.

Beneath an apparent wrangle over who should stand for election lay issues of real substance. The formation of PCS had been the product of continuous, mainly isolated struggle, which had placed enormous strain on activists and members, especially those who were conscious of the wider political and industrial environment. Some activists found it difficult to transition from conditions of oppositional battles against the Moderates in the CPSA to the challenges and responsibilities of leadership in the merged union.

Left Unity had also changed. Its wide influence across the union almost guaranteed election to official lay positions. Inevitably, this resulted in some people joining who were more committed to personal advancement than to transforming society. Meanwhile, its most experienced leaders were serving simultaneously as national and group lay officers. This had some benefits, but the problem was sometimes a diminution of the type of workplace activism that had proved so effective in defeating the right wing. A concrete example was that the drive for campaigns, especially around industrial action, increasingly tended to come from national and group leaderships, albeit grounded in intensive democratic processes. Previously the impetus had been driven more from below, with many key union leaders gaining early experience as local strike leaders. Now the emphasis on national strategies meant that while regular large-scale strikes took place, local disputes, often the catalyst for escalatory action, became relatively less common.

Of further critical political importance was the developing role of the various socialist and communist organisations active in PCS and the wider movement. These had been at the very core of organising the left in the union from the late 1960s, but the years of reaction had tested many of them, not least in their relationship with the trade union movement. Some like the SWP and the Socialist Party, which had played a good role in educating and training militant activists and which had produced some exceptional class fighters, had retreated into competitive 'party prestige' politics, in the process abandoning theory in favour of frenetic activism entirely focused on 'party-building'. In UNISON, their 'rule or ruin' approach weakened efforts to realise the potential for a broad coalition of progressives and the left. Consequently, its skilled and ruthless union bureaucracy – closely tied with the Labour Party's right-wing apparatus – retained firm control.

A critical background factor across the public services and especially within the civil service was the enduring influence of Whitleyism. Habit and tradition had engendered an ideological commitment to this peculiar expression of class conciliation. Whitleyism became almost a shibboleth that existed above and separate from supposedly temporary trends such as the increasingly hostile management strategies employed by all governments since Thatcher. For such activists, Whitleyism constituted an objective natural order of industrial relations in the civil service that would be restored in time. The idea that negotiating skill was the key factor in bargaining had a tenacious hold, although the strongest weapon in the negotiator's arsenal was really a membership organised and prepared to fight. The collaborationist Whitley ethos was a substantial fetter in defending and advancing terms and conditions. Even amongst those who considered themselves socialists or revolutionaries, it had shaped a strand of thinking that prioritised dialogue with management over workplace organisation. The contradiction between class conciliation and militant trade unionism would become the dominant theme in the union's internal crisis.

If these were the political factors behind the PCS conflict, there was also a personal dimension. Individuals are not just bit-players at the mercy of impersonal political forces. Human beings operate in political, economic and social circumstances not of their own choosing, but they can exert decisive influence on events.[4] This was the case with several actors in these events, most notably Chris Baugh and the national leaders of the Socialist Party.

When the dispute first became public, Baugh and the Socialist Party's general secretary, Peter Taaffe, assistant general secretary, Hannah Sell and industrial organiser, Rob Williams, claimed that differences over Baugh's candidacy had come as a complete surprise to them. They presented them as stemming from a 'personality clash' between Baugh and Serwotka, whom they sought to portray as a capricious bureaucrat. Claims that had been made about Baugh's conduct were dismissed as 'character assassination'.

In fact, leading PCS activists like Janice Godrich had raised concerns over Baugh's conduct with senior members of the party, particularly including Taaffe, Sell and Williams, for more than a decade. The main issues had been Baugh's inconsistent orientation on industrial and political matters and his attitude to the PCS left lay leadership and his own Socialist Party comrades. Also problematic was his undermining of Serwotka, whom Taaffe had once extravagantly claimed was a 'main ally' in the trade union movement.

Baugh had fully participated in the collective decision-making structures of the union, including the NEC and senior officers' committees, as well as in unofficial structures like the PCS Socialist Party caucus and Left Unity. He had voted in favour of every single decision made within those structures over the years, without exception. Despite this, he had consistently attacked those same decisions through gossip, rumour and distortion, denouncing the leadership of which he was a part.

The most extensive efforts were made, particularly by Godrich, to counsel him about the negative impact of his conduct, including countless appeals to him to change his behaviour. Socialist Party leaders also repeatedly claimed that they disapproved of Baugh's actions, with Taaffe admonishing him on various occasions. The top priority for Godrich and others in the leadership, including Serwotka, had been to manage the situation, rather than risk a divisive public dispute.

Baugh's approach to industrial strategy was particularly problematic. Beyond minor tactical differences, these involved accusations of open capitulation to the methods of collaborationist trade unionism. There were several instances. In the middle of the first national membership ballot in 2004, called in response to Gordon Brown's job cuts announcement, Baugh had pleaded with Serwotka and senior policy officer John Macreadie, to halt the ballot on the grounds that the union could not risk losing it. This was rejected as it would have left the union's entire strategy in shreds, while demoralising the membership and encouraging further government attacks. During the 2007–8 pay campaign, he had similarly argued that PCS should not embark on its industrial action strategy as, 'we would be taking on the state', a new version of the right-wing argument that the opposition was too strong for strikes to work.

When a union takes industrial action against a government employer over terms and conditions, it does not necessarily imply a threat to the state, nor that the full force of the state would be employed against it. Under certain political conditions, industrial action may well assume such a character, as with the 1984–5 Miners' Strike, which was provoked then crushed by the Thatcher government using the full coercive machinery of the state, including the use of physical violence. In circumstances where these tactics were again likely to be employed in breaking a strike, any serious union leadership, in full consultation with members and activists, would consider all options based on the balance of forces, the potential for building and receiving solidarity from the wider movement and the working class generally. But to start from the self-defeating position that any strike would provoke such a response amounted to an argument for never taking serious industrial action.

Most concerningly, in 2013, during negotiations with the coalition government over redundancy protocols, Baugh proposed that PCS 'needed to show we can do deals' and that it should concede to Frances Maude's demand to waive the redundancy rights of workers in smaller workplaces. Finally, in another long-running dispute over privatisation at the National Gallery in 2015, Candy Udwin, one of the union's most prominent activists, was victimised and sacked. Baugh suggested at the union's national disputes committee that the strike should be wound up as management would refuse to settle, a proposition rejected by the rest of the committee; the dispute continued until Udwin's job was secured as part of a wider settlement.[5]

The common thread running through these episodes was Baugh's lack of confidence in the ability of members to fight and his skittish fear of confrontation with employers. Nor were these isolated concerns; his conduct and behaviour had implications on several levels, including for union democracy itself. When Serwotka, as returning officer, refused a demand from two Left Unity activists to overturn and rerun an election in the Metropolitan Police departmental group, in which there were no irregularities, Baugh advised and encouraged these activists to report Serwotka to the Commissioner for the Rights of Trade Union Members (CROTUM) – claiming it was 'a legitimate tactic to put pressure on him'. There is no objection in principle to a socialist making a referral to the CROTUM. When the union was under Moderate control, John McInally, at some considerable risk from threatened legal action by then general secretary Barry Reamsbottom, did just that and won access to the union's financial records. The Socialist Party fully supported this action on the basis that there was no issue of principle against using the legal system. Rather, it was a question of who was doing so, for what purpose, and in whose interest. But there is a world of difference between using the legal system to defend members' democratic rights against a corrupt right-wing leadership and threatening a socialist general secretary actually defending the union's democracy.

In addition, Baugh made the malicious claim that Serwotka was discriminating against full-time officers who were Socialist Party members. This was uncritically repeated by Taaffe, who described the failure of one full-time officer to receive the posting they wanted as an 'attack on the revolutionary party'. This was an accusation so serious that Godrich demanded evidence. None was forthcoming.

The issue of conduct in a union setting is not a shallow question of good manners or comradely relations. Maintaining the highest possible standards of integrity is essential in building trust with members. In 2010, Mark Serwotka had contracted a virus that almost led to his death, requiring him to use a battery-operated machine to keep his heart beating.[6] He won tremendous sympathy and great admiration as he returned to work and continued to lead the union under such difficult conditions. In 2016, he was admitted to Papworth Hospital to await a heart transplant. During this time Baugh resurrected an issue that he had raised intermittently over the years – the removal of the general secretary's powers, specifically over the allocation of staff. In this case, he argued that full-time resources should be moved from organising to bargaining, while the NEC, consisting of over forty annually elected lay officials, should take over staffing allocations.[7]

The suggestion was universally regarded as idiotic. Problems over staffing, especially in the years following the government's withdrawal of check-off, did exist, but were best resolved through discussion, compromise and agreement. His frivolous proposal was a caricature of ultra-leftist posturing, counterposing 'grassroots democracy' with 'union bureaucracy'. Godrich, Fran Heathcote and others argued that removing Serwotka's powers as he was undergoing a heart transplant would be an act of political insanity. Nevertheless, Baugh continued to push the matter in open defiance of the Left Unity conference, which had rejected the proposal, as had the Socialist Party itself.

Every ultra-left excess disguises betrayal in one form or the other. The issue over bargaining and organising resources exposed the real ideological forces represented by Baugh and those opposing his outlook – the chasm between those conditioned by Whitleyism, and those seeking to build a militant, democratic trade union. Bargaining and organising are complementary and interconnected processes whose effectiveness is contingent on the development of workplace strength. Baugh's opportunistic creation of a false antagonism in the union between the two was a manufactured difference. Incapable of understanding or adapting to the new hostile conditions within civil service workplaces, he represented the view that, despite all the evidence to the contrary, it was possible to negotiate a path out of conflict. This was a delusion that would inevitably end in concession bargaining and proposals – such as selling redundancy rights to 'do deals'. It was no coincidence that some of the most conservative forces within the union also supported him. Although formally opposed to such a collaborationist industrial viewpoint, the Socialist Party leadership also backed Baugh in a contortion explicable only in relation to the differences of method, principle and politics that would emerge later in full glare.

Rule or ruin

The leaders of the Socialist Party supported Baugh's bid for re-election in the full knowledge that the issue had already caused a public split in the PCS left. Their internal discussions give some insight into how they had become so divorced from the wider union context, displaying a personalised 'rule or ruin' sectarianism that prioritised the party's standing above all else. As Peter Taaffe had expressed it: 'I will tear the lot down before I give an inch to Serwotka'.

In these inner-party debates, Taaffe defended Baugh on the redundancy sell-out proposal, arguing it was part of 'a legitimate tactical discussion', while claiming that he could not remember details of his threat to report Serwotka to the Commissioner for the

Rights of Trade Union Members. His main political theme though, parroted by their full-time officials who constituted the party's National Committee, was to view it as a 'direct attack on the party'; he went on to insist that, 'the party would not allow Serwotka dictating to us, [as] nobody tells us what to do, and nobody tells us who our candidate can be', as it is 'a matter of prestige'. Meanwhile, Hannah Sell tried to provide an ideological basis for their actions declaring, 'what is in the interests of the party is in the interests of the working class'. This allowed for summary expulsions of Socialist Party members, including Godrich, who were branded as 'renegades' who had, 'placed themselves outside the party'. Their initial position that the dispute was merely a 'personality clash' had become so unconvincing that the leadership were now obliged to construct a 'Marxist' analysis, which relied on the false accusation that dissident members had 'capitulated to reformism, opportunism and the union bureaucracy'.

Taaffe had previously upbraided Baugh for using the term 'bureaucracy', to describe the PCS full-time structure, correctly preferring the term 'left officialdom'. In CPSA and PCS under the Moderates there had been no less than forty-six appointed Senior National Officers, the highest paid grade other than those elected to senior positions. This became a corrupting edifice entirely reliant on the grace and favour of the right-wing leadership. Under Serwotka's general secretaryship, this was reduced to seven. This process took time – a strategic decision was taken not to invite an expensive and time-consuming internal war, or risk expensive employment tribunals, but to transform the union's internal culture.

The elements that constituted the previous leadership's 'Praetorian Guard' found the new conditions uncongenial, and a new working environment emerged with full-time officials more accountable both to the national leadership and to lay officers in the departmental groups. Full-time officers were thenceforth largely recruited from among union activists, proven organisers and strike leaders. The conscious aim was to develop a culture in which full-timers and lay officials worked together to prioritise the implementation of conference policies, programmes and strategies, under the day-to-day direction of elected national and group leaderships, not as politically antagonistic forces. Building such a tradition and culture inevitably presented many problems, but thankfully few people assuming full-time positions exhibited the high-handedness, routinism, indolence and careerism of the professional bureaucrat.

Nevertheless, the 'bureaucracy' narrative would be increasingly deployed by the Socialist Party during the dispute. This, alongside Baugh's creation of a false antagonism between 'bargaining' and 'organising' constituted a reactionary attack on the PCS leadership's strategy of building union democracy and workplace strength, designed to deliver militant, participative campaigns, including effective industrial action. It also demonstrated the inevitable interconnection between sectarianism and opportunism. The Socialist Party's decision to publicly justify and defend Baugh was an effective denial of the party's militant traditions, but this was a secondary consideration when compared to the need to defeat the 'enemies of the party'.

It may appear quite baffling as to why the Socialist Party leadership could indulge Baugh's behaviour and outlook. But there is no mystery. The party, like other groupings who were unable to adapt to new conditions of struggle during the extended period of reaction, had abandoned Marxist theory and method in favour of a frenetic activism which led to distortions like its surrender to prestige politics.[8] As embodied in Taaffe's oft-repeated 'no-one tells us what to do' phrase, the status of the party came first, even if this meant a rewriting of history for factional advantage.

An article in August 2018, by Rob Williams and Hannah Sell entitled 'PCS: the real issues at stake' made the claim that Serwotka and the PCS leadership – which they forgot included Baugh at the time – were responsible for downplaying 'co-ordinated strike action against austerity' in the wake of the pensions sell-out of 2011. They had allegedly failed to make 'any serious attempt to create a "coalition of the willing"', beyond 'appeals to the TUC and bilateral discussion with some general secretaries'.[9]

None of these criticisms had been raised prior to Chris Baugh's candidacy. They also ran contrary to the public record which showed that the union had actually been the prime mover in calling for continued coordinated protest, including joint strike action. Indeed, the positive role of Serwotka and the PCS leadership in this respect had even been highlighted in a double centre page feature in *The Socialist* newspaper in 2016, which listed Williams as co-author.[10] The accusations were particularly egregious as it was the union's militant industrial response to the coalition government during the period that had brought down the wrath of Francis Maude. Many activists were incredulous that the Socialist Party seemed prepared to deny the contribution of their own activists, just to secure Baugh an elected union position. One Socialist Party dissident, Mark Baker, commented: 'For a so-called Marxist party to downplay and rubbish the role of workers and activists who stood up and fought in regard to pensions and other attacks, and bizarrely in the process trash their own record, demonstrates the madness of sectarianism'.

The Socialist Party's internal discussions also exposed the political concerns that really underpinned their decision to support Baugh. Taaffe and others claimed that, since both Serwotka and Jeremy Corbyn were 'reformists' and as 'betrayal was inherent in reformism', then a Corbyn-led Labour government would inevitably capitulate to pressure from the capitalists, while Serwotka would sell out PCS members and the working class. Given Serwotka's record, this was political slander rather than Marxist analysis. Behind this 'sellout before it happened' position, as it was satirically branded, lay the fact that the Socialist Party had been wrongfooted by the Corbyn phenomenon. It had never come to terms with his election as Labour leader, which not only contradicted its existing positions but also raised the question of how to build the party amid the Corbyn surge, which seemed to threaten their profile and relevance.

Reduced to the sidelines, incapable of orienting to the new political situation in a strategic manner, they now faced a revolt of their key activists in PCS, the only mass organisation in which they exercised any real influence. Moreover, a catastrophic split had taken place in their international body, the Committee for a Workers' International. Ironically, given their criticism of the PCS leadership, the instinctive response of Taaffe and other Socialist Party leaders was to assert their bureaucratic authority. This led to some very cynical manoeuvring, including the demand that the Socialist Party be admitted to the Corbyn-led Labour Party 'on a federal basis', though Taaffe admitted in internal party discussions that if they were allowed to affiliate it would be disastrous and would pose the greatest threat to holding the party together.[11]

During Baugh's candidacy, the allegation of bureaucratism further rebounded on the Socialist Party. It had always argued for the accountability, scrutiny and regular election of full-time officials in the movement, who were expected to abide by the 'worker's wage'. Now Taaffe argued that incumbent senior union officers should only be challenged if there was evidence of 'financial irregularity or inappropriate behaviour', effectively guaranteeing a 'job for life'. Revealingly, he repeatedly described the assistant general secretary post as 'Chris's job', as did Baugh himself. There could be no more bureaucratic formulation, it is the antithesis of genuine democratic accountability and scrutiny and an expression of arrogant self-entitlement. This was compounded by an open letter from Baugh's supporters to union activists stating:

> We think someone has to have behaved pretty badly to deserve being removed from a position, especially when that would also lose them their job. That could only be justified by them no longer supporting the policies of the left in the union, by laziness, incompetence or improper behaviour.

Demanding the regular election of full-time officials had been a key demand of the left, secured in PCS in the face of the strongest possible opposition from the right. Union elections subject candidates to the scrutiny and accountability of members, and in choosing its candidates, so too should the left. Rather than rely on the negative criterion that they have not been guilty of financial irregularity or inappropriate behaviour, the widest range of factors should be considered, including electability, conduct and, critically, industrial and political judgement.

This conflation of an elected senior national officer position with a 'job' from which the holder could be 'sacked' caused genuine anger amongst activists. When it transpired that Baugh did not even abide by the 'worker's wage', as the Socialist Party had implied, it only further exposed the hollowness of the party's allegations of bureaucratism.

Campaigning

The Socialist Party had announced its support for Baugh's re-election before Left Unity was able to organise its internal nomination process. In response, Janice Godrich also announced her candidacy, although, unlike her opponent, she stated she would abide by the decision of the Left Unity election. She was one of the most respected women activists in the movement and had led the union as president for seventeen years. Regarded as a role model, and not only for women activists, her principled commitment to the union and socialism won her many admirers, even among political opponents.

The tone of the Socialist Party's campaign in the run-up to the Left Unity election was set by the extraordinary threat from Taaffe and others that, as far as Godrich was concerned, 'we will put so much pressure on her we will force her to withdraw'. Bad as this was, their subsequent actions revealed how quickly sectarian methods could descend into open class betrayal, with serious consequences for union members. As noted in the preceding chapter, the PCS national pay ballot in July 2018 had narrowly failed to reach the threshold required for industrial action. A rerun ballot in March the following year promised a positive result as careful work had gone into developing workplace organisation in the intervening period. With only weeks to go, Baugh now used his NEC platform to openly reject the previously agreed PCS strategy. Instead, he proposed a 'disaggregated' ballot – holding departmental votes simultaneously – an option that had already been rejected.[12] If adopted, this would have sunk the legal national ballot and allowed the government to divide and rule by offering minimal concessions while avoiding settling the members' most pressing concern – pay.[13]

Baugh claimed to be merely presenting an 'alternative' which offered 'flexibility' and that 'differences are healthy'. Incapable of providing a coherent critique of the original national strategy, he resorted to the type of vacuous phraseology employed by right-wing bureaucrats to sow confusion and avoid strike action. This 'alternative' was another expression of his earlier defeatist postures. It was condemned as 'treacherous', not only because it would have meant the end of the national pay campaign, but also because it flew in the face of a democratic decision previously endorsed at every level of the union.

So shocked were Baugh's closest political allies that they initially distanced themselves from what was widely condemned as 'act of sabotage for electoral and factional advantage', but unforgivably, the Socialist Party continued to back him. The union would eventually miss the 50 per cent threshold in the second ballot, which permitted Baugh's supporters at the 2019 PCS annual conference to make pessimistic speeches, revelling in 'Serwotka's personal failure', which they hoped would provide the basis for a challenge against him in the election for the general secretary later that year.

The forces assembled behind Baugh's campaign to keep his 'job' were of various types; Socialist Party loyalists and allies naturally, but there were also those demoralised elements who hankered for the bargaining routines of the old Whitley system and who had turned inwards away from the new conditions of struggle. Many had only joined Left Unity after the defeat of the Moderates. The Socialist Party industrial organiser had emailed its members, urging them to sign up whoever they could for the upcoming election, including family and friends. It was unfortunately impossible to refuse membership to some of these applicants on the basis that they were 'non-political' or not even socialists. There was even an attempt to recruit people who Baugh himself had previously described as the 'last remnants of the Moderate group in PCS', but this was regarded as a step too far, and their applications were refused.

Although Janice Godrich went on to defeat Baugh by a considerable margin in the election, she withdrew her candidature shortly afterwards on the grounds of ill health. This caused considerable demoralisation amongst activists opposing the Socialist Party, and even a degree of trepidation. As one commented: 'If they could do that to Janice, what else would they be prepared to do to anyone else standing up to them?'.

Taking advantage of the situation, Baugh stood in a re-run Left Unity election in January 2019 against Stella Dennis, a Godrich supporter who was a full-time officer and former president of the DWP group. Typically, his supporters labelled her a bureaucrat, despite her distinguished record as a campaigning activist and strike leader.[14] Baugh won the rerun by eighteen votes. Although this meant that he was in effect the official Left Unity candidate, Mark Serwotka and many activists publicly endorsed the candidature of Lynn Henderson, the union's national officer for Scotland and Ireland, to stand in opposition to both Baugh and the Independent Left candidate, John Moloney.

Standing on a socialist programme entirely in line with Left Unity policy, Henderson ran a strong campaign from a standing start, especially in her performance in the members' debate. The election in May was won by Moloney due to the split in the Left Unity vote; Baugh took second place with only just over two hundred votes more than Henderson. Baugh's defeat was a crushing blow for the Socialist Party. Even up to the last, they were confident they would win, showing little awareness of how appalled many activists were by their recent behaviour.

Aftermath

The Socialist Party attempted to win the Left Unity nomination for the upcoming general secretary election in opposition to Serwotka, but they received little support for their candidate, Marion Lloyd, who then decided to withdraw, alleging 'undemocratic practices'.[15] Citing a 'centralisation of power' and a 'crisis of leadership', the Socialist Party then launched their own 'Broad Left Network' in June 2019, undermining the united front they had done so much to build.[16]

The role of the party and its sectarian rule or ruin prestige politics, which demonstrated their willingness to abandon any principle or employ any method to win a union position, had the most severely negative impact on the left and the union. Maintaining a united front of disparate parties, groups, trends and tendencies on the left requires compromise, discipline, a sense of political perspective and the prioritisation of the union members' interests and of the wider working-class over factional self-interest. Once such imperatives are discarded, the focus of the left on building a fighting democratic union with a united approach in delivering militant policies, programmes and strategies is deeply compromised.

Lloyd went on to stage a Broad Left Network challenge for the general secretaryship with Socialist Party backing, but her campaign illustrated the corrosive effects of sectarianism on left unity. The election in December coincided with the critical 2019 general election. The strategic priority for PCS was the return of a Corbyn-led Labour government, but in her election address, Lloyd attacked this political strategy, implying it had been cobbled together by Serwotka and the leadership alone, rather than having been approved through the union's democratic processes. Indeed, as a long-standing NEC member she had voted for the strategy at every single stage. She declared in her election address, distributed to all members:

Political independence: 'no' to Labour Party affiliation.
I am desperate to see the back of the Tories. I am a

socialist and believe a Corbyn government would improve our pay and conditions. But my opponents in this election have got it badly wrong by telling you to vote for all Labour candidates in England and Wales. We should not support MPs who have attacked our terms and conditions. Mark Serwotka has placed his personal loyalty to the Labour Party above members' wishes. I will ensure that we retain an independent political voice. I oppose Labour Party affiliation unlike my opponents.

This was a calculated appeal to the most conservative and anti-Corbyn elements of the PCS membership – the very social base on which the right wing's support had always rested. The call for selective support of Labour candidates conflicted with the position of virtually every socialist and communist in the movement – and with Socialist Party policy in every other union but PCS. During the 2017 general election, former Labour MP Dave Nellist, chair of TUSC, the Socialist Party's electoral front, had commented, '... defeating the Tory government would be seen as such a victory for Jeremy Corbyn it would inspire and give confidence to millions that a different society is possible'. If this was true in 2017, how much more so in 2019 when the full apparatus of the political establishment and the media was focused on eliminating Corbyn as a political threat? Losing even one Labour seat could mean the difference between a Corbyn or Johnson-led government, with all that implied for the working class. Commenting on the Labour conspirators against Corbyn, Unite general secretary Len McCluskey caustically remarked: 'Even the most demented sectarian on the left has not championed a Tory election victory to win an inner-party argument.'[17] But this was precisely what Lloyd and the Socialist Party were doing, a reckless act in the heat of a major class battle.

Serwotka won the general secretary election, for the fifth time, with 53.3 per cent of the vote, despite facing not only Lloyd but also the Independent Left candidate Bev Laidlaw.[18] In response, the Socialist Party finalised their split from Left Unity. At a conference in Manchester in January 2020, they met under the aegis of Broad Left Network to agree a programme and candidates for forthcoming elections as a first step in 'rebuilding the left in PCS'.[19] In reality, prestige politics reduces everything to political and personal spite, distorts and devalues everything and is incapable of producing unity and solidarity. Wholly subordinate to Taaffe's 'tear the lot down' mentality, their tactics became the type warned about by Lenin in his famous comment: 'Spitefulness plays the worst possible role in politics'.[20]

In March 2020, during the Covid-19 pandemic, PCS members at Jubilee House, a joint DWP-HMRC office in London, complained to the union that the Socialist Party was demonstrating a 'dangerous disregard' for health and safety by selling *The Socialist* outside their premises during lockdown. When Serwotka contacted Hannah Sell requesting that this should not be happening outside PCS-organised workplaces during the Covid emergency, she made the bizarre allegation that he was, 'suggesting that the socialist press should face greater restrictions than those placed on media that do not have the interests of workers at heart'. She went on to claim that the union's real aim was to shut down the workers' press and restrict workers' right to self-organise. Serwotka wrote again, underlining that it was PCS reps in Jubilee House who had expressed their concerns over the risk to members. Revealingly, the party complied this time, but only after publishing the correspondence on their website.[21]

During the massive strike wave that followed the pandemic, most unions pursued their own pay campaigns. The targeted action strategy of PCS put so much industrial pressure on the Tory government that they were forced to make significant concessions. The 2023/24 pay award for non-senior civil service grades was the biggest pay rise in over 20 years, and one of the biggest pay rises achieved during the strikes. This did not win back all that had been lost over the decades of pay freezes and restraint, but the fact that the government was forced into national negotiations was of considerable significance for future struggles. The pay deal was accepted by the vast majority of members on the recommendation of the national leadership.

Throughout the pay campaign, the Broad Left Network had attacked the union more than the employer. It opposed the deal, offering no alternative strategy other than action without strike pay, which the membership had already rejected. The distance between Broad Left Network and their own rank-and-file on this issue could not have been clearer. Of the 363 branches voting, 261 (72 per cent of the total, representing 75 per cent of members) voted by a margin of 90 per cent or more to accept the deal; only three branches representing 1,102 members in total (including 1,003 in one branch) voted No. In the branch in Marion Lloyd's area members voted Yes by over two to one. Not one Socialist Party activist won a No vote in their own branch.

Challenges, both old and new

On Mark Serwotka's retirement in January 2024, Left Unity's Fran Heathcote, a dedicated and committed union organiser and Janice Godrich's successor as union president, defeated a challenge from Marion Lloyd, who had stood as part of an alliance with the same Independent Left grouping that the Socialist Party had condemned for decades.

It appears that sectarian division has produced a seemingly irreconcilable element of instability within the PCS left wing and across the union more generally. This potentially creates the conditions for a possible re-emergence of an organised right-wing force of the type defeated more than 20 years before. As the real issues behind the 2018 dispute become obscured with the passage of time, it may seem to many members that the conflict between Left Unity and the Socialist Party's new alliance is nothing more than a factional squabble for bureaucratic power. Nothing could be further from the truth, as the analysis outlined above demonstrates.

The socialist principles of the original Broad Left and Left Unity were grounded in a powerful belief: the left may have to fight the right wing and deal with internal divisions, but when it comes to campaigning, the defence of members' interests and raising awareness of the structural inequalities rooted in capitalism must come first. It is only by making this a reality that a united left can be rebuilt in PCS.

The Starmer government has launched an attack on public services, with the civil service again first in the firing line. In these circumstances, members will not tolerate seemingly arcane internal disputes. The road to the creation of a new united front may be a hard one, but any left organisation operating within the union that sets its face against such a task will at best appear irrelevant, or at worst become a poisonous force furthering reaction rather than the cause of the working class.

Despite a loss of authority and legitimacy, Britain's ruling elite still pursues its strategy of cuts, privatisation and austerity. Their system has entered a period of irreversible decline with multiple crises in which the public services will remain under constant attack. Public sector workers and the wider working class will resist, and the role of the left in PCS remains to provide militant leadership, ensuring that resistance is organised at every level, while building solidarity in the broadest sense.

The story of how the left came to win the PCS leadership and went on to challenge successive governments on austerity holds many valuable lessons. Understanding how sectarian divisions threatened these achievements is of equal significance for left activists, in whatever mass working-class organisation they operate.

....

Notes & References

1. V.I. Lenin, '"Left-wing" Communism: an Infantile Disorder', *Selected Works*, Progress Publishers, Moscow, 1968, pp.512–585.

2. PCS Independent Left, NEC Elections Bulletins 1 and 2, 2007.

3. 'Socialist Caucus - the Politics of Betrayal, Despair and Cynicism', Left Unity leaflet, 2007.

4. K. Marx, *The Eighteenth Brumaire of Louis Bonaparte*, George Allen & Unwin Ltd, London, 1926, p.23; GV Plekhanov, *The Role of the Individual in History*, International Publishers, New York, 1940.

5. *Art History News*, 2 October 2015; author's contemporaneous note.

6. *The Guardian*, 2 September 2010.

7. Author's contemporaneous note.

8. J. McInally, 'A problem of prestige; the crisis within the Committee for a Workers' International (CWI)', *In Defence of Marxism*, August 2019.

9. *The Socialist*, 20 August 2018.

10. *The Socialist*, 23 November 2016.

11. *The Socialist*, 19 September 2018.

12. Author's contemporaneous note.

13. McInally, 'A problem of prestige'.

14. *The Socialist*, 9 January 2019.

15. 'Marion Lloyd Confirms Withdrawal from LU GS Nomination Process', PCS Broad Left Network Newsletter, July 2019.

16. 'Broad Left Network Launch Statement', PCS Broad Left Network Newsletter, June 2019.

17. *The Independent*, 15 April 2020.

18. *Morning Star*, 13 December 2019.

19. *The Socialist*, 15 January 2020.

20. Quoted in *Kommunist*, June 1956

21. See, *The Socialist*, 27 April 2020.

12. Looking forward – collaboration or militant struggle?

Global crises and Starmer's Britain

This concluding chapter presents a conditional perspective on some of the key challenges facing Britain's wider trade union movement. It is intended as a contribution to debate for the socialist and communist left, especially for those active in the trade union movement.

Elected in July 2024, Sir Keir Starmer's Labour government is committed to maintaining the anti-working-class policies that have been at the heart of over four decades of reaction. Reforms of any significance are entirely ruled out. Simply defending what remains of the gains of past generations will require determined struggle. Those who predicted from the very beginning that the new government would be one of crisis have been proved correct. Although having one of the biggest majorities in British parliamentary history, its victory was achieved with the lowest voter share ever. Popular support for Starmer's government is now wafer-thin. The previous Tory government was universally despised but within months of assuming office, its replacement has scored even worse in the opinion polls. Despite its huge parliamentary majority, Labour could well be defeated at the next general election.

Starmer's attempts to position himself as an international power broker between President Trump and the EU leaders have been exposed as vacuous posturing. Neither he nor his government will escape the gathering crisis and the parlous state of Britain's economy. Already the result is rising discontent and resistance. The electoral implosion of the Tory Party, previously so adaptable as an electoral force, is a striking testament to a world where instability and multiple crises are the new normal.

There is a profound split in the ruling class compounded by the re-election of Trump. The 2008 crash marked the effective end of neoliberal globalism, but political responses always lag behind economic reality. Protectionism did not begin with Trump, but it developed incrementally following the 2008 crash. Trump's latest policies merely represent a qualitative intensification of this process. Europe's political elites, including those of Britain, have nevertheless remained largely committed to the globalist project. Having deindustrialised their economies in favour of finance capital and having pursued imperialist adventures, they are now unprepared for the new realities. They are struggling to respond to Trump's attempts to maintain the USA's global economic and political hegemony in the face of economic decline and geopolitical challenges. We are seeing the end of a unipolar 'rules-based order' and a return to open competition between major imperialist blocs in which national interests come above all else. This will have the most profound consequences for the cohesion of the EU. Even more so for Britain, since it is positioned between the crisis-ridden imperial blocs, it will be particularly vulnerable as American and European corporations compete to divide the spoils.

In this context, a compliant Labour government will attempt the further privatisation of the NHS and other parts of the welfare state in the interests of US capital, with which Britain's own financialised economy is already deeply integrated. Heightened economic and political instability, supercharged by inter-imperialist conflict, has brought intensified attacks on the working class across the West. Ruling elites seek to further divide workers through chauvinism and militarism. As a result, defence spending is set to rise exponentially at the cost of public services, with welfare the main target. Neoliberalism has failed to resolve capitalism's inherent contradictions, nor will Trumpian economic and political nationalism do so. Since the 2008 crash, the prevailing order has precariously rested on a mountain of fictitious capital and ever-increasing debt. The question is not will there be another crash, but when and how destructive.

Both neoliberal globalists and protectionist nationalists agree on one thing. Not only must the historic transfer of wealth and power from the working class be maintained, but it must also be concentrated in fewer and fewer hands. This underpins the three principal imperatives of Starmer's government. These are:

- Intensification of the cuts and privatisation in the interests of capital.
- Unwavering support for US imperialism.
- An authoritarianism beyond what we have seen from modern governments.

The Labour Party and the trade unions

This may be a period of crisis for the ruling class and its government, but so too it is for the trade union movement. How it responds to issues such as welfare cuts, protectionism, war and growing repression will define whether it is able to defend workers' interests. Is the movement capable of building industrial and political resistance? Will it be an advocate for a socialist alternative to capitalist barbarism, want and inequality?

Accelerating deindustrialisation largely explains why union membership has halved since the 1980s. A subjective factor worsening this decline has been the collaborationist 'strategies' pursued by most union leaders. Class collaboration is the main fetter on the working class's ability to defend even its most basic rights. The refusal to recognise the realities of heightened class war has led to a spiral of decline and marginalisation. Starmer's government seeks to continue Blair and Brown's partnership strategies with compliant union leaders. This is on the firm understanding that they police their members, hold down expectations and never dare organise serious campaigns to oppose cuts in living standards. Starmer correctly calculates that if the organised labour movement can be held in check, then he will have a free hand to wage war on the disabled, sick, unemployed and all of those on state benefits. Even the meagre pre-election commitments made to the trade unions have been diluted under pressure from the rich. Commitments to guarantee stronger employment rights have been whittled away as a result of caveats and demands from employers. They will now be virtually worthless in practice. Labour's promises on employment rights were used to justify the benefits of continued affiliation to the party. The very limited concessions that remain will not seriously shift the workplace balance of power.

Labour's belief that artificial intelligence and other technologies will revolutionise public sector delivery is more likely to result in chaos on a greater and more dangerous scale than even Brown's huge cuts programme.[1] Cutting costs and 'waste' to secure 'value for taxpayers' money' will be the mantra of the profiteers tasked to deliver new technology. Inevitably, as in the past, it will be ill-considered, badly planned and ultimately ineffective. The consequences for those dependent on a whole range of public services, not just benefits, but justice, transport and the environment will be severe.

For many decades, wage restraint in the public sector has greatly reduced workers' living standards. The effect, as always, has been to demoralise workers, despite some fierce resistance and fightbacks over the years, creating the conditions in which cuts, closures and privatisation can be more readily achieved. There will be no respite under Labour; public sector pay will be held down just as it was under previous governments. But there is a limit. The 2022–3 strike wave was not, as politicians and even some union leaders hoped, a unique event in which limited concessions brought an extended period of industrial peace.[2] The relatively benign economic conditions before the 2008 crash, which allowed compliant union leaderships to keep members' grievances in check, no longer exist. Ultimately, every worker expects their union to protect living standards and conditions. With little on offer from Labour, union leaders will now come under stronger pressure to deliver. The biggest danger to Labour is a coordinated fightback by the unions, a threat capable of both encouraging and unifying resistance and dissent across society.

A real contradiction is developing between what the general mass of the population and the government consider the duties and responsibilities of the state to be. People expect the state to provide those services that make for a civilised way of life; support for a national health service free at the point of need is the best example of this. Although the findings of studies like those by Channel 4 of the views of so-called Gen Z (13- to 27-year-olds) should be treated cautiously, they are still worthy of consideration as they reveal opportunities for both left and right. 52 per cent thought, 'the UK would be a better place if a strong leader was in charge who does not have to bother with parliament and elections', with 27 per cent believing that, 'the entire way our society is organised must be radically changed through revolution'.[3] Clearly economic, political and social instability is politicising people who know something is badly wrong but have no clear idea of how to remedy it. The question for the trade union movement is this: who will win the support and confidence of not just this demographic, but also the growing disaffected population of all ages. A failure to respond to the desire for something better will only strengthen reactionary forces, enabling them to fill the vacuum left by the absence of a clear socialist alternative. One obvious expression is the Reform UK breakthrough. If the trade union movement, which remains the most potentially powerful unifying force of the working class, proves incapable of mounting effective resistance to the ongoing onslaught on their members' living standards and security, workers will look elsewhere.

Trade unions and their leaders face a stark choice: acquiesce with the oligarchs and 'liberal democratic' politicians, or defend working-class interests by fighting for an alternative. Bureaucracy and class collaboration inevitably grow in trade unions during periods of reaction. Union bureaucracies extend far beyond the full-time cadre. In some unions there exist extensive and highly developed lay bureaucracies, whose self-interest can become indistinguishable from that of both right and left-reformist leaderships. As noted in Chapter 1, these relationships often produce an outlook in union representatives that is more closely tied to the central bureaucracy's priorities than to those of their fellow workers. The 'union room' activist, comfortable with 'personal cases' and partnership working can be as strong a force for collaboration as the hardened full-time bureaucrat. In some unions certain reps receive so-called 'honoraria' for their roles; this can involve quite considerable monetary sums over and above legitimate expenses. The result is financial dependency and an impetus to avoid conflict with both employers and incumbent union leaderships. Taking up positions in the union and spending more time on committees can divorce activists from the workplace. It can also block the progression of new members, not just militants but also frequently women. And while retired members can play a very useful and important role in developing activists and other union work, some unions allow them to hold on to positions long after they have left the workplace. The now ubiquitous use of electronic communication can also create a situation in which the 'union room' is disconnected from members – nothing can effectively replace face-to-face communication in union organising. All this frequently leads to low levels of activity among the general membership. Unions can only build effectively by focusing on building in the workplaces and developing effective reps and activists. This is a necessity, not an option.

Few union leaders or activists disagree with the principle of the 'organising union'; but this is often disconnected from a socialist political understanding that the purpose of organisation is to transform each workplace into a bastion of militant unionism. The bureaucratic method approaches organising as an abstract concept, perceived almost as a technical matter. Many books have been written on the subject, with some authors achieving a guru-like status. It is inaccurate to suggest that all these writers ignore the political dimension and concentrate exclusively on recruitment techniques. But it is also true that such issues are often relegated to optional status in union discussions and courses, if considered at all. New activists are usually eager to learn about the movement's industrial and political history, but it is in the interest of collaborationist bureaucracies to ensure they do not acquire more than a routine trade union consciousness.

The main obstacle holding back the development of fighting trade unions is not primarily organisational but political. It is the task of militants in each union to tackle this.

Coordinated demands and campaigning

In terms of the tasks confronting the trade union movement and its leaders, the gap between what is and what necessity demands has never been wider. Without effective campaigning, unions will retreat and contract. The decline in collective bargaining from 82 per cent in 1979 to around 20 per cent in 2025 is largely explained by the failure of union leaderships to uphold our class interests during the intervening decades. This will only be reversed by coordinated campaigning, including joint industrial action. Under membership pressure, left reformist leaders may well be pushed towards a militant response in the coming period. But if such militancy simply means the continuation of isolated struggles, it will become clear that those leaders cannot move far beyond established collaborationism. The recent uncoordinated strike wave may have won certain concessions of a very temporary nature in specific sectors, but such strategies are utterly incapable of halting the general assault on our class. This is not to suggest such struggles are wasteful – no struggle is – but they are simply inadequate to the scale of the crisis facing unions and their members.

Despite the scale of attacks on the public sector, it remains the strongest area for the trade union movement. Significantly, it is also one that most closely interconnects with the lives of the working class, who rely on the services it provides. A strategy to challenge the assault on our class must be expressed through simple concrete demands that workers see as affecting both their working and everyday lives. To win support for such bread-and-butter claims, these must be linked to ones of a wider political nature to build the greatest solidarity. The issue of what common demands should be raised in the workplaces is central for socialists and communists. In other words, how do we go beyond handwringing, to organising the class as a whole.

And there is no shortage of pressing material demands, including, at minimum, if not exclusively:

- Defend and improve living standards.

- Oppose all cuts and privatisation.

- End austerity and tackle endemic inequality.

- A nationally coordinated council house building strategy.

- Nationalisation of all the major utilities.

- A fair and equitable welfare system based on principles of universality.

- Opposition to racism and fascism.

- Repeal of all anti-union laws and repressive legislation.

- Oppose war and all imperialist wars and interventions.

- A national plan to tackle climate change.

- Nationalisation of the banking and finance industry.

Campaigning against the coalition government's austerity assault, unions and campaign groups came together in the People's Assembly Against Austerity. This demonstrated the potential to organise beyond the unions themselves and build wider support around common demands. Out of opposition to the 2003 Iraq invasion, a parallel mobilisation against war and militarism, and for defence spending to be redirected into socially useful services has developed. This has once again taken on a mass character with current demonstrations against Israel's genocide in Palestine. The movement for action on climate change may develop along similar lines, but if the trade unions do not seriously raise concrete demands for a just transition protecting jobs and communities, there is also potential for division and isolation.

In contrast, there are those on the left who dismiss a concentration on such basic demands as 'economism'. They should perhaps spend more time talking to workers to understand their chief concerns, worries and aspirations. It is the task of socialists and communists to raise such demands uncompromisingly in their unions since they remain the only organised forum where this can be done. Many workers will draw the conclusion that their demands are worth fighting for; many will go on to grasp the nature of the profit system and why it should be challenged politically as well as industrially.

Long experience tells us that reformist leaders will find a multitude of reasons why the movement cannot take such a course. They will plead for a 'rational' approach and demand that socialists and communists 'live in the real world'. These 'realists' must be challenged and exposed at every opportunity and pressed on the consequences for workers if they do nothing. The Labour government will try to neutralise any potential opposition by accommodating compliant union leaders where it can. At the same time, it will try to isolate or even smash unions prepared to fight. Whilst bemoaning anti-union laws, reformist bureaucrats and elected leaders will do little to resist them. Every effort will be employed to depress activity and stop strikes, including distracting reps with tokenistic 'equality' campaigns that actually undermine real action to achieve equality. But with little or nothing to offer in terms of concessions, the tolerance of union members will wear thin, and provide the driving force for potential militancy, if effectively galvanised by the left.

Marketing-style recruitment can raise membership on a short-term basis, but on its own, it is incapable of strengthening workplace unionism – principally because this model places little or no importance on finding and developing reps. In such an environment, the targeting of union activists, usually over spurious and concocted 'disciplinary' issues, will be used to silence dissent and suppress militancy when all else fails.

Repression – the state and the unions

Starmer has largely succeeded in crushing dissent from the left within the Labour Party itself; discontent from Labour MPs over welfare legislation is driven more from fear that they will lose their seats and careers. It would be wrong to focus too intently on the personality of the current prime minister. While he is a particularly repellent example of the British political class, with strong links to the state security forces, any successors too will be entirely loyal to the prevailing consensus on enforcing the race to the bottom, imperialism abroad and repression at home. In times of crisis and instability, a principal strategic goal of the ruling class is to bring union leaders onside and cleave them ever closer to the interests of the state. This necessitates waging a war on the left and on socialist ideas generally.

The Labour government has shown no hesitation in using its powers to limit resistance, whether from the trade union movement or from the climate crisis and anti-war movements. This raises the issue of how the campaign for trade union freedom is linked to other movements. In the sharpest conflicts, especially in relation to imperialism, union leaders are forced to take sides. When they either take no action or worse, capitulate, the consequences are not just division but far more dangerous. They act as a spur to reaction itself.

Britain already has some of the most repressive public order and trade union legislation in Western liberal democracies. Labour now intends to strengthen the Tories' Public Order Act. With endemic instability, the loss of legitimacy and authority inevitably leaves the state with few options but to silence dissent. Starmer's role in attacking the pro-Palestine movement provides a clear warning as to how the state will act against any serious resistance. Revulsion at Israel's genocide in Gaza and its enablement by the USA and Britain has prompted numerous mass demonstrations since 2023. These peaceful expressions of opposition, jointly organised by the Palestine Solidarity Committee, Stop the War and many other organisations, have been systematically denounced by both Tory and Labour governments. In particular, the demonstration on 18 January 2025 was subjected to the most provocative harassment by the police. Chief steward Chris Nineham – whose record in organising peaceful demonstrations goes back decades – was violently arrested; and along with Ben Jamal of PSC and others, including an 87-year-old Holocaust survivor, Stephen Kapos, a former National Education Union (NEU) NEC member Alex Kenny and CND secretary Sophie Bolt, was subsequently charged under the Public Order Act. In a very serious development, MPs Jeremy Corbyn and John McDonnell were also interviewed under caution by the Metropolitan Police and, despite opposition to such repressive measures, the Labour government, fully supported by the state apparatus, has now banned the protest group Palestine Action under anti-terrorism legislation.[4]

This is a development with the most serious implications for all protest groups, as the government and state are seeking to conflate legitimate protest with terrorism. Inevitably, the labour and trade union movement itself will be targeted at some point, most likely on the basis that industrial action in the public services represents a threat to 'national security'. It was very encouraging that 22 union general secretaries signed a statement in defence of the right to protest in the wake of these events, including PCS general secretary, Fran Heathcote and TUC general secretary, Paul Nowak.[5] Pressure must be applied to ensure others follow.

The *Morning Star*'s Andrew Murray summed up the reason why the government, and no doubt Starmer himself, demanded such a use of force against peaceful demonstrators: 'They have done so because of the sustained scale and anger of the demonstrations. And because they know they have lost public opinion on this issue by an overwhelming margin'.[6] Incapable of convincing the majority in society on a key issue of political concern, the government has no reliable method of silencing criticism other than bringing into play the full power of the state, including the use of violent police repression, the legal system and a compliant media.

Instability has created conditions in which mass resistance

and dissent will arise, not least over issues apparently unrelated to the day-to-day concerns of workers. Some union leaders have essentially argued that questions of war and repression are not trade union issues. This goes straight to the heart of what unions are for. The government aims to pull union leaders ever closer to the state and its interconnected corporate and imperial interests. But if trade unions leaders refuse to condemn genocide, many workers will reasonably ask, what precisely are they prepared to speak out against? A young woman protestor was asked by a television reporter why she was on the Palestine demonstration against the genocide simply said: 'If they can do it to them, they can do it to us'. This comment is a profound expression of how class consciousness develops, especially among youth. War and oppression, even thousands of miles away, are a class issue. And the enemy is at home.

As well as leading the struggle on basic trade union questions, an unhesitant solidarity with the victims of imperialism is the ground upon which the trade unions must stand if they are to appeal to the millions searching for a way to build a better world. But the opposite is also true. Capitulation to chauvinism and warmongering will lead many to recoil if unions seem to stand with the oppressor.

The ruling class and the government now demand increases in defence spending that can only be delivered by cuts in services and living standards. To defend such increases, as some major unions and the TUC itself have done, requires union leaders to uncritically regurgitate the militaristic rhetoric of politicians. They may claim that increased defence spending is beneficial for members' jobs, but this is a direct act of collaboration with the capitalist class, the state and imperialism. It is directly inimical to the interests of both the victims of oppression and workers. Defence expenditure creates few jobs compared to investment in useful production and services. In the final analysis, defence industry workers themselves cannot remain insulated from the disastrous consequences of cuts on their communities and from the effects of war itself.

There is no fixed barrier between the industrial issues that concern workers, and questions of war and oppression. The new period of great power competition, exacerbated by tariffs, will inevitably result in war, just as such antagonisms caused the first and second world wars. As the battlelines of class antagonisms and interests are laid bare, the fundamental question workers will ask of their union leaders is this: whose side are you on, the arms manufacturers and the warmongers, or ours?

There is now an almost universal distrust of traditional political parties that offer nothing but austerity in one form or another. Workers increasingly view the government and much of the state apparatus as entirely lacking in legitimacy. An uncontainable reservoir of rage is developing among the working class that will find expression in one form or another.

As governments in the liberal democracies haemorrhage authority, increasingly, they will turn to state repression to maintain control and retain power in the interests of capital.

Liberal democracy and reaction

It is a measure of capitalism's irrevocable decline that liberal democracy is incapable of confronting, let alone resolving, the many challenges facing humanity, including some of an existential nature like climate change. This has the most serious implications for Britain's major political parties, including the nationalist ones. If governments are perceived by most people to be 'all the same', if their policies cannot be altered through the ballot box, and if they refuse to put the interests of the people above profiteers, then many workers will draw the conclusion that voting is pointless, or turn to right-wing opportunists of the Farage stripe.

With no clear socialist alternative on offer, the increasingly powerful nationalist wing of the ruling class exemplified by the right-wing 'anti-elite, anti-deep state' populism of Trump and Farage's Reform UK present themselves as alternatives. The conspiracist idea of the so-called deep state has gained considerable purchase precisely due to the unbridgeable chasm between liberal democracy's claim to be based on the will of the people and the reality – the rule of unelected corporate elites whose aims are dutifully enacted by whatever government holds power.

Liberal democracy has been a highly successful method of governance and political control in the more advanced Western capitalist countries. At the height of the Cold War in 1947, Winston Churchill said: 'Many forms of government have been tried in this world of sin and woe. No one pretends democracy is perfect or all-wise. Indeed, it has been said that democracy is the worst form of government except for those other forms that have been tried from time to time'. Churchill's defence of liberal democracy is purposefully conditional; if it is incapable of defending the hegemony of private property, then other methods of governance and control must be considered. History shows that when profit is under threat, the sanctity of 'democratic values' is placed to one side in favour of open repression and violence. The overthrow of the democratically elected Chilean government in 1973 is one of the most notable instances.

Liberal democracy is the cheapest form of governance, as it usually does not require the same enormous expenditure on policing the general population as dictatorships. Even so, all democracies have been consistent in focusing considerable state resources on combating the 'enemy within', whether this be defined as socialists, communists, trade unionists, or in the current period, climate change and Palestine solidarity activists.

Liberalism in its essential form extols the rights of the individual, freedom of speech, the right to property, religious tolerance and equality. These were the ideological and political expression of the demands raised by revolutionary progenitors of capitalism in their struggle against the forces of absolutism. These 'ideals' often coincided with demands from the early workers' movement. The contradiction between these high-minded principles and their practical application was revealed decisively in the class struggles that followed. A central tenet of liberalism is that the state should never encroach on individual human rights and personal liberty, but should instead stand above politics and class antagonisms. This was exposed as a sham when the new working class sought to secure political and industrial rights. The liberals stood foursquare with the capitalist class against the masses and did not hesitate to use state power to crush them.

The individual right to own private property and extract profit, rent and interest remains the key ideological justification for capitalist exploitation, imperialism and the neocolonialism that flows from it. Any notion that the collective rights of the vast majority in society outweigh the freedom of the ruling class to exploit workers is an anathema to the liberal. When class struggles intensify during strikes or mass protests, liberals step forward to become the most steadfast defenders of the status quo. In today's disorientating period of reaction and multiple crises, liberalism is a qualitatively more destructive influence than at any other time in history, both in Britain and across the Western capitalist world.

Liberal ideology is interconnected with the ubiquitous tendency of reformism within the labour and trade union movement. Reformism developed from a material and pragmatic reality that from the super-profits generated from the empire, it was possible to extract concessions from the capitalist class, if always on the basis of struggle. There are two things that explain the continuing influence of liberalism in our movement, one general and the other specific. First, it is the ideology of the ruling class, nurtured and enforced through the entire apparatus of the state, and the institutions and culture of society. It develops a tenacious hold on consciousness – as Marx commented succinctly: 'The ideas of the ruling class are in every epoch the ruling ideas'.[7] Second, for the labour movement, liberal ideology inevitably underpins the view that reforms and concessions can be won on a permanent basis under capitalism. Liberal ideas like human rights seem indistinguishable from the demands raised by trade unionists, while liberal democracy itself, for all its faults, still seems to have the potential to advance workers' interests. What reformism cannot see though is that liberalism's adherence to its stated values remains wholly contingent on the ruling class *ruling*. If this is in any way threatened, liberal freedoms give way to restrictions and ultimately coercion.

As we witness capitalism's deepening degeneration, liberal democracy's progressive elements are systematically stripped away as multiple crises leave no option but to enforce compliance. Features that liberalism may once have rested upon, and which reflected the working class's own interests, are now rapidly turning into their opposite. It is an irony of the current political reality that it is socialists and communists who must now defend 'liberal' values like free speech, freedom of assembly and so on in the face of growing authoritarianism.

Whilst rejecting and exposing liberalism, the left will be obliged to defend these now threatened freedoms. As it opposes authoritarian liberalism, the left must be the strongest advocates for democracy, including demands for proportional representation, local and devolved democracy, and the right to national self-determination. Ultimately, these correspond to the wider interests of the working class in promoting a socialist alternative.

In attracting workers to a united front, socialists and communists must focus their energies on those yet to be won to their ideas. In this context, the trade unions and the workplaces where they organise, rather than committee meetings, offer the best opportunities to build militancy, alongside increasing campaigning work in the communities.

The left must also step away from 'left-liberal' echo chambers, those opinion-formers, journalists and social media personalities who, as they have always done, play the most parasitical role and will always betray working-class interests. We saw this with Corbyn and now with the Palestinian solidarity movement. This is not to suggest that we do not work with others to oppose fascism and racism, and the intensifying assaults on the welfare state. What it does mean is that socialists and communists are not led by the nose by such people, as has too often happened in the past. Instead, the left must campaign with a clear independent position and voice, and with clear socialist demands which fundamentally challenge the ruling order.

To do so, we need socialists and communists who are prepared to work consistently in the unions and win the confidence of the workers they seek to represent; and who become real militant workers' leaders presenting an independent class position stripped of liberal and reformist cant. It is these activists who must be heard if we are to build confidence in the ideas of solidarity, struggle and socialism. However, there are also powerful new liberal ideological tendencies that, if not defeated, will prove stubborn barriers to the re-emergence of class politics.

Identity politics

Every extended period of reaction brings economic, political and social attacks on the working class. It is accompanied by ideological offensives aimed at undermining and defeating any idea of class struggle and, of course, attacking Marxism. These ideological offensives are invariably based on new iterations of idealism; the concept that reality is constructed on the basis of ideas independent of material reality itself. Initially popularised by liberal academics, such ideologies are now deployed with increasing stridency to undercut and discredit the materialist analysis of history and society central to Marxism. This is not some abstract intellectual discussion, it has very real consequences for the labour and trade union movement and any thought of an advance towards socialism.

It is in this context that concepts such as 'self-identification' are seized upon by reformists, liberals and downright reactionaries as a diversion from unified class struggle. Where has the determined fight been from the TUC and many unions to overturn anti-trade union laws? Where has been the concerted resistance to the ruling class stripping away workers' civil rights as they defend their own interests?

The capitalist elite is not of a wholly homogeneous nature. There are liberal and conservative wings. The former attempts to manage society with a progressive face through the language of equality.

The latter, more honestly, sees little need for such subterfuge. From the liberals though, has come the near all-pervading ideology of identity politics. It aims to bamboozle workers with false ideas that achieving social justice can be divorced from any notion of class struggle and ultimately the socialist transformation of society. It takes root with ease in the liberal and reformist collaborationism that still dominates the trade union movement. Identity politics elevates the individual above all else. It offers no opposition to capitalism and is, in fact, a product of its neoliberal form. Indeed, it seeks to provide it with an ideological underpinning through its hyper-individualism. Identity politics does not unite, rather, it separates workers from what should be their common interests. Such ideas have been seized on by some right-wingers who denounce them as 'cultural Marxism'. There is no such thing of course, it is a contradiction in terms. But the right wing is given free rein to ply such distortions by left liberals, some of whom even 'identify' as communists and Marxists but are the most zealous culture warriors in their promotion of identity politics.

Socialists and communists are opposed to all forms of discrimination and oppression. Every single gain for under-represented or oppressed groups in society, including for women who make up its majority, has been won by campaigns on streets, on picket lines or through political action. Identity politics parades its concern on issues of race and gender, but under its faux radicalism expunges the centrality of class and class struggle from the fight for equality. Fostering division, it has achieved not one material gain for those whose interests it claims to represent. In many trade unions, identity politics has allowed liberal authoritarian ideas and methods an insidious entry point. Ironically, it has been driven by the 'left', even supposed revolutionaries, who have provided cover for witch-hunting reformist bureaucrats.

The view that certain opinions are inviolable and must be accepted without criticism and brook 'no debate' is utterly incompatible with the democratic traditions on which the workers' movement was founded. It is also totally inconsistent with the concept of independent and critical thinking. Worse, it is an effective endorsement of authoritarian methods that will, and already are, being used against trade unionists, socialists, communists, anti-war activists and anyone else challenging the status quo. The ruling class needs no lessons in how to silence and censor 'unacceptable' opinions. They can now argue that the use of such methods in the workers' movement justifies their own suppression of ideas. Once discussion is censored or silenced, witch-hunts follow. This is most clearly the case with socialist and communist women who raise legitimate concerns about the regressive nature of gender ideology and the loss of single-sex services and spaces.[8] Those left activists who adopt the methods of reactionary liberal authoritarianism simply strengthen the grip of bureaucratism. They tacitly justify repressive measures generally and facilitate liberal policy capture by stifling real debate, alienating women, and undermining trade union activity and even membership. All these questions must be clarified through open democratic debate in the interests of the working class as a whole. Quite separate from those union activists working for genuine equality, supporters of this reformist trend provide political cover for passivity and class collaboration. Through performative virtue signalling, they produce little but the alienation of those whose interests they pretend to advance.

The trade union movement is in crisis, as are the disparate forces of socialists and communists. At a time when Marxist ideas have never been more necessary, the left is at its most demoralised and disorientated. Broken by decades of reaction, some once influential revolutionary organisations have abandoned Marxism and materialism itself in their capitulation to identity politics. Having already surrendered to 'rule or ruin' politics, they are now even more incapable of playing a serious role in building left unity in the face of heightened class struggle.

But there is nothing new in this. In an earlier period of reaction, Lenin had the measure of these fads and trends, and those who surrendered to them:

The years of reaction (1907–10). Tsardom was victorious. All the revolutionary and opposition parties were smashed. Depression, demoralisation, splits, discord, defection and pornography took the place of politics. There was an ever greater drift towards philosophical idealism; mysticism became the garb of counter-revolutionary sentiments. At the same time, however, it was this great defeat that taught the revolutionary parties and the revolutionary class a real and very useful lesson, a lesson in historical dialectics, a lesson in an understanding of the political struggle, and in the art and science of waging that struggle. It is at moments of need that one learns who one's friends are. Defeated armies learn their lesson.[9]

A mass working-class party cannot be built on identity politics. For socialists and communists who have not capitulated to liberalism and sectarianism, the forces to build a genuine class movement will be found in the workplaces and working-class communities.

The left and working-class political representation

The great betrayal on the eve of the first world war saw the Second International and leaders of the mass working-class parties, including erstwhile Marxists, capitulate to chauvinism and national bourgeois interests. The result was the industrialised slaughter of millions of workers. This catastrophe plunged even the most resolute Marxists like Lenin into despair, albeit temporarily. Yet three years later, the working class grasped and held state power for the first time in history in the October Revolution. As a result, the more astute ruling-class strategists knew that their inability to resolve capitalism's contradictions produced not only war and fascism but also a working-class response. In the advanced capitalist countries, mass membership of workers' parties and trade unions led to state welfare programmes and to major extensions in civil rights, especially for women.

During the current period of reaction in Britain and internationally, the capitalist class has won back much of the power it had ceded in the face of such struggles. The fault lines between collaboration and militant struggle have also been exposed. Other contradictions have emerged which may impede the struggle to defend workers' interests. Although today's multiple crises are of an objectively deeper and of far more dangerous nature than in the past, the debilitating effect of reaction also opens the door towards new forces and expressions of class struggle.

The trade union movement and its leaders should be a critical and positive factor in the struggle for the liberation of the working class from capitalist exploitation, and for a socialist society. Any dismissal or refusal to recognise such potential would be a serious error and a reflection of ultra-left defeatism. However, they can also play at best an indecisive indecisive, and at worst a reactionary, role. This is the central issue facing the movement – collaboration or militant struggle. As the contradictions within capitalism intensify, so too do the antagonisms between advocates of these two tendencies. Right-wing and even some left-reformist leaders and bureaucracies may well respond by conducting internal wars against socialists and communists, even in conditions of heightened class struggle – in fact, especially in such conditions.

Objectively, the conditions for ending the barbarism of capitalism have never been more advantageous, but the subjective factor – the socialist and communist movement – is pitifully underdeveloped. Extending the influence of Marxist perspectives in the trade union movement requires first a re-orientation towards class politics.

As the Labour government fails to deliver, demands for disaffiliation by union rank-and-file activists will intensify. In defending the link to Labour, union leaders now have little to offer in mitigation, other than the argument that it is better to have some influence with the government, rather than none at all. Workers' patience in the face of 'lesser evil' appeals from union and political leaders has reached a point of exhaustion. In this context the debate over the formation of a new workers' party must develop beyond discussions limited to left activists. There are at least two conditions that will determine how far the demand for such a new political formation can successfully develop. First, debate around the issue of working-class political representation must extend beyond the activist layer and into union branches and workplaces. Such a broadening of debate is necessary to confront the growing attraction to right-wing populist formations among wide sections of our class. Second, we need the development and popularisation of a clear socialist alternative, reflecting workers' material needs and aspirations.

In those unions still affiliated to Labour, it is necessary to demand disaffiliation as a crucial first step towards building a new party. If socialists and communists are to rise to the task that history has placed upon their shoulders, there must be the most rigorous analysis of why their ideas are not being translated into an effective mass force. The question of rebuilding the Marxist left is deeply interconnected with the question of building effective working-class political representation. The formation of the Labour Party and the transfer of working-class allegiance away from Liberalism were largely driven by the industrial militancy of New Unionism. Likewise, the founding of the Communist Party in 1920 from a disparate group of organisations and campaigns arose in conditions of large-scale industrial militancy when the British ruling class seriously feared revolution.

Campaigning for a new workers' party is, among other things, a struggle to build a coordinated united front in conditions of struggle. The re-establishment of effective working-class political representation is an imperative, not an option or mere aspiration. It is rightly acknowledged that the road to a new party may be a complex and drawn-out process. But it is also true that this is an urgent task. Building a united front on the electoral plane does not mean waiting for the formation of a new party, but it does require agreement now on key policies reflecting the most pressing material and political concerns of workers.

A new workers' party will not win those millions of workers looking for a real alternative to austerity and growing threats of repression and war by echoing outworn ideas now shown to be inadequate by the historic failure of labourism as exemplified by today's Labour Party. The demand that unions should simply disaffiliate from Labour and then affiliate to a new and untested party would be a recipe for a 'mark 2' Labour Party with Labourism embedded at its core. Any new workers' party must advocate and fight for more than a reformist redistribution of wealth, which implies a common interest with our class enemies. In this period of multiple crises in which the capitalist state and establishment wage unremitting class war, any new workers' party must unequivocally call for, and fight for, the socialist transformation of society. Nothing less will do.

The rise of right-wing populism in Britain is a consequence of austerity and the wider crisis of capitalism, but also of the failure of the labour and trade union movement to represent the interests of the overwhelming majority in society – the working class. Reform UK is not at this stage a stable political formation, but it is drawing in many who are attracted to it in the absence of a socialist alternative. As the class struggle intensifies, it may be that the same workers voting for or joining Reform today will leave as it fractures along class lines. Dismissing such people, some who will be union members, as fascists or racists, or characterising Reform UK itself as a fascist party, is not just wrong in itself but a serious tactical error. Doing so is also a consequence of the ubiquity of liberal ideas on the left, which has led to the term 'fascist' being thrown around as an insult rather than a serious designation. Farage and Trump, for that matter, may employ some of the rhetoric and methods of fascism but are not fascists – they are establishment to the core; notwithstanding the fact the social composition of society is now heavily weighted in the working class's favour, the ruling class is unlikely to repeat the historic error of handing over state control to fascists as in the inter-war years, liberal authoritarianism is their weapon of choice. The danger is that workers who are not in any sense fascist but have an initial attraction to Reform are alienated from the only force that can represent their interests – socialism. In conditions of growing instability, these workers can most effectively be won to socialist ideas by the formation of a new workers' party.

Socialists and communists must be at the centre of debate in the workplaces, as well as in communities and on the streets, to build resistance and solidarity and provide the impetus to fight for a socialist alternative. In doing so, they must consciously disentangle themselves from liberals and reformists and be a clear voice for militant struggle and socialist transformation.

The lessons of Marx should be reiterated in setting the tasks for socialists and communists in the trade unions. The central task is to forge these workers' organisations into a movement that transcends narrow sectional interests to become a beacon for the struggling millions. This is a question of both necessity and survival.

....

Notes & References

1. *Civil Service World*, 10 March 2025.

2. J. White, 'Thinking about the British strike wave: class, class struggle and consciousness in 2022–3', in E. McFarland and J. Whiston (eds), *What history is for*, Manifesto Press, Croydon, 2024, pp.47–53.

3. Craft research agency, *Gen Z: Trends, Truth and Trust*, Channel 4, London, 2025.

4. *Morning Star*, 18 January 2025.

5. *Morning Star*, 16 July 2025

6. *Morning Star*, 22 January 2025.

7. K. Marx and F. Engels, *Critique of the German Ideology*, Lawrence and Wishart, London, 1970, p.64.

8. Susan Dalgety, *The Scotsman*, 15 February 2025.

9. V.I. Lenin, '"Left-wing" Communism: an Infantile Disorder', *Selected Works*, Progress Publishers, Moscow, 1968, p.517.

Glossary

CSCU Civil Service Clerical Union – *see CSCA*

CSU Civil Service Union

ACA Assistant Clerks Association

ARC Association of Revenue and Customs

ASLEF Associated Society of Locomotive Engineers and Firemen

ATL Association of Teachers and Lecturers – *see NEU*

BERR Department of Business, Enterprise and Regulatory Reform

BL Broad Left – *CPSA rank-and-file socialist organisation, became LU*

BL84 Communist-led grouping formed in 1984 following split from the existing BL

BLN Broad Left Network – *SP-led organisation which broke from LU*

CBI Confederation of British Industry

CCC Conference Campaign Committee

CCSU Council of Civil Service Unions

CDMT Campaign to Defeat Militant Tendency

COA Clerical Officers' Association – *see CSCA.*

CPSA Civil and Public Services Association – *name change from CSCA in 1969, see also PCS*

CSCA Civil Service Clerical Association – *amalgamation of CSCU and COA in 1921, see also CPSA*

CSCS Civil Service Compensation Scheme

CWU Communication Workers Union

DE Department of Employment

DEFRA Department of Food and Rural Affairs

DHSS Department of Health and Social Security

DLA Disability Living Allowance

DPAC Disabled People Against Cuts

DTI Department of Trade and Industry

DWP Department of Work and Pensions

DVLA Driver and Vehicle Licensing Agency

EETPU Electrical, Electronic, Telecommunications and Plumbing Union

EIS Educational Institute of Scotland

ES Employment Service

FBU Fire Brigades Union

FDA legal name since 2000 of the former Association of First Division Civil Servants

GCHQ Government Communications Headquarters

GMB legal name since 1987 of the former General, Municipal, Boilermakers and Allied Trades Union

GPMU Graphical, Paper and Media Union

HMRC HM Revenue and Customs

IL Independent Left

IPMS Institution of Professionals, Managers and Specialists – *see Prospect*

IRSF Inland Revenue Staff Federation – *see PTC*

ISU Immigration Service Union

LU Left Unity – *CPSA and PCS rank and file socialist organisation, previously BL*

J30 public sector industrial action on 30 June 2011 to defend pensions and retirement rights

MT Militant Tendency

MYVC Make Your Vote Count

N30 public sector industrial action on 30 November 2011 to defend pensions and retirement rights

NATFHE National Association of Teachers in Further and Higher Education—*see UCU*

NATO North Atlantic Treaty Organisation

NCA National Crime Agency

NDC National Disputes Committee

NEC National Executive Committee

NEU National Education Union – *amalgamation of ATL and NEU in 2017*

NHS National Health Service

NIPSA Northern Ireland Public Service Alliance

NMG National Moderate Group – *known as the 'Moderates'*

NUCPS National Union of Civil and Public Servants – *amalgamation of CSU and SCPS in 1988*

NUM National Union of Mineworkers

NUT National Union of Teachers – *see NEU*

PCS Public and Commercial Services Union – *amalgamation of CPSA and PTC in 1998*

PDS Performance Development System

PFI Public Finance Initiative

PLP Parliamentary Labour Party

POA Prison Officers' Association

Prospect amalgamation of IPMS and the Engineers and Managers Association in 2001

PTC Public Services, Tax and Commerce Union – *amalgamation in 1996 of IRSF and NUCPS, see also PCS*

RCTU Revenue and Customs Trade Union

RMT National Union of Rail, Maritime and Transport Workers

SCPS Society of Civil and Public Servants – *see NUCPS*

SNP Scottish National Party

SP Socialist Party

SSP Scottish Socialist Party

SSTA Scottish Secondary Teachers' Association

STUC Scottish Trades Union Congress

SWP Socialist Workers Party

TGWU Transport and General Workers Union – *see Unite the Union*

TRUMID Movement for True Industrial Democracy

TUC Trades Union Congress

TUCETU Trade Union Committee for European and Transatlantic Understanding

TULO Trade Union and Labour Party Liaison Organisation

TUSC Trade Unionist and Socialist Coalition

UCU University and College Union – *amalgamation of the Association of University Teachers and NATFHE in 2006*

UKIP United Kingdom Independence Party

UNISON amalgamation of the National and Local Government Officers' Association, the National Union of Public Employees and the Confederation of Health Service Employees in 1993

Unite the Union amalgamation in 2007 of Amicus and TGWU, commonly known as 'Unite'

Bibliography

Primary sources

PCS Internal documents
PCS Annual Returns to the Certification Officer
PCS National Executive Committee Papers

PCS Publications
Alternative Vision for HM Land Registry (London: PCS, London, 2014)
Anti-racist and anti-fascist strategy (London: PCS, 2014)
There is an alternative: The case against cuts in public spending (London: PCS, 2010)
Welfare: An Alternative Vision (London: PCS, 2011)

Parliamentary Papers
Civil service pensions – developments to 2010, SN 3324 (London: House of Commons Library, 2013)

Demographic and voting patterns in Scotland's independence referendum, S. Ayres (London: House of Commons Library, 2014)

House of Commons Debates (Hansard)

Ministry of Reconstruction. Commission on Relations between Employers and Employed. Final Report. Cd, 9153 (London, 1918)

The Parliamentary Pensions (Amendment) Regulations 2002, UK Statutory Instruments, No. 1807 (2002)

UK Parliament, Employment Law (Beecroft Report), vol. 545 (12 May 2012)

Official Reports
Building our Future: Transforming the way HMRC serves the UK (London: HMRC, 2015)

Committee of Enquiry into Civil Service Security Procedure (Radcliffe Committee) Report (1961–2)

Establishment matters; First Report of the Civil Service Inquiry Commission, Playfair Commission (1875)

Fraud and Error in the Benefits System: 2010/11 Estimates (Leeds: DWP, 2012)

Report of the Masterman Committee on the political activities of Civil Servants, Cmd. 7718 (1949)

Report of the Organisation of the Permanent Civil Service, Northcote-Trevelyan Report (1854)

Reps in Action: how workplaces can gain from modern representation (London: BERR, 2009)

The Civil Service Reform Plan (London: the Cabinet Office, 2012)

Campaigning materials

'Defend Your Union' leaflets

PCS Broad Left Network newsletters

PCS Independent Left, NEC elections bulletins

PCS Senior Officers' election addresses

'Socialist Caucus – the Politics of Betrayal, Despair and Cynicism', Left Unity leaflet (2007)

'Striking Against Market Madness' (Militant Labour leaflet, October 1993)

Magazines and specialist journals

Art History News

Civil Service World

Kommunist

Labour Research

Nursing Times

Personnel Today

Public Finance

Reader's Digest

Newspapers

Aberdeen Press and Journal

Belfast Newsletter

Belfast Telegraph

Birmingham Daily Post

Birmingham Mail

Bristol Evening Post

Chorley Guardian

Cumbernauld News

Daily Express

Daily Herald

Daily Mail

Daily Mirror

Evening News

Financial Times

Leicester Daily Mercury

Leicester Evening Mail

Liverpool Daily Post

Liverpool Echo

London Daily Chronicle

Mail on Sunday

Merthyr Express

Militant

Morning Star

Newcastle Journal

Northamptonshire Chronicle and Echo

Nottingham Guardian

Reynold's Illustrated Newspaper

Scottish Socialist Voice

Socialist Worker

The Courier

The Guardian

The Herald

The Independent

The Scotsman

The Socialist

The Sun

The Times

West Lancashire Evening Gazette

Western Daily Press

Western Morning News

Published secondary sources

Brown, W.J., *So Far...*, (London: George Allen & Unwin, 1943)

Clifford, Ellen, *The War on Disabled People: Capitalism, Welfare and the Making of a Human Catastrophe* (London: Zed Books, 2020)

Craft research agency, *Gen Z: Trends, Truth and Trust* (London: Channel 4, 2025)

Curtice, John, and Ormston, Rachel (eds), *British Social Attitudes 32: The verdict on five years of coalition government* (London: National Centre for Social Research, 2015)

Freud, David, *Reducing dependency, increasing opportunity: options for the future of welfare to work. An independent report into the Department of Work and Pensions* (2007)

Gerth, Matthew, *Anti-Communism in Britain During the Cold War: A Very British Witch-Hunt* (London: University of London Press, 2023)

Halpin, Kevin, *Memoirs of a Militant: Sharply and to the point* (Glasgow: Praxis Press, 2012)

Henderson, Lynn, 'Defeat Government Union-Busting', *Scottish Left Review*, 86 (April–May 2015)

Henderson, Lynn, 'Public and Civil Service: Transformed by Trade Unionists' in Bryan, Pauline (ed.), *Keep Left: Red Paper on Scotland 2025* (Edinburgh: Luath Press, 2025)

Humphreys, Betty Vance, *Clerical Unions in the Civil Service* (London: Blackwell & Mott, 1958)

Lanning, Hugh and Norton, Richard, *A Conflict of Loyalties: GCHQ 1984–1991* (Cheltenham: New Clarion Press, 1994)

Lenin, V.I., 'On Strikes', *Collected Works*, vol. 4 (Moscow: Progress Publishers, 1964). First published in *Proletarskaya Revolyutsiya*, No. 8–9 (1924)

Lenin, V.I., '"Left-wing" Communism: an Infantile Disorder', *Selected Works*, (Moscow: Progress Publishers, 1968)

Marx, Karl, *The Eighteenth Brumaire of Louis Bonaparte*, (London: George Allen & Unwin Ltd, 1926)

Marx, Karl and Engels, Friedrich, *Critique of the German Ideology* (London: Lawrence and Wishart, 1970)

McAlpine, Robin, *Some thoughts on the first minister's lecture*, The Jimmy Reid Foundation (30 January 2013)

McInally, John, 'A problem of prestige; the crisis within the Committee for a Workers' International (CWI)', *In Defence of Marxism* (August 2019)

Milne, Seumas, *The Enemy Within: The Secret War Against the Miners* (London: Verso, 2004)

Newman, Bernard, *Yours for Action* (London: McCorquodale, 1953)

Nunns, Alex, *The Candidate: Jeremy Corbyn's Improbable Path to Power* (New York and London: OR Books, 2016)

Plekhanov, Georgi V., *The Role of the Individual in History* (New York: International Publishers, 1940)

Ramsay, Robin, *The Clandestine Caucus – Anti-socialist campaigns and operations in the British Labour Movement since the war*, (Hull: Lobster, 1998)

Seifert, Roger and Sibley, Tom, *Revolutionary Communist at Work: A Political Biography of Bert Ramelson* (London: Lawrence and Wishart, 2012)

Serwotka, Mark and Gall, Gregor, *The future of public services under Labour*, Working Paper, University of Hertfordshire (2007)

TaxPayers' Alliance, *Taxpayer Funding of Trade Unions*, Research Note 97 (25 November 2011)

White, Jonathan, 'Thinking about the British strike wave: class, class struggle and consciousness in 2022–3', in Elaine McFarland and Jim Whiston (eds), *What history is for* (Croydon: Manifesto Press, 2024)

Wigham, Eric, *From Humble Petition to Militant Action: A History of the Civil and Public Services Association, 1903–1978* (London: Civil and Public Services Association, 1980)

Index

A
Adams, Terry 67, 69, 113–4, 115
Air Traffic Control 50, 60–1, 125
Alderson, Ray 51
Alexander, Danny 174, 185, 187
Alternative Vision for HM Land Registry (2014) 178
Anti-Waste League 24
Armstrong, Robert 73–4
Assistant Clerks' Association (ACA) 29
Associated Society of Locomotive Engineers and Firemen (ASLEF) 116
Association of Irish Post Office Clerks 29
Association of Revenue and Customs (ARC) 202
Association of Tax Clerks 29
Association of Teachers and Lecturers (ATL) 186
Attenborough, Richard 58
Attlee, Clement 38, 42

B
Baker, Mark 278
Balls, Ed 187
Bannister, Roger 191
Barber, Brendan 162–3, 173, 189, 193
Baugh, Chris 60, 269, 270–82
Baxter, Arthur 27
Beaverbrook, Lord 38
Bedminster 1, 87–96
Beecroft, Adrian 192
Belfast 126, 135, 177
Better Together 228, 230, 231, 234
BL84 68–9, 72, 82, 85, 86, 101, 102, 103–4, 105–6
Black Activists Against Cuts 191
Black Triangle 223
Blair, Tony 112–3, 118, 123, 124, 125–6, 127, 128, 130, 132, 141, 143, 149, 153, 154, 160, 246, 291
Bolt, Sophie 299
Bonner, Frank 50, 100
Brexit 169, 237, 239–40
Bristol 1, 87, 90, 91, 93–96, 132, 177, 179, 181, 188
British National Party 212
British Telecom 60
Broad Left 5, 12, 45, 55, 56–7, 58, 59, 60,

63–5, 66, 67, 68–9, 70–1, 72, 73, 76, 79, 80, 81, 85, 90, 99, 100, 101, 105–6, 107, 108, 286
Broad Left Network 269, 283, 284, 286
Brown, Gordon 24, 122, 123, 124, 126, 128, 129, 130, 131, 133, 136, 139, 141, 143, 149, 150, 153, 154, 156, 161, 162–3, 165–6, 169, 174, 184, 196, 212, 232, 251, 260, 271, 291, 292
Brown, W.J. 28, 29, 36–7, 38, 39
Bruinvels, Peter 73
Burnip, Linda 222
Byers, Stephen 127

C
Cabinet Office 73, 74, 133, 144, 151, 158, 164, 184, 186, 195, 197, 202, 204, 208, 250
Caerphilly 11, 107, 247
call centre workers 130, 136, 153–4
Callaghan, James 45, 50, 133
Cameron, David 128, 165–6, 170, 171, 173, 175, 182, 188, 193, 217, 227, 234, 235–6, 249, 252, 258, 260
Campaign to Defeat Militant Tendency (CDMT) 80, 81
Campfield, Brian 242n.
Cardiff 1, 135, 179, 185, 247
Castle, Dawn 85
Catholic Action 51
Caton, Brian 116
Cavanagh, Martin 254–5
Cawkwell, Steve 85
Chacko, Ben 241
Chambers, Marion 70, 71, 76, 80, 82, 83, 84, 85, 91, 94, 99, 103, 112
Chapple, Frank 50
Check-off 75, 196, 198–201, 206, 207, 235–6, 237, 254, 259, 274
Civil Aviation Authority 60
Civil Service Clerical Association (CSCA) 36–7, 38, 39, 41–3, 49
Civil Service Compensation Scheme (CSCS) 134, 143, 162–5, 181–2, 206, 247, 249–50, 251
Civil and Public Services Association (CPSA) 1, 11, 12, 13, 14, 45, 49, 54, 55–8, 59–65, 66–76, 80, 81–4, 87–96, 101, 106, 108, 109–12, 115, 116, 150, 151, 269, 276
Civil Service Clerical Union (CSCU) 46n.
Civil Service Federation 29
Civil Service Reform Plan (2012) 195–6, 203

123, 133, 135, 46, 175, 179, 190–1, 202, 219, 225, 239, 260, 268, 271–2, 274, 275, 279, 282, 286.
Goldfinch, Steve 88, 90, 92, 95, 96, 97n.
Gordon, Alex 198–9
Graham, Alistair 66, 69, 70, 71
Graphical, Paper and Media Union (GPMU) 87, 94
Green, Guy 58
Green, Nigel 118–9
Griffiths, Mike 90

H

Hammond, Philip 126
Hampton, Colin 222
Hayes, Billy 116
Heath, Edward 50, 52
Heathcote, Fran 2, 254, 274, 286, 299
Henderson, Lynn 299, 282
Hewitt, Patricia 127
HM Revenue and Customs (HMRC) 125, 157, 174, 175, 185, 201–5, 224, 246, 248, 254, 285
Holbourne, Zita 191
Home Office 74, 180, 200, 248, 253
Homer, Lin 204
Hoon, Geoff 126
Hutton, John 127, 181–3

I

Immigration Service Union (ISU) 192
Independent Left 267–8, 282, 284, 286
Inland Revenue Staff Federation (IRSF) 52, 54, 62, 90, 109
Institution of Professionals, Managers and Specialists (IPMS) 109, 181
Irish Congress of Trade Unions 228
Ironside, Mike 177

J

J30 186–7, 191
Jamal, Ben 299
Jim Conway Foundation 51
Johnson, Alan 140, 144–5
Johnson, Boris 240, 284
Jones, Digby 146

K

Kapos, Stephen 299
Kelly, Emily 155
Kendall, Bill 49, 82, 83
Kenny, Alex 299
Kerslake, Bob 236

Kinnock, Neil 67
Kirk, Christine 69–70, 72

L

Lamb, Peter 112
Land Registry 56, 178, 258
Lane, Amanda 88, 90, 91–6
Lanning, Hugh 112, 113, 114–6, 119
Lavery, Ian 196
Lawn, Barney 242n.
Left Unity 1, 99, 100, 105, 107–8, 109, 110–5, 117–8, 121, 130, 134, 138, 146, 147, 190, 211, 213, 214, 232, 252, 254, 266, 268, 271, 273, 274, 280-1, 282, 283, 284, 286
Lenin, V.I. 20, 29, 264, 267, 285, 307, 308
Lewtas, Geoff 69
Lloyd, Marion 283–5
Lloyd George, David 39
Losinska, Kate 52–4
Lowe, Robert 25
Lucas, Caroline 239
Lynn, Billy 242n.

M

Mackney, Paul 116
Macmillan, Harold 44
Macreadie, John 14, 62, 67–8, 69–76, 81, 84, 99, 101, 108, 118, 120, 272
Magee, Brian 242n.
Magistrates' Courts 157
Mahony, Peter 81
Major, John 123–4, 125, 126, 129, 235
Make Your Vote Count (MYVC) 160, 212–3, 215–6
Malone, Gerry 242n.
Manasseh, Leslie 206
Manchester 60, 113, 135, 188, 285
Mandelson, Peter 123, 127
Martin, Terry 81
Marx, Karl 6, 7, 30, 303, 312
Masterman Committee (1949) 43
Matthews, Gayle 242n.
Maude, Francis 184, 186, 195-9, 201, 203-4, 206, 208-9, 233, 237, 272, 278
Maughan, Alan 81
May, Teresa 237, 239
McCloskey, John 242n.
McDonnell, John 160, 191, 222, 238, 239, 299
McGirr, Louise 92
McHugh, Kevin 202
McInally, John 1, 11, 85, 188, 273